THE
FRIGHTENERS

THE FRIGHTENERS

A Journey Through our Cultural Fascination with the Macabre

Reverend Peter Laws

Skyhorse Publishing

For Emma and Adam

This book—about scary things sometimes being fun—ended up as a celebration of self-acceptance. But it takes thousands of words to get there, and there are some pretty freaky bits along the way. So, for now, you can just read the shorter, nine-word version of the book.

Here it is:

Be who you want to be, okay? Be *you*.

CONTENTS

THE
FRIGHTENERS

CHAPTER ONE

THE SINISTER MINISTER

I'm in Luton airport, and the guy on security is rummaging through my bag. He keeps squeezing and prodding stuff. Checking if my pants are ticking or if my toothpaste contains a nerve agent. He asks me where I'm off to. *Finally!* I've been hoping he would ask that because I get punch-the-air excited when anybody does. I beam at him and I say, all chipper, "I'm going on holiday."

"Yes, but where to?"

[mental drum roll] "Transylvania!"

He drops the toothpaste, frowns, then eyes me up and down. "Really?"

"Yep."

"It's a real place?"

"Course! It's in Romania."

"You're going to vampire land?" He tilts his head. "On *holiday?*"

I want to slap my hands together like a sea lion. "I'm staying in a spooky old Saxon village. It's gonna be amazing."

He does something next that I've seen other people do in this situation: he slowly glances at my wife, as if she'll explain this anomaly. It's not like he's found cocaine in my bag, or a severed limb. He's not horrified by me, but I can tell he's confused. My wife shrugs: "He likes morbid stuff, and he's wanted to go since he was a kid." She looks apologetic. "It's his 40th birthday present."

His eyebrows spring up. "Yes, but why on earth would anybody *want* to go there?"

To be honest, it's the same reaction I've had from most people this last month, when I've told them where I'm headed for five days. I say the five-syllable word and they do a double take . . . *Transylvania*. They don't exactly cross themselves and stumble backwards, like the gasping, creeped-out innkeepers from the first ten minutes of a Hammer Horror movie, but it's close. A mate of mine had a similar frown last week. All he could say was: "Why? Is Benidorm shut?" Another told me about her upcoming break in France, and when I mentioned *my* trip she burst out laughing, right in my face. "Wow, Peter," she said. "You are *so* weird."

I'm used to these sorts of looks. Like when folks come round my house and see my home office; they can't avoid the huge vintage drive-in posters of 70s movies like *Dracula's Dog* (1978) and *Nightwing* (1979). Or my badass *Grizzly* (1976) poster that screams *18ft of Gut-Munching Fury!* Or maybe they spot my bookshelf, which is bulging with titles like *Dreadful Pleasures*, *Ghoul Britannia* and *Everyone Loves a Good Train Wreck*. Maybe they spot my signed collection of the complete soundtrack to all of the *Friday the 13th* movies (about a guy in a hockey mask who chops up teenagers), or if they're *really* observant, they might recognise a chunk of stone that I nicked from a supposedly haunted church, famous for grave desecrations in the 60s. I have a piece of it on my window sill. Next to that are the original storyboards from an 80s horror movie called *The Mutilator* (1985). And piles of magazines and books with real-life tales of the paranormal.

When guests see these morbid items, as I politely take their coats and offer them Earl Grey, they sometimes give me a look that says: *Is it wise to accept this tea?*

I've had the *you're-a-bit-kooky* glance a fair bit because I've loved creepy and macabre things pretty much my whole life. And by that I mean I've *really* loved them. The dark, the mysterious, the weird, the scary, they're *valuable* to me. They matter. I reckon if you slice my brain open, there'd be a whole section dedicated to the gothic and strange. Or more likely it's threaded all over, like when you spill coffee on your laptop and it gets everywhere.

One of the earliest places I noticed my love of the dark side was at theme parks. I'd always slap open the map and search for the ghost train first. The big rollercoasters? The thrill rides? I skipped them, because I get spectacularly motion sick. I braved the waltzer once just to impress a girl and ended up puking on her shoulder and chest. Yet I'll giddily push through cobwebs and hanging fake tarantulas in a fright ride because it clicks a pleasure switch in me that I don't always understand; I just know that it's there.

When Halloween comes around, I'm the fella in the supermarket lurking in the tacky novelty fang aisle. I'm trying on masks and chasing my squealing kids down the ready-meal section. I've got this compulsion to squeeze and prod every single prop to see if it makes a ghostly scream or a blood-thinning cackle. Often I set them all off at once, just so I can unleash 30 wailing witches through an otherwise jolly store.

My humour cortex has a little horror spilled on it too. I saw a photo the other day of a plastic baby-changing unit, one of those drop-down ones you get in public toilets. Somebody had written on it: *PLACE SACRIFICE HERE.* I'm not exactly "pro" baby sacrifice, but man, I laughed hard at that. When I showed it to others, they looked at me like I was insane. Which made me chuckle even more. So I looked even . . . um . . . insane-*er.*

Yeah, I'm *that* guy.

In the car, I sometimes listen to electro, sometimes kitsch lounge music—the type you'd hear in a 70s supermarket. And sometimes I even listen to normal everyday music that plays on low-number radio stations. But *often* it's the soundtrack to films like *Creepshow* (1982) or *Tenebrae* (1982), *Don't Look Now* (1973) or *Pet Sematary* (1989). And as the violins squeal (minor chords, naturally) I'm popping to the shops or doing the school run. Not feeling glum or depressed at all, just living my life like everybody else, only threading it with a little spook.

Now, other fans of the morbid don't have any issue with this at all. They slip into the passenger seat, hear the music and say, *Wow! This is* The Omen *soundtrack, cool.* But let me be frank, and perhaps obvious: most other people don't say "wow" or "cool." When they gather in my kitchen for my 40th birthday and see the cake has meticulous icing replicating the hotel carpet from Stanley Kubrick's 1980 film *The Shining* (complete with sugary axe embedded in the centre) they say *Oh yeah, you like those things don't you?* And there's a nervy little twitch behind the awkward smile. A flicker that makes a statement: *Maybe it's not just odd to love morbid culture, maybe it's odder than odd. Maybe it's twisted, dangerous even, to be so into the dark side of life.*

Thing is though, I've been like this my whole life. I even remember the reports from my Parents' Evenings. They consisted of a lot of "yes . . . , but . . ." phrases from my teachers:

English: *Yes he's good, but does* every *story have to have a werewolf in it?*

Art: *Yes, he tries hard, but aren't there other things he'd like to draw apart from skulls with chomping fangs? Plus, we're running out of red crayon.*

Music: *Yes, I appreciate he's teaching himself the glockenspiel, Mrs Laws, but he's eight and he's playing the theme from* The Exorcist *over and over. It's creeping Mrs Bates out.*

My mum even says that when I was born (during a storm that blew the lights out, apparently—how ominously cool is that?) I grabbed a pair of scissors and held them aloft. She immediately decided I'd either be prime minister or a mass murderer. Thankfully, her bizarrely polarised prediction never came true, but, at the same time, I have always felt a bit different. But then, doesn't everybody? You probably feel odd sometimes, in those quiet moments in a coffee shop when you wonder if you're the only person in town listening to *that* piece of music, reading *that* particular book, thinking *that* specific thought.

Some people use culture to make them laugh, others only watch tearjerkers that'll guarantee a good cry. I'll take those too—I'll happily watch a romcom. But my heart beats fastest when I read a spooky tale of hauntings or watch a scary movie, or when I sit on a plane that's slicing through the clouds towards Transyl-bloody-vania! My wife Joy sits next to me. She's watching some BBC crime drama on her tablet while I devour *The Bedside, Bathtub & Armchair Companion to "Dracula."* I'm reading a wild fact about the *real* Dracula (and national hero) Vlad the Impaler. He once nailed turbans to the skulls of a group of Turks because they refused to take them off in his presence. He got all sarcastic and said, "I'll *help* you keep your custom," and then the whacking began. It's a barbaric incident, and I despise real-life violence, yet for some reason my brain notes the long passage of time since this incident happened, then files the story under "cool."

Saying that out loud probably sets warning bells off in some people's heads. For example, I recently read about a vintage issue of *Cosmopolitan* magazine which told women that the "video store" was a great place to meet men . . . *unless* they were in the horror aisle. In which case, such a man would obviously have "questionable feelings about women" and would be clearly, "a man to avoid."[1]

Is that *really* what people think? Is it what *you* think—that there's a monster crouching inside me, waiting to unzip my chest and climb right out? And what about the other fans of the macabre, the millions scattered across living rooms, trains and airport terminals, libraries and swimming pool loungers, watching or reading grisly forensic crime dramas, or playing out ghostly visitations or murder in video games? Are all these people death-obsessed freaks? Violent time bombs, even?

I'm especially conscious that people's frowns deepen when they hear my profession. I might be wrong, but I suspect that it's this that makes people think I'm *really* off base.

You see, I love darkness, but I'm also a church minister.

We've landed in the Transylvanian city of Sibiu.

The airport has strip lights, clean floors and industrial strength hand dryers which shine little blue lights on my wrists before trying to blow all the skin off. It's like any other airport I've been in. I'm not sure what I expected really: large oak doors creaking open? A shuffling hunchbacked man with a sheet over his arm, holding a candelabra and grunting: *Passport, sir? Did sir pack his satchel hisself, sir?*

I'm not disappointed though, because as we're collecting our bags from the conveyor belt all I keep thinking is: *I'm in Transylvania, I'm in Transylvania.* I catch Joy's gaze. She winks at me. This is a cosmic wormhole away from her ideal holiday. She'd rather be on a city break, eating fish in a glam restaurant, but she knows this matters. She understands that I have a bucket list like anybody else, only mine's scrawled with Gothic swirls and thunderbolts.

There are supposed to be three other English couples on the same trip as us, but we haven't seen them yet. I start scanning the crowd looking for people who look like they'd choose scary castles over poolside karaoke. There's no guy with studded boots and a long leather jacket striding about; no top-hatted pseudo-Goth, creeping to the Coke machine in a "dark and epic" way. Everyone just looks normal. But that's the thing about us fright fans. We can blend in. Some of us even wear fleeces. We lurk in unexpected places.

We brush past the rest of the world on the Tube; we write prescriptions in the doctor's office; we help kids finger-paint at pre-school; and we serve skinny lattes with dainty sprinkles. We clean public toilets, and we own multinational corporations. You'll even find us wandering the corridors of power and running the country, like the Conservative MP John Whittingdale. During his time as Culture Secretary, he admitted that he liked "really nasty films."[2]

Whittingdale cited stuff like Eli Roth's *Hostel* (2005), which is a pretty brutal movie. One scene has a Dutch businessman cheerfully drilling holes into the legs and chest of an American backpacker. Then the Dutchman slices the guy's Achilles tendons, followed by his throat. It's a film that centres on lingering, protracted violence. But get this: Whittingdale didn't admit to watching this stuff after some sort of police sting on his property. He wasn't contrite about it. He happily admitted his morbid tastes to a newspaper journalist, and the public didn't seem that bothered—perhaps because so many of them had gone to see the film themselves. It was a multiplex hit, across the world. The fact that a high-profile politician can publicly admit he's into films like this, without being socially lynched, suggests that we're living in a world where even extreme horror is slipping into the mainstream.

Take Halloween, for example, Christmas for spooky folks. It's more popular today than ever. I grew up in the 1980s, in the North East of England. Back then I'd be lucky to find a set of glow-in-the-dark fangs in a high-street shop. I'd trawl the streets searching for Halloween masks, but it'd always be those crappy plastic ones with the twangy white elastic. They came in three flavours: Witch, Frankenstein's Monster and Dracula (or the Mummy if you found a really swanky place). Yet the plastic would often crack apart, and it'd cut lines into your cheek. It felt less like Halloween and more like "the annual strapping of a margarine tub to your face."

But there was another world, a horror Shangri-La: the seaside town of Blackpool and its joke shops. I stood in one of them during a break at Pontin's Holiday Camp, when I was ten. The shop had this amazing latex werewolf mask hanging from a high hook, with crazy big fangs and a mass of wild grey hair. The type of get-up Michael Jackson might wear on a date. I was desperate to buy it, but the price was so high my parents nearly vomited. At £70 I couldn't blame them. Remember this was mid-1980s money. Back then you could probably buy a hovercraft for that. As a British kid, I quickly learned that decent, morbid merchandise was a "speciality" product. A mail-order thing. It certainly wasn't mainstream.

Today though . . . *wow.*

You can buy proper werewolf masks in Asda supermarket for twelve quid, along with a *mahoosive* range of screaming skulls, rubber knives and fake severed hands. As a kid I was so itchy for scares that I swapped a cardboard box *full* of rare comics for a single, floppy, chopped-off hand prop. That box could have probably paid my mortgage off these days, but it wasn't stupidity that made me do that deal, it was the era. In my hometown, fake severed limbs were rarer than a Sasquatch. Not anymore. Asda do a super-cool hand for £10, which crawls by itself. Tesco do a severed zombie's foot for £2.99! Morbid kitsch is a lot cheaper these days, and the reason for this is simple: demand. In 2015 Asda met this demand by tripling its stock of Halloween costumes. They upped their supplies of scary makeup by 60 per cent. Sainsbury's creepy costume stock went up 30 per cent that same year.[3] UK marketing analysts have even claimed that Halloween is now the third biggest sales "event" for retailers—behind Christmas and Easter.[4]

For some, just dressing up in white sheets and trick-or-treating doesn't cut it. Growing numbers want more intense, scarier Halloween experiences. Something's been quietly exploding these last few years in the tourism and leisure world that's not just scratching the world's horror itch, it's tearing it open and digging deep inside. Theme parks, farms and warehouses are being converted into seasonal horror houses so that visitors can crawl through pitch black mazes while live actors with fake knives hunt them down. This is the "Scare Attraction Industry," where people are paying real-life money to be petrified.

A few years ago, events like this would have been incredibly niche. These days, you could visit one and be back home for bedtime. The continual growth of the scare attraction industry means it's even breaking free from the Halloween season. Scare events are cropping up all year round, with names like "Night of the Killer Rabbit" at Easter, or "Jingle Hells" at Christmas.

I tried one in March called "The Pit." For £3 some bloke yanked a sack over my head and I was forced to clamber through a maze while people grabbed and pushed at my body. Unseen mouths of actors screamed into my ears, saying they were going to kill me. Two hissing women dragged me down saying, "Oooh, we like you. We're gonna keep you here . . . *forever*!" To which I said, "At least buy me a drink first." It was all quite fun really, although I saw others come out of The Pit shaking and unable to speak. The same company helped organise much more extreme events like Survival: Cracked, where paying guests have their heads rammed into troughs of water and are force-fed slop. Yep, this is happening today. This is a thing.

Horror conventions are also on the rise. There used to be a time when *Star Trek* fans were the only ones who had those. Now events celebrating scary movies are cropping up all over the place. In May 2017, I was a presenter at the biggest one in the UK: HorrorCon in Sheffield. The place was rammed with thousands of fans over two days. There were constant streams of people lining up to pay big cash to get posters signed by sadistic onscreen killers. Merchandise tables sold teddy bears with entrails hanging out and severed witches' heads in glass bell jars, ready for the mantelpiece at home.

At these conventions, everywhere you look you'll see ordinary people dressed as zombies, werewolves and fictional murderers—and the skill level of these make-ups is sometimes Hollywood-level, with thousands of pounds and hours invested in getting them right. I chatted with an entire family of zombies once. One of the little girls had half a Coke can rammed into her gore-soaked eye. "I made sure she could see out of the drinking hole," her mum told me. So I looked down it, and, sure enough, there at the bottom of a soft drink can was a little blinking eye.

So, in the world of Halloween and horror, business is good—and the cinema box office is no exception. In 2016, the *Guardian* reported that horror movies are "the most profitable genre in the industry and it's booming. This year is set to be horror's best ever."[5]

Here in Transylvania, the travel operators don't hide the horror heritage: they actively celebrate it. Multiple companies now offer a Dracula-themed holiday experience. Of course, there's a lot more to Transylvania than vampires—it has stunning mountains, and wild bears, and pints of beer only cost a pound. Yet these are all just a wonderful bonus to me. The *prime* factor that has enticed a bundle of English men and women to holiday in a former communist country is our love of the undead.

As we scan the airport for the others, our host Jez arrives. He looks like the Red Baron. He's wearing a bomber jacket with a huge fluffy collar; though he has ditched the long white scarf, blowing out at a 90-degree angle. He's gripping a clipboard bearing the company name, Secret Transylvania, and the sight of it makes people shimmy out of the crowd to form a group. We check each other out. Everybody's a similar age. There's a grinning couple from the Highlands, plus a Greek girl and her bearded English boyfriend. The latter two cuddle *a lot*. A third couple appear. They're from Essex. We stood right behind these two in the security queue way back in Luton and had no idea we'd be in the same vampire clan. All eight of us shake hands and introduce ourselves. As we head to the cars, I hear nervous giggling because none of us is quite sure what to expect. The website said we'd be looked after by an English couple who run a small travel business in an old Saxon village away from the city. This is all in a country notorious for blood and mystery. It sounds like a horror movie plot, right there.

We lug our bags across the car park, and Joy leans into me, whispering, "How do we know they're not just going to take us to the woods and kill us?"

"I think Trip Advisor would have mentioned that," I reply.

We bundle into a car with the Scottish couple, Kenny and Lorraine. He's smiley, she's giggly. Turns out they have five kids, so I guess any time out of the house makes them ecstatic. I quickly like them.

"So . . ." Joy clicks her belt in the back seat. "Whose idea was it to come to Transylvania?"

"Lorraine's," Kenny says. "She's got a thing for vampires."

Lorraine chuckles and nods. "True."

"And you, Kenny?" I say. "Are *you* into all this vampire stuff?"

"Nah, but it's her 40th, and she's always wanted to come here."

Joy and I erupt into laughter, and I give Lorraine an immediate, mental high five. As the engine sputters into life, I'm reminded that maybe I *am* weird, but, hey, that's not such a big deal when you're walking through a world that's filled with weirdos.

Night's falling and we're heading for the traditional Saxon village of Cisnădioara. On the drive from Sibiu Airport, I look out the window and spot a woman pushing a pram. Stood under a street light, she's frantically crossing herself. Is there a vampire clinging to our car roof? I almost hope that there is . . . but nope. Turns out that's just what religious people here do whenever they walk past a church or a shrine. I keep seeing wooden crucifixes by the side of the road. Some have ornate shelters over them to keep them dry. There are a lot of these crosses, so if you're a vampire and you fancy coming here to find your roots, I suggest you use the back streets.

It all looks like a film set, which reminds me of how many people think Transylvania (meaning "beyond the woods"[6]) is a fictional place—like Orwell's Oceana or Thomas the Tank Engine's Sodor—but it's very real. The region has a rich and complicated history, going back, as far as written records tell us, to 1075. Yet in the global mind, it's the land of forbidding castles, howling wolves and vampires. I mean, Brussels probably has a rich and complicated history, so does Kazakhstan, but I have no desire to celebrate my 40th there. Or even my 50th. (I've got Salem, Massachusetts pegged for that.)

We reach our village and it ticks my creepy-boxes instantly. The winding, sloping streets are mostly made of dirt, and the creaking Saxon houses have gates just wide enough for a horse and cart to trundle through. Grizzled-looking farmers in tracksuits and woolly hats rock gently on the back of horse-drawn carts, which make the sort of clip-clop sound you hear in old movies. I see the men chewing, and rubbing tired hands across their brows. The fields are stacked with hay. I can smell it in the air, and right next to where we're staying, up on a high hill, I spot a fortified church, bold against the growing night. It's not exactly a castle, but it's brooding enough for me to paint it as Dracula's little holiday home (for when he comes to feed on the villagers).

We arrive and dump our stuff in the bedrooms where the ceilings are low and the floors creak like old witches wailing. I'm chuffed about these little details and get even happier when I open my bedside drawer. There's a wooden crucifix in it, as well as a head of garlic and an Egyptian Ankh: the hieroglyphic symbol that means "life." I guess the owners aren't taking any chances. We nip to the tiny residents-only bar and try out a local brew called Tuica. It's a fast-track-to-tipsy drink, so soon we're all giggling and chatting through our itinerary. Conversation eventually gets to the classic question when meeting new people: *What do you do?* We've got PR execs, managers in software firms, housewives and lawyers. Then someone hands me a pint of local lager and asks, "How about you, Peter? What do *you* do?"

"Well, technically," I take a quick sip, "I'm a church minister."

Ta-dah!

There it is, that look again. Only this time even the horror fans are frowning.

Someone snorts. They don't believe me. "Are you *really?*"

I nod again, because I really *am* ordained. I've done the whole Bible College thing: three years' study and three years' probation. I tick the "Rev" box on government forms, and I've trained and served in various churches. I've conducted weddings, I've buried people (officially and legally you understand—when you say you love the macabre it's always important to clarify that), and I've preached sermons on the Bible and prayed for world peace. These days I spend most of my time writing, so I'm not in charge of a particular congregation, but I still regularly lead church services across the country. I don't tend to wear a dog collar though, so I guess, like my love of horror, my profession isn't so easy to spot for the passer-by.

"And you're *here*?" one of them says. "That's . . . unusual."

This combo *is* hard to compute. I get that. God's into forgiveness, while horror loves vengeance; washing away sins vs bathing in blood; the Holy Ghost vs spooks in the attic. Which means the worlds of faith and fright aren't often mentioned in the same breath. In fact, they're usually treated like those awkward guests you get at parties, who should never be seated together in case they kick off: *Faith, you sit on that table, and, Fright, you are waaaay over in the corner. Don't you* dare *look at each other, and you must never, ever dance . . . at least not together.*

In my line of work, I've seen this clash between faith and fright a fair bit. The vast majority of my Christian colleagues have accepted my interests, but I've also had my share of Christian books thrust into my hand by concerned believers. They say things like: *Horror movies are portals for Satan!* I've heard sermons against the demonic power of heavy metal power chords, and once, when touring England and Germany with a band, we played in a church where the vicar insisted we put the drum kit under the cross, "to sanctify the beat." I've had a friend get shouted at for reading Stephen King's *It* at a Christian festival. And I was recently interviewed by a Christian radio show host, who asked for a prayer before meeting me—just in case I was demonically possessed.

It's this sort of reaction that explains why many horror fans would never dream of setting foot in a church. They assume they'll be told to burn off their Freddy Krueger tattoo or to stop dressing like a vampire. It's the same for those interested in the paranormal. I've met serious ghost hunters and parapsychologists who tried out church, only to reject it because the vicar told them an interest in spooky things was a no-no. A comment that ironically suggests God has no interest in the supernatural. So, yes, in many people's heads, faith and fright don't mix.

Just look at how Christians reacted when the movie *Black Christmas* came out. This 2006 remake about a psychopath chopping up women in a sorority house on Christmas Eve had the Christian Coalition of America spitting out their eggnog. They objected to the content, like the bit when a girl gets scalped with an ice skate. But they especially despised the release date: *Black Christmas* opened in cinemas on the 25th of December. Dimension Films pitched it as "the ultimate slay-ride." Geddit? Christian campaigner and Catholic mother-of-nine Jennifer Giroux saw no place for horror in the holidays. "It's not enough to ignore and omit Christmas," she said in an interview with Reuters, "but now it has to be offended, insulted and desecrated. Our most sacred holiday, actually a holy day, is being assaulted."[7]

Is that what all this morbid culture is? An assault on decency? I personally know a hundred Christians who'd applaud that statement and say: *Too right, Jennifer!* I also know plenty of atheists who have similar concerns about my interest in scary culture. Maybe even *you* might glance up from these pages and think: *Hang on, Reverend. I'm a pretty cool cat and all but . . . an ice skate scalping a woman at Christmas time . . . and you're down with that?*

The assumption is that when I say "Horror rules!", people think I *actually* mean to say "real-life murder is the tops!" or "I genuinely want to eat a Frenchman's brain." Something psychotic, anyway. They see me preaching a sermon and shaking the hands of the congregation afterwards, but then picture me going home to watch people's heads getting hammered in, while I rub my knees like a homicidal pervert. Let me settle this once and for all. I do not rub my knees when I'm watching *anything* on TV. That's weird, and people who do that should be avoided. But do I sometimes curl up on the sofa like a regular person, while watching wince-inducing grisly content? Yep.

Case in point: I watched a slimy horror movie recently called *Contamination*, from 1980. In it, Martian eggs spurt green goo at people, which makes their stomachs explode in bloody slow-motion. There's a scene where scientists test this deadly alien yoke on a white lab rat. It scurries inside its Perspex container while the scientists watch and wait, the camera lingers, the viewer leans in, and then . . . *Boom!*

The white rat turns bright red in an explosion of blood.

It's hokey, it's daft, and it's not a *real* rat, but do I rewind just to see it one more time? I do.

Now bear in mind that I *hate* real violence. Actual uninvited pain-infliction troubles me deeply. Real violence *scares* me. I even suspect it freaks me out more than it does others. I sometimes skim-read newspapers because I hate starting my weekend thinking about some real guy getting stabbed in a nightclub doorway. So, instead, I'll watch a film in which an actor gets stabbed in a nightclub doorway. Or I'll turn off a news report about someone being shot in the head because it makes me sad. Then I'll play a video game shooting zombies in the head.

To me, examples of real horror and their simulated, morbid counterparts are two completely different phenomena. And to love one does not imply love of the other. But not everybody sees it that way. For many, macabre entertainment and evil behaviour are a dangerous, inseparable double act.

On the 14th of December 2012, Adam Lanza shot and killed his mother in Newtown, Connecticut. Then he drove her car to Sandy Hook Elementary School and killed twenty children and six adults. I, along with everybody else, was appalled. In the bleak days that followed, the usual narrative kicked in: scary films and violent video games were the real culprits. His online "kill" count was printed on the *Daily Mail* website (83,000 gaming kills including 22,000 "head shots").[8] Twenty-year-old Lanza was just another in a long line of school shooters supposedly programmed by sick, morbid entertainment. David Duke (the former member of the House of Representatives, conspiracy theorist and former Grand Wizard of the Ku Klux Klan) wrote a blog post four days after the Lanza shooting with the title: "The 20 school-kids at Sandy Hook: Murdered by Hollywood, Not Guns!"[9]

It came as a surprise to some then, when it was discovered that Lanza obsessed over family-oriented video games like *Dance Dance Revolution*. He spent hours in a cinema lobby playing it, perfecting his moves.[10] Yet he *did* have some violent games, too. Also, in an age where all online content gets stored, we can access Lanza's posts on internet forums where he discusses, among other things, centipedes, school shootings and movies.[11] He lists his favourite 25 films and they're almost all obscure horrors from the 70s and 80s. I read the list and recognised almost all of them. In fact, two of my personal favourites are on there: *Let's Scare Jessica to Death* (1971) and *Pin* (1988), two surprisingly touching stories of lonely individuals gradually going mad.

I remember reading through Dr Duke's blog post feeling it all seemed a bit knee-jerk. Yet the idea of horror warping people doesn't go away easily, and there was something about the blog post that I found hard to shake. It wasn't so much what he said but a photograph he used at the top left of the post. A sweet little girl with a cute smile and long blonde hair tumbling over her cardigan. Next to it Duke had written a single line in bold:

Charlotte Bacon, six years old, one of the 20 children murdered at Sandy Hook.

I think of my own daughter who's nine. Even as I balk at the idea of mass censorship, I wonder: it's not unreasonable, is it? For people to worry that all this morbid culture might warp society? That all these tales of vampires, ghosts and killers might just be making us humans homicidal and cruel? No, it's not unreasonable at all, and many assume that the answer is simple—macabre culture is bad for us. Yet what about the voices that we rarely hear? The ones which say that morbid interest is a natural, even *desirable* human behaviour. Aren't they worth considering too?

Tonight in Transylvania, we've eaten well and drunk great beer. We've laughed a lot and now everybody's gone to bed. We need to be up early because we're heading to the Carpathian mountains in the morning. We're taking a cable car up through the snow-thick peaks to sleep in a hotel made of ice. Not exactly Dracula's style, but an added extra I opted to go for because the pictures I've seen look so much like one of my favourite horror movies, John Carpenter's Antarctic classic, *The Thing* (1982). While the others settle into their rooms and brush their reassuringly blunt teeth, my wife snuggles in bed to store up warmth for tomorrow.

She catches my eye: "Aren't you coming to bed?"

"Soon. I just want to pop outside for a minute."

She yawns and turns over, while I creep out the back door. I head down some rickety wooden steps and stand alone under the stars. It's been snowing tonight. The streets are covered in unbroken white. There's an icy breeze in the air which is fingering my hair.

I'm here, in Transylvania, and it looks and feels the part. When we drove in earlier there were stray dogs in the street, padding up and down and circling the lamp posts. Now it's almost midnight and most of them have gone, but I spot a few still wandering near the corner of an old house. They see me and start coming closer, punching silent paw holes in the snow. They look me over as snowflakes fall in slow motion. Then they do something that makes me jump: they start barking high into the night. But I don't leave. I just stand there in the white street, watching *them* watching *me*. I listen to the snap of their barks and look up to the hill where the fortified church glows under a spotlight.

I wait here for a long time because one of the other guests was out here earlier and said they could hear wolves up on those wooded hills, near Dracula's holiday chalet. To hear howling here, as dogs pad around, would freak many people out, but for me it's like seeing a treasured gothic movie scene that I've watched again and again. Only now I've climbed into the screen to stand in it for real. I wait for a long time but don't hear any wolves.

I hear something else instead.

The low growl of a dog.

I flick my head and stare into the darkness. It sounds close. There's a long, unused garden behind the place we're staying in. It's lined with thin trees and upturned rubbish. There are lots of shadows at this time of night.

I frown but decide to follow the growling. I walk past my room where my wife is sleeping and head into the dark garden.

My eyes adjust and I stop dead. Is that a bush quivering in the dark or an animal crouching?

Some common-sense chip in my brain says: *Go back to your room, idiot*, but my instincts are in charge now. I stand there in the dark, hoping for howls, looking for the unseen animal, because now the mood's so Hammer Horror, I half expect the dog to become the Count himself, morphing from the shadows to introduce himself.

Ah, Peter, he'll whisper: *I've been waiting for you for such a long, long time. Welcome.*

I love this feeling.

It's a world away from standing in a pulpit, as I did just two days ago—something I also love doing. Yet as I stand listening to the barking, I get this odd impression that if God really is up there, he's probably smiling because if anyone *gets* me, he does. He gets all of us, after all. And he's been kicking around so long that he knows full well that faith and fright really *do* dance sometimes. And they make the strangest, most beautiful moves, if you take the time to watch.

For a moment, I wonder if I'm just telling myself what I want to believe, and that he may be up there tearing his hair out, flicking the demons away from me like I'm some dumb character in a tablet game.

Nah. He digs this, I decide, and head back to the room.

I creak across the boards and climb into the warm bed, leaning in to kiss Joy goodnight. "How great is this?" I whisper, but she's asleep.

Even as I revel in this moment, questions about *why* I like it try to surface, like the relentless dogs outside, calling out for an answer.

Why *are* millions of humans fascinated with the morbid and macabre? How might I explain it?

When I get back to England, I think to myself, I'll try to address these questions. Maybe that security guard who gave me an odd look deserves an answer. Maybe the people who fear for me need a decent explanation. Maybe my kids need one. And maybe the family of that little girl from David Duke's photo, whose image I struggle to shake—maybe they especially need to know why some humans can be both fascinated with dark things and heartbroken by her death. And, you know what? Maybe *I* need that answer too.

Somewhere deep in my subconscious, an idea is seeding: that tonight is the start of a journey to map this freaky terrain out. To get to the heart of why humans would do something so odd as to love monsters, ghosts, death and gore. And to understand why lying here, in Transylvania, feels like this particular church minister's pilgrimage. This little boy's Holy Land.

That *is* a little weird isn't it?

That journey for those answers is coming. I sense it. It's seeping into the room like a luminous mist.

But tonight . . . Tonight I sleep in the shadows, smiling.

CHAPTER TWO

THEATRE OF BLOOD

I'm in the woods at night, staring at a woman in agony. She's called Mia, and I met her about an hour ago. Even then, I had a feeling she'd end up like this.

Her hand is trapped beneath an upturned car, and she's desperately trying to yank it free, because *another* woman is coming. The maniac. I see her sliding on her belly through the wet grass. Mia sees her too and screams. It's lashing down with red rain.

With a pitiful sob Mia yanks her arm as hard as she can. Skin splits, bones crack. She's free, but the hand stays under the car, severed and twitching. Mia somehow gets to her feet while the slithering woman slides close and pushes herself up. She growls: "I'll feast on your soul."

A chainsaw chugs on the wet grass. Mia stuffs her spurting stump into the handle for ballast. "Feast on this, motherfucker!" She shoves the spinning blade straight into the maniac's forehead.

Boom!

It's a volcano of blood. It's Mount Vesuvius spewing up innards from a body in spasm. This is the moment that makes me stop and look away from the screen. It's not because I'm disgusted (though it is pretty disgusting). It's not that I'm shocked (though the intensity of it is startling). The reason I turn away is because something is happening in the cinema, something that might be considered even more terrifying than the images on the screen.

The audience is cheering.

It's Tuesday night and we're in the Vue Cinema, Leicester Square, London. It's a press screening of the remake of *The Evil Dead*, an 80s horror classic about crazed demons who torment and murder Americans in a secluded cabin. At one point, a woman gets raped by a tree.

The chainsaw hacks through the woman's head for a whole seventeen seconds, which gives me ample time to watch the watchers. The cinema is full of newspaper journalists, magazine columnists and online reviewers. They probably got decent grades at school. They're civilised types. Some are slapping hands across eyes, but most of them are smiling so much I can see their teeth flashing in the light. They laugh into fists. One guy whoops in delight. Ultraviolence flashes onto their eyes and most people look . . . happy.

Back onscreen, Mia is sobbing now, as she finishes her epic sawing. The carnage finally stops, and the cinema fills with applause.

The last time I saw a cinema audience slap their hands together like this was when E.T. made those BMX bikes whiz over the heads of baffled grown-ups. Even now, when I watch that Spielberg moment, I want to hop out of my seat and shout: "YES!" Only right now, it isn't a lovable, big-eyed alien that's pressing everybody's life affirmation buttons. It's this young woman, drenched in blood, towering over a body that jerks and trembles then peels apart. I watch one half of the corpse flop to the left, the other half to the right.

Fffffft.

This film has given us something rare: a sense of communal exhilaration. People feel alive tonight as they spill out into a cold Leicester Square. And it was a chainsaw to the face that did it.

I write a monthly column for a British magazine called *Fortean Times*. Heard of it? Don't worry. It's often lurking on newsagents' shelves, tucked behind the better-known titles. The magazine has explored "The World of Strange Phenomena" since the 1970s, and it's inspired by the work of Charles Hoy Fort (1874–1932). He was an American writer and researcher with a thick, strong-man moustache. Fort worried that scientists were actively suppressing anomalous data, or at least playing it down, so he set out to log and chart "the freaky stuff" in life. The aberrations of human experience. Essentially, that's what the magazine still does today.

Think Fortean and you're under the lights of a UFO or you're seeing the face of a ghost, hovering in a family photo. You're measuring the forest footprints of Bigfoot, or logging which religious statues weep the most milk. In recent months, we've covered the surge in homeless cannibalism, the recent boom in church-sanctioned exorcism, and the growing number of murder cases inspired by the fictional internet meme known as "Slenderman." Yes, we've run jokey sounding articles too, like "50 Shades of Grey: The Hidden History of Alien Sex Pests," but this is scholarly, well-researched investigation into strange and unusual news stories.

I write articles for them, but I'm also the *Fortean Times*'s regular horror guy. Squished into the back pages, I review scary movies each month. It makes sense that the mag covers horror films since their themes are so often Fortean: it's a genre that thrives on the supernatural.

In the light of my *Evil Dead* experience, Fort is making me wonder about the audiences of these films. And the makers too. I saw a few hundred people applaud a chainsaw murder tonight. In the case files of normal human behaviour, might that not be filed under "anomalous data?" Could those seventeen seconds be classed as "unexplained?" Or weird, at least?

I was a kid when the original version of *The Evil Dead* hit video stores. This was the early 1980s and, if you saw the mainstream response to it at the time, the answer was clear: people who enjoyed this sort of film were swivel-eyed sickos. Major newspapers, appalled at the influx of these so-called Video Nasties, led the fight to wipe them from society. In July 1983, the *Daily Mail* ran their famous front page with the call to: "Ban Video Sadism Now!"[1] The government agreed and, for a while, shop owners who stocked the uncut version of the *Evil Dead* had their copies seized under the Obscene Publications Act. They could face prison. Seventy-one other films were also deemed too extreme for the public to see.

In 1993, a second wave of horror-panic hit Britain with the horrendous murder of the toddler, James Bulger. The case was famously (if tenuously) linked to the film *Child's Play 3* (1991), about a homicidal doll called Chucky. The outcry was so great that a few MPs even told Parliament that any film over a PG certificate should be banned on home video—even for adults.[2] This radical solution was never put into motion, but horror films were still routinely cut or even banned outright—because the public (and especially children) needed protection.

But that was the 80s and 90s, which feels like ancient history. Now you just have to wander down the DVD aisle of your local supermarket to see how much we've changed. Today you can buy the original, uncut *Evil Dead* in garden centres. I've seen kind old ladies in charity shops hand it over to shoppers. This 2013 remake (which is way more brutal and *way* bloodier than the original) has had no hint of a ban. The British have relaxed over *Child's Play* too. At one point, it was the most hated film in Britain with the power to re-program children into killers. Yet I just tapped "Chucky" into the Tesco Direct website to find that you can buy a full character costume on there. The website shows a picture of the *Child's Play* killer, waving a blade in the air, alongside the item description:

INCLUDES: Top, Dungarees and Mask

MATERIAL: 100% Polyester

EXCLUDES: Knife and shoes

REVIEWS: Sean, 14. *Great! This product was great value for money. And much better than I was thinking it would be.*

THEME: Disney

SUB THEME: Disney Frozen

Next I scroll through Google and find all the Hello Kitty versions of Chucky, which come as either a toy, a shoulder bag or a box of spicy corn treats. The gore that shocked and appalled society from the early 80s to the late 90s doesn't cause anywhere near the same fury as before.

Yes, some voices do still complain about violence in modern entertainment—but general audiences seem to have become acclimatised to onscreen carnage. Gore-laden TV shows like *Hannibal* and *Game of Thrones* revel in a level of brutality that up until recently wouldn't have even been *legal*. Yet today you'll find them advertised on billboards and supermarket shelves. The TV show *The Walking Dead* features genuinely shocking scenes of violence, like when a zombie bites into a dude's eye and rips it from the socket, with no cutaways. Hasbro now do a *Walking Dead*-themed Monopoly set.

Those folks who love simple answers are going to come to a swift, easy conclusion about all of this: the human race is growing more perverse. It's the whole pigs-in-their-own-filth argument—the dirtier we get, the less we notice how polluted we are. But what if the presence of all this horrific drama isn't a sign that we're getting more uncivilised? What if it's a symptom of the exact opposite? What if this genteel audience cheering at a chainsaw death isn't a display of growing depravity, but is actually a sign of ingenious human progress? I can see your face twitching a little. You look confused. So for this to make sense, we're going to need to go back.

Way back.

Human beings are funny. They believe things that don't reflect the facts. (I'm a Christian, so, believe me, I get that accusation a *lot*.) For instance, it's not hard to spot the idea that: *the world is getting more depraved and violent.* Listen in to coffee shop conversations, leaf through newspapers, or scroll through Facebook feeds. It won't be long until you find the "What the hell is this world coming to?" line buzzing from old and young. Conservative American radio talk-show host Dennis Prager makes this notion crystal clear on his website: "I cannot imagine any thinking person who does not believe the world is getting worse."[3] He argues that the number of refugees and terrorist attacks are growing out of control today, and sees that as slam-dunk evidence that the planet is descending into violent anarchy.

Millions would agree with him, and maybe you do, too, because it's hard *not* to think that the world is getting more screwed up. Our screens are filled with rolling news images of death. We even have video games like *Grand Theft Auto 5*, which lets players mow down pedestrians with their car, or beat people to death with a baseball bat. It seems natural to turn to one another, and shudder, saying: *The human race is growing drunk on blood; the planet is more dangerous than ever.*

Cue wistful looks and a projector flicking up sepia images of the past. Ah, if only we could get back to the 1980s, when PacMan just gobbled up ghosts—he didn't beat their brains out with a bat. Or we reach for the 1960s, when everybody was kissing geraniums and dancing to Leonard Nimoy albums. *That was the time of love*, we say. *No rapey trees there!* Or we go back to the pretty, pastel tones of the 40s and 50s when police didn't hunt for suicide bombers or break into crack dens—they helped you find your lost cat instead. We pine for the years when, even in wartime, our country was one of the good guys. TV shows fuel this nostalgia bubble. We watch *Downtown Abbey* or *Call the Midwife*, where everybody's just so darn lovely, and we think: *Life used to be simple, innocent and safe, back then.*

As we reminisce like this, we might also spot what seems to be a growing darkness in our world. The 20th and 21st centuries brought us the misery of big-hitters like Hitler, Stalin, Pol Pot, and ISIS, and wars in Rwanda, Darfur, Iraq, and so many others. Add these stats to our two World Wars, throw in a dollop of modern terrorism and a dash of school shootings and serial killers, and many agree: the human race is more homicidal than ever. Therefore, this mainstream embrace of violent entertainment might not just reflect this decline, it might even be helping to fuel it.

This whole argument rests on the idea that the world is getting more violent today, but there's a teeny tiny issue. What if it isn't? What if it's actually getting better?

Steven Pinker, an American cognitive scientist, psychologist and a two-time Pulitzer Prize finalist, makes a surprising case in his widely praised 2011 book, *The Better Angels of Our Nature*. He argues that, despite what millions of us think, violence in human societies continues to decline steadily; in other words, the world is getting *safer*.

Pinker contrasts modern societies with the tribal societies of our ancient past and shows that 10,000 years ago life was way more dangerous. With no permanent settlements or any sort of governmental system, your chances of being violently killed were somewhere between 15 and 60 per cent. Compare that with twentieth-century America and Europe, where it's only 1 per cent. If that old tribal death rate had continued, it would have delivered 2 billion violent deaths in the twentieth century, rather than the 100 million we actually saw during that time.[4]

Swedish academic Johan Norberg came to similar conclusions in his book *Progress: Ten Reasons to Look Forward to the Future.* Statistically, he says, we're living in a golden age—particularly in recent years. For example, the European murder rate has halved in the last two decades.[5] Of course, wars and conflicts still continue today—nobody is suggesting they don't—and we were rightly appalled when, for example, 650,000 people were killed in the recent wars in Afghanistan and Iraq. Yet Norberg says we have short memories. We forget that in the 1980s, *2 million* people died in conflicts in those same countries.[6]

Our nostalgia for (or ignorance of) the past has a tendency to cloud our view of its flaws. It's like when people say men were more respectful to women in the 50s because they'd hold the doors open or tip their hats. The door and hat bit might be true, but let's not forget that back then it was also legal for men to beat their wives, and marital rape was only made fully illegal in the UK and Australia as late as 1991, and the US as late as 1993.

We're getting better.

In September 2017, former US President Barack Obama echoed this optimism when he told a gathering of activists, artists and royalty that human society is healthier, more tolerant, better fed, better educated and "demonstrably less violent" than ever before.[7] We're killing each other less.

World trade has helped contribute to this decline in violence. We buy and sell goods and services from across the globe now, so, to be blunt, our fellow humans are usually worth more to us alive than dead.

Consider too how our systems of crime and punishment have changed. In late medieval England, about 80 per cent of executions were for *non-violent* offences. Mainly it for was property crime. These felons were sometimes mutilated too, before execution. Eyes were gouged out and tossed into the crowd; testicles were used as footballs by onlooking kids. The corpses of criminals became toys for the crowd.[8] Some parts of the globe may continue these techniques today, but when the wider world gets wind of it, we tend to call that stuff barbaric.

Have you ever heard a politician or newspaper call for a return to "old-fashioned law and order?" Of course you have, but you know they probably refer to tougher prison sentences, or perhaps the humane execution of the very worst criminals, rather than torture and public executions. Do you honestly think there'd be serious, *majority* support today for hacking off scrotums in the street for low-level crimes? Or publicly hanging eight out of ten shoplifters? I doubt it. That sort of uber-violent response doesn't seem to fit with the majority view anymore. It's no longer *us*. As a species, it's like we're growing out of brutality. Even by the fifteenth century, the English public were finding this sheer scale of torture and execution unpalatable. Particularly as literacy grew and cases could be assessed in more depth.[9]

This new wave of optimism has its critics. Some say Pinker doesn't take into account the billions who could die in a nuclear strike. He's also been accused of not paying enough attention to present-day tribal societies, who still have high homicide rates. Yet the stats for most of the world are persuasive: the punishment we sanction for crimes is way less sadistic than in generations past, and our risk of encountering everyday violence is lower than it used to be. For example, in 1993, 80 out of every 1,000

Americans over the age of twelve was the victim of violent crime. By 2015 this figure had dropped to 19 in every 1,000. It's still too many of course, but that's a decline of almost 77 per cent.[10] If we look at domestic violence, in 1994, out of every 1,000 Americans over the age of twelve, 13 to 14 people became victims of non-fatal domestic violence. By 2013, this figure had dropped to 5 in every 1,000; that's a decline of 64 per cent.[11]

Funnily enough, this is probably the reason why some people are so shocked by modern media violence—we're simply not used to seeing such things in our relatively peaceful present.

This is good news. We should be cracking open the champagne and celebrating our progress—and just because our mainstream entertainment is more morbid than ever shouldn't put a downer on the party. Because what if morbid entertainment is *helping* this decline, by giving us a safe channel for our dark side?

I believe it is, and this channelling of dark desires is a skill we humans have been trying to perfect for millennia.

If you want to approach the puzzle of modern violence attraction with a Charles Fort mindset, you don't want to begin by labelling anything "wrong" or "right." The true Fortean seeker doesn't ask whether a gore-hungry movie crowd is "evil." They ask: *Is this a deviation from the standard, historical experience?* Or in other words, is this behaviour really *anomalous?*

All you have to do is crack open a history book to get your answer. Humans finding value in horrible, morbid spectacle isn't anomalous at all. It's kind of our *thang.* In fact, you even see it at work in that great shaper of human thought: religion. Flick through the major faiths of the world and you'll see the principle of blood sacrifice at work. In Islam, the festival of Eid al-Adha, meaning "Feast of the Sacrifice," can involve the ritual slaughter of animals. In Judaism, believers may not sacrifice animals anymore, but they venerate the scriptures of the Tanakh (sometimes known by Christians as the Old Testament), which contains animal sacrifice. The practice also features in some forms of Hinduism. The idea is that one creature will have its blood spilled on behalf of the rest of the community.

We see this principle at work with the ancient Aztecs, too. They performed human sacrifice. Most of the time, they'd carry out the ritual slaughter at the top of a huge stone pyramid, where the heart of a human was removed and offered to the Sun. Afterwards, they'd roll the corpse down the steps where a priest was waiting at the bottom to cut the head off. After carefully preparing the skull, he'd place it in a skull rack known as a *tzompantli*, which could display thousands of skulls belonging to men, women and children.[12]

Modern folk might gag at this and say morbid ideals should *never* have resonance in religious thought—yet look at what dangles from the necks of millions of people today, both believers and non-believers: a crucifix. Have we forgotten that the cross was the cruellest form of execution the Roman Empire could invent? The weight of the victim would pull the shoulders out of the sockets, putting lethal pressure on the body. The lungs were slowly crushed until the victim could no longer breathe. It's the sort of grotesque, elongated torture that you'd find in a horror movie, and today we have it as a symbol on tea towels and neon signs. Imagine instead that we bought necklaces for our spouses with tiny nooses on them, or electric chairs. You get my point. And that's not even to mention the idea that Christians drink and eat the flesh and blood of Jesus in a communion service.

What I'm saying is that the idea of blood sacrifice is shocking and grotesque, but it holds value in religion. Perhaps this idea resonates with us because it presents us with a tantalising principle: that it might be possible for someone *else* to suffer so that we don't have to.

This idea was so attractive to us humans that you see a similar sacrifice principle developing in the sport of ancient Rome. I've stood in the massive Colosseum in that great city, where, during the height of the Roman Empire, thousands of spectators cheered the slaughter of humans and animals. On one level, the battles took place for sheer spectacle and entertainment. Yet there were other benefits too. These institutionalised examples of cruelty began during a time of relative peace. They were thought to acclimatise soldiers (and citizens) to the horrors of real war. For those taking part, the price was extremely high—they could, and did, lose their lives. Yet the majority of citizens could watch others do battle in a controlled way, without being hurt themselves.

Rather than stoke up violence in the crowd, the horrors of the arena seemed to subdue it. One feature of the spectacle, the gladiator fight, became cathartic and helped the audience purge their own aggression. Most crowd fighting tended to break out at the chariot races instead, which were relatively light on violence.

People were encouraged to attend these events, with poets like Ovid urging women in particular to "go and look at the games, where the sands are sprinkled with crimson."[13] As the popularity of the games grew, the carnage level was turned to the max. Emperor Trajan, for example, celebrated one of his war victories by ordering the public slaughter of 11,000 wild animals. Emperor Commodus even had crescent-shaped arrows made, so that ostriches could be decapitated when the arrows hit. It's said that the birds kept on running for a while after they lost their heads. Audiences loved it.[14]

Church leaders criticised the games as sick and debased, but even *they* sometimes struggled to resists the charms of the ring. Saint Augustine writes of his young disciple Alypius, saying that he would often visit the amphitheatre, transfixed:

> Seeing the blood he drank deep of the savagery. He did not turn away but fixed his eyes upon the sight. He drank in all the frenzy, with no thought of what had happened to him, revelled in the wickedness of the contest and was drunk with lust for blood.[15]

In time, Alypius broke his addiction to the games and became a bishop, but there were millions of others who struggled to leave the blood and gore behind. Even today, thousands of people *still* flock to the Colosseum to hear stories of the horrors that went on there.

Augustine might have been shocked at the savagery of the games, but he would have had to accept that his most sacred text, the Bible, contains shocking moments of horror too. The New Testament book of Revelation is a torture-gore-fest which features people partying over rotting corpses, a woman getting drunk on the blood of Christians, and a demonic dragon crouching at the legs of a pregnant woman, eagerly waiting to devour her newborn baby. Secular author Will Self is known for his provocative novels, but even he describes the book of Revelation as a "sick text . . . a portentous horror film."[16]

Our history is littered with examples of us making space for the morbid. Like the Bayeux Tapestry which kids study at school. This colourful, 70-metre-long embroidery depicts the Norman Conquest of England in 1066, and it's filled with soldiers having their guts cut out or their heads split in two. You'd think we would want to forget this stuff—but we don't. We hang it on a wall to help us remember. Or what about the European miracle plays of the Middle Ages? These vivid re-creations of the fates of the martyrs were a huge hit with audiences, and they pulled no punches.

In 1536, for example, the people of Bourges performed an elaborate shock-show called *The Mystery of the Holy Acts of the Apostles*. The performers took the depiction of Christian martyrdom so seriously that, for the decapitation of Simon of Magus, they switched the actor with a live sheep, who provided the onstage blood.[17]

In 1583, Pope Gregory XIII tried to capture the grisly deaths of the martyrs forever, by commissioning a series of frescoes about them. Faith heroes who were boiled alive or bled to death while being crushed by stone could now be pondered for hours.[18] Many other religious leaders did the same in following years. Just walk through the churches of Rome and you'll see graphic paintings of martyrs stretched by the rack, flayed alive or—in the case of *Martyrdom of St Simon the Zealot* by Pomarancio— sawn in two. You can see the guy's exposed brain.

Or just cast your eye over our most distinguished works of literature—many of them are dripping with gore. If you're at a trendy dinner party, just mention you've been reading Homer's *The Iliad*. People will look at you like you're the cleverest, most cultured person in the room. What they might not realise is that this poem, written in circa 750 BC, is filled with tongues being torn out and fellas getting stabbed in the nuts. In one gratuitous moment, a Greek man, Idomeneus, rams a bronze spear into the mouth of a Trojan called Erymas, which smashes his teeth, shatters bone and fills his eyes and nostrils with spurting blood.[19]

If that scene were in a computer game, some would call it sick exploitation. Yet *The Iliad* is a treasured work in Western culture, violent death and all.

What about Shakespeare? He's the calling card of sophistication, but I'm hardly the only one to have been horrified by *Titus Andronicus*, in which a woman is raped, then has her hands chopped off and her tongue cut out. Later on, the culprits get dismembered and baked in a pie, which gets fed to the rape victim's mum. I mean, come on. This stuff is *brutal*, and the classics are filled with it: *Beowulf, Crime and Punishment, The Divine Comedy*. All require a strong stomach.

These are the stories that have lasted in our collective memory . . . but *why?* The American literary critic Leslie Fiedler says they endure not in *spite* of these horrible plot-points but precisely *because* of them, because their presence helps us to explore our potential savagery in safe ways. Better to trap murder in a novel or theatrical re-enactment, than to let it run rampant in the streets.[20]

Skip to the nineteenth century, in which Dime Novels and Penny Dreadfuls thrilled readers in the UK and US, with hideously graphic tales like that of Sawney Bean and his incestuous family of cannibals (which was presented as a true story). They wound up getting their penises cut off and thrown into a fire while the Bean women were forced to watch, before being burned to death themselves. At the Grand Guignol theatre of nineteenth-century Paris, audiences paid to see fake eyes scooped out and faces pressed into red-hot stoves.[21] It finally closed doors in 1962, which wasn't a sign of waning morbid appetite. It's just that, by then, people were getting their gore fix from elsewhere, like Hammer Movies in the cinema.

I share these little horrible homilies to make a simple point. The cinema audience that cheered at the chainsaw death are *not* anomalies. Not historically speaking. We've always sought safe ways to experience horror and violence. From scary campfire stories and grisly "games" in gladiatorial arenas, to Gothic novels and knuckle-biting cinema experiences, the voluntary consumption of scary, distressing or violent material is one of culture's great constants. We love stories of death in which *we* don't have to die.

The best part is that we've invented ingenious ways to scratch our itch for violence without actually sacrificing humans or shedding real blood.

It might seem natural to say that cheering at a big-screen chainsaw death is a sign of modern depravity—but compared to the ancient world, where people would cheer *real* faces being hacked? I'd call that progress.

Yet this still begs a simple question.

Why do we like the morbid in the first place? Why are human beings drawn to it at all?

To answer that, we need to dive into the brain.

CHAPTER THREE

WIRED FOR FRIGHT

They've strapped me to a chair in a wood-panelled room. Electrodes are taped to my forearms and the wires trail across the floor. They lead from me to a man called Dee. He's wearing a wide-brimmed black hat and eye-liner, and is sitting next to a box of dials. He's grinning. There are three other victims with me, all strapped to their chairs with leather belts, like I am. We're about to take a quiz, and if any of us gets the answers wrong, that person gets an electric shock. Each round, they'll turn up the inten-sity dial.

We're in a stunning thirteenth-century manor house, surrounded by a sprawling 2,000-acre estate. This isn't some freaky S&M weekend, by the way. Honest, it's not. I'm taking part in a BBC documentary about fear. It's called *Meet The Humans*, and so far we've been forced to watch films of rotting animals and insect hordes. We've been made to sit in a candlelit bathroom while a Victorian ghost stared at us through a mirror. We've been locked in a room while the fire alarms went off and the place filled with smoke. A creepy old woman took us into the graveyard by moonlight and told us tales of the dead. Then she grunted and ran off into the woods before we heard massive growls coming from the trees. In between takes, we've been served crisps and dips from a one-eyed butler in an ornate room of stuffed animals, weapons and insects. While all this happens, TV medical celebrity Dr Michael Mosley has been monitoring our vital signs in a hidden room.

I'm having a blast.

Strapped to the electric chairs we hold three paddles each—with the letters A, B and C on them. We lift them in response to multiple-choice questions.

"What was the real name of Sweeney Todd?"

I pick Benjamin Barker, which turns out to be right. Half of the participants get it wrong and Dee shrugs. He flicks the switch. They squeal and jerk in their chairs, teeth clenched. The guy next to me spasms, shouts "Shit!" and drops his paddle on the floor. Dee keeps rattling through the questions, and people keep getting zapped . . . but not me. I seem to be getting them all right. Normally I'd be pleased at this, but I notice that when the others scream, it's quickly followed by their laughter. So, for the final five questions I try a new tactic. I try my hardest to pick the *wrong* answer.

It works.

"You *want* to be shocked?" Dee says, frowning, noticing my change in tactic.

"Yep," I brace myself. "Do it."

"Well," he lifts his finger over the switch, "who am I to argue with a man of the cloth?"

Dee blasts me with an electric shock, and I spasm in the chair.

He does this multiple times, each with increasing intensity. My heart rate goes through the roof. The build-up is the scary part, waiting for the switch to click and then the sharp, toe-clenching pain. That and the panic that I might wet my pants on national TV. But I'm laughing too. When it's done, they unstrap us and, thankfully, I still have a dry crotch. We head to the next room for dinner and I just keep thinking: *Phew, that was a lucky escape. Thank heavens I started to get them wrong.*

Otherwise I'd have missed out on fear.

A doctor pushed my baby daughter over once. On purpose. She wasn't even a few hours old but her life was already filled with hassle. Her nine-month stint in the liquid spa resort was over. She now had stark electric light and the new phenomenon of unmuffled sound. Little wonder that she screamed and curled into a ball, while giant, leering aliens boomed out their terrifying war cries of "Koochy-Koo!" It can't have helped when a nurse—at the *precise* moment she was born—announced "Is everyone okay with Abba?" and the delivery room exploded with the sounds of "Knowing Me, Knowing You." That wasn't in the birth plan, by the way. An important point.

So my daughter's first few hours were intense enough, but later on a doctor came to examine her. He wanted to see if she was semi-human, I guess. Check the scalp for 666 tattoos. Scan for Illuminati chips. The usual stuff. But as he was checking her over he did something totally bizarre that I hadn't been expecting. He sat her up, settled her into a sitting position and smiled like he was going to tell her a cute story. Then, knowing full well that she had neither the physical strength nor psychological know-how to stay sitting up, he took his arms away and let her drop backwards like a little sack of potatoes.

Timber!

They call them micro-expressions: faces that display a brain full of information in one split second. Right in that moment her infant brain was screaming: *Craaaap!* She keeled backwards, arched her spine and jerked her arms out. Thankfully the doctor grabbed her at the (very) last minute, set her down on her back and nodded, with a pleased look on his face. He scribbled something on his notepad while she curled up in a ball, like she was waiting for the womb to snap back into place and take her home. When it didn't, she filled the room with chilling banshee screams.

"Er . . ." I nodded at his doodling pen, "Why did you just do that?"

"Moro reflex," he tapped out a full stop. "Some people call it the startle response."

I learned later that this comes from the Austrian paediatrician Ernst Moro, who was famous for a bunch of baby-related breakthroughs. He coined the phrase "first trimester," for example, and in 1908 he invented Professor Moro's Carrot Soup, which cut infant deaths related to diarrhoea by almost 50 per cent. But perhaps his most famous contribution to science is the understanding of the Moro reflex, which proves that human beings have at least one inbuilt, unlearned fear. Honk an industrial air horn directly into a baby's face (actually, don't) or sit them up and let 'em drop, and you'll see instant, panicked terror, followed by a spasm of arms and legs. Nobody teaches us that dance move. *Sesame Street* episodes on this are *not* required. This fear button is hardwired into our system.

I asked the doctor, "What if she hadn't freaked out?" I had a proud image of her falling back, palms together, super-chilled and brave.

"That'd be bad if she hadn't reacted. She could have a motor-system disorder, or her central nervous system might not be functioning right," he smiled. "But she *did* freak out, so that's good. She's normal."

Normal.

Remember that, reader. Being scared by certain things is *normal*.

In fact, more than that, it's vital. Evolutionary theorists reckon we evolved the Moro reflex to help infants stay close to their protectors. Drop a baby and it automatically reaches for an arm to grab. It's a kind of automatic, pre-loaded wisdom software. Without this reflex, we'd crash to the floor and break the spine we never knew we had. The presence of this fear from birth, is an excellent advantage.

Imagine if we *didn't* have it. How long would we have lasted? Picture our ancestors acting all chill when a deadly animal leapt out to attack. They'd look brave and cool for a few seconds—*Hey, panther friend, whatcha knowin?* But they'd look remarkably less suave two seconds later when they lacked a throat. See, it's the *Holy crap, RUN!* response that ensured our species didn't plummet down the food chain. In other words, we felt the fear and we embraced it as a tool. Fear helped us survive.

Singers may well croon into mics, yearning for a world without fear, but we must never let their dream become *fully* true. And if some clever dick invents a pill that removes all fear from modern humans, we *must* ban it. A world without fear may sound nice, and prompt clapping in political speeches (*We're gonna stamp out Project Fear!*), but in practice, fearless humans would skip onto the motorway during rush hour, and when a gunman started shooting in the shopping mall, we'd keep on eating our burritos and wink at him, even as he raised the barrel.

Constant bravery is not a good idea. Not at all.

Just ask the few hundred people in the world who don't feel fear, because they *can't*. Like the 44-year-old mother of three, referred to as SM, who suffers from Urbach–Wiethe disease.[1] This is a condition that destroys the amygdala, the almond shaped structure in the brain which some scientists see as the "hub in the wheel of fear."[2] Without this hub, SM's fear wheel can't turn, so she's as chilled as they come. She was held up at knifepoint once, but didn't call the police because it was no big deal to her. Her attacker jabbed the blade at her throat and said he was going to cut her. She simply said: "Go ahead and cut me." Her first husband almost beat her to death, but she takes that memory in her stride because it lacks any trauma. Neuroscientist Antonio Damasio, who studies Urbach–Wiethe disease, explained: "If you have no fear, more terrible

43

things will happen to you, but you don't personally experience them as terrible."[3] In other words, banishing fear means you notice danger *less*, which means you experience danger *more*.

Of course, I'm not suggesting we should live in *constant* fear. Bravery and courage are desirable, honourable goals. But as a million self-help gurus will tell you: courage isn't the absence of fear, it's acting in the face of it. We need it so that we know when to stand our ground and fight . . . but also when to run screaming with our arms flailing. Our ancestors chose to embrace the klaxon of fear, and it's one of the best choices they ever made.

In fact, our fears are *so* ingrained, the things you flinch at might just be little memory-blasts of your ancestors' sensible freak outs. Consider how many of us are petrified by spiders: it's the world's most common phobia. Australians have to cope with some of the deadliest spiders in the world—so it makes sense for them to be cautious.[4] Yet what about the millions of us who have small, harmless spiders in our houses? Why do we still break into a skittish dance at the sight of them? Partly it's nurture: we've seen adults freak out at spiders, so we learn to do that too. But the fear may well be deeper than that.

According to psychologist Joshua New, deadly spiders were well established in Africa long before humans turned up. For millions of years, our ancestors shared the same space with genuinely dangerous beasts.[5] We learned that the bite of the spiders, such as the black widow, could leave us paralysed for weeks or even kill us. Handily, our brains logged this and in response we kept our distance. Millions of years later, that reasonable memory lives on whenever you spasm at a spider crawling out of your plughole.

When Charles Darwin visited the London Zoological Gardens, he put his face up-close to a thick plate of glass, the only barrier between him and a puff adder. This hissing, venomous snake is thought to be responsible for more deaths in Africa than the black mamba. Darwin faced off with this killer, "with the firm determination of not starting back if the snake struck at me." But Darwin couldn't be a badass even if he'd wanted to. "As soon as the blow was struck my resolution went for nothing and I jumped a yard or two backwards with astonishing rapidity. My will and reason were powerless against the imagination of a danger which had never been experienced."[6]

So this fear response is an ingrained advantage. It's kept us alive for millions of years, and yet something very important has changed, particularly in the West. These days, most of us don't hear the padding of panther feet behind us. Millions of us have sturdy houses we can lock securely. We rarely worry about psychotic tribesmen from the next village. Spiders may well lurk inside those houses, but they're *not* poisonous on the whole. We know that, deep down.

In other words, modern life is surprisingly *unscary*, compared to that of our ancestors. Wars happen, but—for most readers of this book— mainly in other countries. People get murdered and disasters ruin lives, sure, but the majority of us have the good fortune to avoid being victims. Undoubtedly, the world continues to hold its horrors, especially if illness strikes close to home, but our day-to-day fears aren't genuinely deadly. For some of us, our biggest concerns may be whether the hotel has Wi-Fi or whether we look podgy in our swimming shorts.

The relative safety of modern society is obviously a great thing. I love the fact that sabre-toothed tigers don't lurk behind my Nissan every morning. But the side effect of all this safety is that our amygdala doesn't get to flex its fear response much. Perhaps the reason we tell one another scary stories or watch horrifying movies is because the ghosts of our ancestors keep sending us messages, bobbing down the ancient streams of our DNA. *Dear future offspring*, these messages say. *Don't lose fear—you need it. You need to keep that hub greased, ready to spin the wheel of fright that has kept us alive this long. Lose it, and you're history. TTFN.*

Author Stephen King has long been stimulating the amygdalae of millions of modern humans, and he knows the instructive value in it. When he was younger, he was both frightened and fascinated by the 1950s serial killer Charlie Starkweather. He even kept a scrapbook of his crimes. It's the kind of behaviour that'll get a guy funny looks, but in a newspaper interview in 2000 he explained why.

"Well," King said, "it was never like 'Yeah go, Charlie, kill some more.' It was more like 'Charlie, if I ever see anyone like you, I'll be able to get the hell away.' "[7]

You see, there's a reasonableness to this interest in scary things. A sort of dark wisdom. We pass a car crash on the motorway, and decency tells us to look away, but survival says: *Stare and learn*. See what they did wrong, so you can avoid it yourself. Call it ghoulish or creepy, but rubbernecking at motorway accidents is one of the world's most predictive behaviours. In 2012, the UK Department of Transport invested £2.3 million into buying 105 large "incident screens" to block car crashes off from passing motorists. It wasn't to protect them from horrific sights. It was to stop the traffic clogging up when they all slowed down to look.

And we *do* look, because something primordial says the data is useful. If we ever see a corpse in the road, our speedy journey suddenly feels less important. We slow down. We don't feel like texting at the wheel anymore. The horror shocks us into wisdom, and we even get evangelical about it—we want to share the fear with others. Shaken by the sight, it's one of the first things we tell our friends and family when we finally make it home. We throw our keys on the table and slump into a chair, asking for a stiff drink while we tremble.

I saw something truly horrible today . . . let me tell you about it.

Some advice. Don't type "Crush Videos" into Google.

Of course, you're going to do that now I've mentioned it. In fact, you've probably tossed this book aside in giddy abandon and are already tapping away. But for the record, when you come back and pick me up again and you feel all crappy inside, know that I *did* tell you not to do it.

I read about crush videos during my research for this book. I heard that it was some sort of morbid fetish that was growing in popularity. I looked it up on the internet to figure out what was so morbid about it. To be honest, my guard was down because the word "crush" made me think it would be videos of obese ladies sitting on men's faces. I'm not sure why that was my first thought, but I think I saw a news report about it once. I think it was in Japan. Men were paying hefty naked women to use their heads as chairs, and I figured it'd be kind of funny to see that. I thought the morbid part might be the suffocation risk. I was wrong.

First, the crush video I watched had no big women in it. All I saw were the bare legs of three women standing shoeless and sockless, and in the middle of the floor was a white and grey puppy. It's kind of immediate, that sense of dread you get. When your brain unhooks the word "crush" from a big woman and a Japanese businessman, and applies it to women and a tiny dog. And all the time you wonder, why aren't they showing their faces? Why are they protecting their identity? They started prodding and pushing the dog around with their bare toes, playfully at first, then more forcefully.

My hand hovered over the escape button.

They gave the dog a little kick. And then one raised a foot.

"Oh . . ." I clenched my teeth.

One of them stood on the dog's neck, with both feet. Another girl did the same on the body.

Crush.

I clicked it off quickly and exhaled a jittery breath, shocked at what horrors await, a mere two mouse clicks away.

Crush videos turn out to be a sexual fetish, in which people get off on seeing objects squashed underfoot. Apparently, there's the Soft Crush crowd. They like seeing food and balloons being squished. Unless you're into balloon rights, that's not such a big deal, but the "soft" label also covers the crushing of small insects, spiders and snails. According to the website Motherboard, it'll cost you $6 to buy a "sexy" clip of a beetle being crushed through bare toes.[8] Cheaper than a Barry White album, I guess.

Then there's the Hard Crush crew, who find vertebrates more alluring. They like to see birds, dogs, cats and reptiles die. The legality of these animal snuff movies varies, depending on where you live. In the UK, hard crush videos are illegal, but insect crushing is allowed, which is sadly consistent with the way we humans think. Life is often valued in levels of cuteness, or attractiveness.

At a dinner party, I once asked the guests if, for an all-expenses-paid trip around the world, they'd pull the wings off a butterfly. (Don't judge me—it was a question in an old psychology book I had.) Most were horrified. They said no and got back to their wine. So, I asked if they'd step on a cockroach for the same deal and people looked at the floor and said, "Yeah, okay. Maybe." Though one guy did have alternative answer— when I asked him if he'd pull the wings of a butterfly off, his response was immediate. "All expenses paid? Around the world? I'd pull the wings off a frickin' *bird* for that."

So the legality of the crush movement has a certain hierarchy of beauty—insect death is less offensive than birds, it seems. Though in China it's a bit more equal across the board. They have no animal cruelty laws, so you can crush kittens until the cows come home. Then presumably, you can crush the cows too.

Who are these people who get a buzz from seeing other creatures die in front of them? For many in the crush movement, the thrill is a sexual one, and perhaps we could dismiss it with a thump on the pulpit and a loud shout of the word: *PERVERTS!* The sooner we get that stuff shut down, the sooner we can get back to watching cute dog movies while eating a factory-farmed chicken burger after crushing an irritating moth into oblivion with our leather shoe.

Who are we kidding? While crush videos leave us in a shivery sort of disgust—which is right and proper—let's not act as if we're devoid of cruelty ourselves. Stamping on dogs is an extremely morbid act (which, in case you were getting worried, I think *should* be banned), but the impulse that lies behind it—to dominate what we perceive as a vulnerable, less powerful being—is more widespread than we like to admit. Just think about reality TV, and in particular talent shows. The humiliation and obliteration of fellow humans is the source of many of our TV hits today. Okay, it's not nearly as bad as stepping on a dog, but the psychology behind it is strangely similar. We can't seem to stop watching people who can't sing being reduced to quivering sobs by powerful judges.

Crush.

These talent shows, along with puppy stamping, are another example of the dominance games we humans like to play. From gladiatorial sports to political elections, there's this streak in us that likes to categorise everybody into winners or losers, predators or prey. And, shock horror, the role of the winner or predator tends to be the more attractive to us.

In fact, we're so desperate for dominance, we even draw strength when our *friends* fall on their faces. "It's not enough to have achieved personal success," Somerset Maugham once said. "One's best friend must also have failed." In isolation, this sounds cruel. I mean, who chuckles when their friends screw up, get demoted at work, or can't afford that huge house they were banging on about all summer? But in practice, we know that

Maugham's words have a ring of truth. School reunions, slimming classes, Facebook walls—they're filled with people sharing their success. But they're also prime hunting grounds for seeking out others' *failure*. Because when others fall, we can place ourselves higher in the pecking order, and none of us wants to be at the bottom.

What if the reason our culture is full of art and stories depicting cruel murder, humiliation and violence is not *just* because we're exercising our vital fear muscles but because we're incredibly insecure, and one of the only ways we can feel safe and strong is to see others become the very opposite?

When an animal hunts, it's in a state of high arousal. Just check out chimpanzees tracking down a meal of monkeys. They go *berserk*. The forest fills with screams and shrieks as they puff themselves out to exaggerate their body size. They grab tree branches and shake them like crazy, totally psyched for the hunt. Then, when they chase the monkeys down, they tear those poor little fellas apart before eating them. It's relentless. Scary, to be honest. There's a lot of blood. And sometimes, when resources are threatened, chimps will even turn on each other. A 2014 study examined chimp-on-chimp homicide in the wild. The results challenged the idea that they were only aggressive towards one another as a response to human interference. The study suggested a more basic reason. In regions of limited resources, chimps killing other chimps came naturally to them.[9]

Funnily enough, when I first planned this book, I had this grand idea of watching *King Kong* with a chimpanzee on my lap. We'd eat popcorn together, I thought, and I'd write down what he made of what is surely a simian's favourite horror film. It'd be my clever segue into this very chapter, and it'd make for a cool picture on my Twitter feed. Me and chimp holding a remote together: *Another day at the office, Lol.* But the scientists and zoo-keeper I suggested it to were completely horrified. They said I was an idiot, and told me I'd get my face ripped off. So, I dropped the idea. Sorry.

What I'm saying is that chimps, along with a great many predators, are occasionally *enthusiastic* about violence and cruelty. There's an academic paper on this called "Cruelty's Rewards: The Gratifications of Perpetrators and Spectators."[10] In it, psychologist Victor Nell argues that throughout the animal kingdom, predators are energised by all aspects of the hunt. When the prey runs away, or shows pain, the predator is filled with strength and energy. Yet one of the most *powerful* triggers of gratification is the sight of blood. When the hunter, let's say a lion, sees red gushing from the gazelle, it's a glorious welcome sign, a quick indicator that death is coming, not for the lion but for the other guy. The chase will soon be over, and the lion and its family will be fed. Blood is a key symbol that tells the creature it's winning. It's a sought-after sight.

We've seen so far that our culture continues to value violent stories and death-tinged entertainment, that when we see a character die it can shock or move us, but it offers a weird, primordial reassurance too. It's the people onscreen who die, while *we* keep living. It's not like we enjoy them dying so much as we rejoice that we're still standing. This lights up an old emotional circuit in our head. *We survived!*

Perhaps that's why many horror fans feel super pumped after watching an extremely violent film. It's empowering because we feel the fear, but we also know we can switch off or walk out of the theatre. This safe-scare combo has proven irresistible to us. Psychologist Jeffrey Kottler says that watching violent entertainment can raise testosterone and adrenalin levels. This appeals to us because we're on a constant quest for stimuli, especially considering our relatively safe lives. The sheer novelty of seeing, let's say, a zombie's head explode helps to feed our neurological and endocrine systems with safe excitement, as well as a reassurance that *we're* alive.[11]

This sense of relief leads to positive emotional states—which is one of the unexpected attractions of morbid entertainment. I asked people to describe how they felt after watching films filled with scares and bloody death. Andy, a shipping clerk and horror festival director said, "After violent films I often feel exhilarated and strangely energised, almost like having a big hit of caffeine." Another said he leaves a horror movie like he's "riding out on a chemical high, and leaving the fictional world slightly giddy and usually smiling and chatty." Actually, several respondents said they found themselves smiling after a scary, violent movie. They felt *pleased*.

Critics of morbid culture are going to swing in right there and say: *Aha! I knew it. You sickos get off on death.* Well, maybe the creepy crush video crowd do, but your general horror movie fan is doing something a little more complicated. They aren't experiencing pleasure constantly throughout a horror movie. For most horror fans, they have as much shock and revulsion as anybody else. Andy described a recent viewing experience in which: "for the first hour I had a knot in my stomach and felt physically ill. Yet by the end I was light-headed and felt almost on another level."

What's going on here? How can a genuinely horrible experience end up creating positive feelings?

Clues might lie in a recent study by researchers at the University of Oslo, who compared the MRI scans of people experiencing different levels of pain. These were created by applying various levels of heat to their arms. Moderate pain was registered as unwelcome. Yet after intense pain was applied, the moderate pain was seen as pleasurable. The researchers concluded that: "A sense of relief can be powerful enough to turn such an obviously negative experience as pain into a sensation that is comforting or even enjoyable."[12]

We see a related principle in our everyday lives. Remember that terrible family holiday you went on, when everything went wrong? The car broke down and the insect-infested hotel stank of stale urine. Your kid puked on your suitcase and you all had to stand in the rain at 3am, when the fire alarm went off for no reason. At the time, those experiences are miserable and you're relieved when they're over. A month later, you're at a dinner party, and everybody's sharing their holiday stories: *We had a marvellous time in the Algarve* or *Austria is stunning at this time of year.* Then you tell them the tale of the holiday from hell. It's the funniest, most enjoyable tale in the room. Now you don't leave out *any* of the nasty bits; you keep them in. You might even exaggerate how bad they were, because in the retelling, your atrocious experiences are transformed into the most interesting, amusing and pleasurable details of all.

Morbid entertainment can be, therefore, a complicated mix of negative and positive feelings. We feel shock and empathy for onscreen victims but also relief and exhilaration that it's not us up there. That part about empathy is important and might explain the initially baffling patterns in audiences for scary movies. Kottler says that fans of violent films "seem to match the dominant victims, that is, young women tend to frequent slasher films in which their counterparts are the ones who are slaughtered; teenagers prefer films like *Scream* in which their age group is a target for killers; young men go to see war movies in which people who look like them are the ones who are killed."[13]

We hunger for the most relevant information. Therefore, material that has "people like us" in peril feels like the most instructive of all. Perhaps that's why many Westerners appear more shocked (and interested) when disasters hit California or London than in Pakistan or Malaysia. I used to think this was pure racism or selfishness—a lack of empathy for people we might label as different. This is probably true to some extent. But it's also linked to having brains that value efficiency.

When we see someone of our own "tribe" suffer (whether that be people of a similar ethnic, religious or cultural background to us) it disturbs us more than any other. Their deaths also hold the most relevant information to us. We ponder these things to avoid the same fate, to remind ourselves of our good fortune in still being alive, or perhaps, because we simply care about these people, and so our being drawn to their tragedy is our way of sharing in their suffering.

We're not supposed to respect violence. That's a given. Ask any teacher, politician or priest. They'll tell you that violence is dysfunctional and morally repugnant.

I agree. Remember I *hate* real-life violence. I wouldn't call myself an all-out pacifist (if you tried to shoot my family, I'd probably hit you with a shovel), but I do rejoice that by and large we've managed to make physical conflict an unnecessary element of day-to-day life. When the waitress brings us the wrong dessert, we might complain or tap out our bile on Trip Advisor later that night. But what we don't tend to do these days is thrust a fork in her eye.

We've conquered the natural world; secured our food and built sturdy shelters; we've subdued the animals and cordoned off our countries and land. Very few of us genuinely want to kill our fellow humans anymore. This is good. I'm all for it. We've created a world in which *The New York Times* columnist Charles M. Blow can write articles titled "Violence is Never the Answer," and we nod sagely and say: *Quite right, Charlie, it never is.*

But that's not to say it never *was*.

When our distant ancestors ran squealing from the stronger animals, they used fear as a tool. But that didn't stop them working out ways they might come back the next night and gut those suckas. They embraced the wisdom of fear, but they recognised the power of aggression too. It was a nifty solution for many of life's problems, from taking the resources of others to defending our homes and deterring rivals from coming back and killing us.

I'm not suggesting that we return to a world with those ideas, but it would be foolish to forget that violence has been *functional* in our history. Brute force has determined which nations survive and what land they keep. It has turfed some people from their land and kept others in power over others. And it has kept different kinds of violence at bay. Political science professor Benjamin Ginsberg puts it this way: "The meek, in short, have not inherited very much of the earth. Indeed, the West's global dominance for most of the past millennium is in large part a function of its capacity for violence."[14]

Like it or not, violence has sometimes worked in our favour, even in very recent times, and even though modern societies are getting better at eradicating the need for it, our capacity for seeing aggression as a potential solution still echoes in our subconscious. And they are loud echoes, at that. Even in our polite society, violence is sometimes lurking, just under the hood of respectability.

Ever had somebody cut you up on the motorway, and you just want to scream or slam your car into them? Ever had your kid cry and wail so horribly loudly that you've put them into the buggy a little more forcefully than your conscience allows? Ever punched an inanimate object, or swore at it? I was never a fighter as a kid, but I did have a ZX Spectrum 48K home computer that refused to load a game once. I was desperate to play *3D Ant Attack*. Who wouldn't be? Yet after multiple tries to load the cassette, my mind heard the squeal of the loading tone and it unlocked my primordial violent personality. I shouted "Damnit!" and slammed my fist into the keyboard, screwing up the rubber "H" key. I must have been a proper weakling since it still switched on afterwards. Yet despite the feebleness, according to my brain, I was out for blood. Even if, in this case, all I would have got would have been a bunch of wires.

I asked various people if they ever had violent thoughts. One woman, who works as a literary agent, told me: "If I see a cyclist not stopping at a Zebra crossing to let someone cross, I might fantasise about kicking them off the bike." She admitted she also thought about hurting her mum sometimes. On her phobia of crowds, she said: "I fear being squished and trampled upon and usually fantasise about violence when I'm scared or in danger." She never acts these things out, but the thoughts still pop into her mind from time to time.

The Apostle Paul, one of the key leaders of the early Christian church, said that such fantasies are indicative of our "sinful nature," while Jung called it "the Shadow." It's the part of us responsible for the wild thoughts of aggression, the melancholic swings towards self-destruction.

I've spoken to mentally balanced, normal people who wait on a Tube station platform, imagining how easy it would be to throw themselves onto the tracks. I've also had people admit that their bored brain sometimes imagines pushing someone *else* onto the tracks, too. Neither the Apostle Paul nor Jung is suggesting we let the Shadow run riot in the real world (nor am I) because we embrace the violence-is-not-the-answer rhetoric. Yet at the same time, people create fantasy worlds in which it really *is* the answer. The real trick is knowing the difference.

Some find this compromise distasteful, and argue that the real solution is to ignore the shadow self completely. The secret to peace and harmony, they argue, is to develop societies that leave no space for morbid, violent culture.

Would removing our outlets for the macabre really be a good idea?

In 1980, anthropologist Bruce Knauft began studying a remote New Guinea tribe called the Gebusi. They appeared to have impressive moral standards, at first. The men were self-effacing and never opposed or bullied other men. They settled issues by consensus not competition. Anger was seen as a negative, individualistic emotion. Kids were never punished; initiation rites were pain-free; the skin was never cut for ritual purposes. Violent stories and aggressive drama were forbidden forms of entertainment.[15]

Sounds like a haven of safety, right? Wrong.

The Gebusi tribe have the highest homicide rate of any known culture. Psychologist Jeffrey Kottler says the problem is that they have "no alternative outlets for aggression such as violent entertainment. In spite of their goal of eliminating physical aggression within their culture, the behaviour has just gone underground."[16] Other groups, like the !Kung Bushmen of Southern Africa and the Semai of the Malay Peninsula, have a similar aversion to confrontation in social life—and, relative to their population size, both also have high homicide rates. These tribes hide violence and act as if aggression doesn't exist. Yet without an outlet, it can explode at shocking levels.

The Gebusi tribe with its smiley surface culture and frequent wild killings remind us that the shadow self tends to surface in one way or another. Better to acknowledge it on our own safe terms, before it explodes. Morbid, even *violent*, cultural expressions can give humans the space to ponder our fears and our potential for violence—our shadow side. Acknowledging our dark and light sides is, according to Jung, the key to self-awareness and mental balance.

"To confront a person with his shadow is to show him his own light," he says. "Once one has experienced a few times what it is like to stand judgingly between the opposites, one begins to understand what is meant by the self. Anyone who perceives his shadow and his light simultaneously sees himself from two sides and thus gets in the middle."[17]

Our culture loves to stand in the middle. We have a compulsion to consider the two sides of our nature, the good *and* the bad. It's why, in a world where we deplore real-life violence, we can still honour the violent warrior heroes in our stories, who prove their worth by striking down the baddies. We take our kids to superhero films in which the finale isn't decided by a pithy war of words but by a full-on, twenty minute CGI duel of pure, physical aggression. Kind and gentle churchgoers watch James Bond pistol-whip a henchman and think: *Hmmm, nice move.* Teenage girls watch a film in which a woman is trapped for months in a maniac's cellar. If she gets out and calls the police, the audience is relieved. But if she sets the guy on fire before she grabs the phone, we're filled with respect. If she stamps on his nuts, even better. She did it! She won. And violence *was* the answer, in the end.

This fiction satisfies something in us, something old. And by us, I don't just mean men. Horrible culture is not just relevant for males. As we're about to see, the world of the macabre is an equal opportunities venture.

In 2017, the University of California developed an algorithm to identify onscreen genders. After analysing 100 of the most successful live-action movies from the past three years, the software found that women appeared on screen only 36 per cent of the time. In Oscar-winning films, that figure drops to 32 per cent (or 27 per cent if you concentrate on speaking-time on screen).[18] Pitiful stats such as these led actresses like Nicole Kidman and Reese Witherspoon to call out Hollywood for limiting female expression in the cinema.[19] But there is one genre that seems to buck the trend: horror.

The study found that only scary movies gave women more screen time than men, with female characters featuring for 53 per cent of the time. Critics of horror flicks might assume those onscreen women were just naked screamers running from an axeman. Yet a closer look at fright films shows a surprisingly diverse array of female roles. Yes, women play the victim sometimes, but they also play the heroes as well as the villains. For example, some of the biggest horror hits of recent years like *The Witch*, *The Babadook*, *It Follows* and *Get Out*, had both critical acclaim and an impressive box office. And they all hinged on strong and complex female characters.

Perhaps that's why women sometimes outnumber men in the audience for horror films. In 2013, some of the biggest hits of the genre had a majority female audience like *The Conjuring* (53%), *The Purge* (56%) and *Mama* (61%).[20]

Female horror fans can be found in numbers outside the cinema too. The organisers of the UK's biggest horror convention in 2018 are women, and female crime fiction writers dominate the market, with explicit tales of murder, rape and abuse. A string of male crime writers even admitted recently that they wrote under women's names, because female crime authors seemed to sell the best.[21] In 2014, crime fiction author Melanie McGrath remarked that 80 per cent of the audience at the Theakston Old Peculier Crime Writing Festival were women. The same proportion attended writing workshops, so that they could write stories of murder for themselves.[22]

To me, the idea that women can also enjoy morbid, spooky and violent content is kind of a non-story. I grew up watching scary films with my sister, and we both had a blast. But in a world that says "chick lit" can only mean pastel book covers and gentle romance, it's worth saying that sometimes "chicks" dig decapitations too.

Perhaps the reason why violent and macabre culture appeals to so many women is because it does something that few other outlets do. First, it lets women experience their fears, particularly the fear of being a victim of sexual or violent assault by men. As they grow up, girls learn about the prevalence of violence towards women. So what do women do? Some watch (or make) movies and read (or write) books where women are the victims of men. It's a way of greasing the amygdala again, using that fear as a learning experience in what to avoid. It does something else too: it empowers them to fight back and defeat the monster—or to even become the monster themselves.

In slasher movies, for instance, teenagers are systematically murdered by a killer in a mask. For decades, these films were written off as misogynistic trash because a lot of bare-breasted women got stabbed. What critics failed to appreciate was that those films acknowledged women's fears while also giving them space to be kick-ass too, because the one who defeats the killer in these movies is, more often than not, female. The so called "Final Girl" usually saves the day while the jock-hero or wise older man ends up with an arrow in his head.

These female heroes frequently defeat the villain in gruesome fashion too. They deliver machetes to the head or axes to the face. Where else in culture are such actions by women seen as positive and appropriate? Horror and crime fiction can give women a chance to face their fears, but also a way to defeat and control them, by using not only their intelligence, but also the aggression society tells them to hide.

For men, scary culture can offer a similar confidence boost. Boys are brought up on action figures and cartoon superheroes. They quickly learn that men must be the brave, tough saviour: the one who saves the princess and takes out the baddie, not the one who wets his jeans and weeps in the toilet. The result? Many men grow up and think if a crisis ever did occur, *I* need to be the one to show courage. *I* need to be the protector.

These stereotypes may be insidious and unfair, and we may take great delight in dismantling them. My favourite example is of the activists who switched the voice boxes on some Barbie and G.I. Joe toys. When kids played with them, Barbie said "Eat lead, Cobra!" while the G.I. Joe said: "Let's go shopping."[23] Scary culture, with its ass-kicking heroines, can challenge these gender stereotypes. Yet, at the same time, it can give us the option to play at stereotypical gender roles too.[24] For 90 minutes we can (if we want) slip into the parts of "the brave one" or "the scared one." I've chatted to independent women who get an odd kick out of going old school for two hours, gripping their boyfriend's arm. Equally, I've seen it the other way around, where men embrace being a scaredy-cat, while their girlfriend goes all alpha.

It happened to me recently. I was in a scare attraction called Tulley's—The Howl one Halloween night. I was creeping around a freaky maze with wailing and flashing lights. I'd just been chased through a giant fridge by a man with a chainsaw. Corpses hung from hooks and I had to push through them to find my way out. A strobe was flashing; it was hard to see.

I happened to be with a group of women in their twenties who were screaming and laughing. We all turned a corner when a crazed clown with a machine gun burst out of a jack-in-the-box, and all of a sudden I felt a woman's hand grab me. Then another. Eventually they all hid behind me as we pushed through to the next corridor. If this had been for real, and there was an actual clown gunman on the loose, I'd have probably been hiding behind them. But it was fake and it was fun, and it was our own little crisis through which *I* was playing the brave one, even though there was little to be actually scared of. When we got out of that place, they laughed and apologised for grabbing me, but I strolled off into the mist like some old echo of an A-Team hero figure I played with as a boy. It felt pretty great, to be truthful. Fake, but great.

We humans are insecure, and so we can't resist the type of tribal dominance games our ancestors used to play. For them, it was about being the best hunters, the strongest fighters, the wisest innovators—and violence was often a key tool to win. We just have different signifiers now—the bigger house, the cooler car, the slicker Facebook photos. To find success in these modern games of significance is hard work, and we often fail to match up. But there's always a pixelated zombie waiting to let us shoot them, meaning there are still arenas in which even the weakest among us can be heroes for a while. And when we blow those brains out, whether we're men or women, our shadow comes into focus, applauding like an eager little puppy. Then when we're done with feeling our fear and letting out our aggression, it fades away once more, its stomach now full, and we can just get on with our lives. And the best part?

In our system, nobody actually gets hurt.

Back in the dining room of our thirteenth-century manor house, the electric shock game is over, and the BBC have laid on a three-course dinner. We're sitting around a circular table when the one-eyed butler puts the final course in the centre of the table. It's a covered silver dish. We theorise about what's under it. I'm convinced we're going to have to eat something horrid, like sheep's eyes or bull testicles. That's par for the course on TV these days. We grit our teeth and wonder if we'll puke. Then someone whips the cover off.

Everybody screams.

Live spiders come scuttling out across the table. They're fast, and are throwing themselves into our laps. I fling my seat back and gasp. Everybody does. We're all on our feet.

A few weeks back the producers had a psychologist interview me. I admitted that it's insects that really push my fear buttons. So, I suspect the spiders are for my benefit. But then I notice one of the women in our group. She's called Zoe, a hip writer and a fellow horror fan. She's been on some of the most extreme scare attractions in the UK and loved them. She's braver than me in almost everything else, but she *loathes* spiders. I don't think I've ever seen anybody more scared in my life. She is *petrified*. She's crying and shaking, and the presence of her fear does something totally unexpected. It makes me brave. The fact that I'm not the most scared in the room floods me with courage. I even move towards the spider and try to pick one up. It's a moment for me.

Later, poor Zoe finally calms down and we head into the plush front room of the mansion. It's two in the morning and through the window pane we see a fire outside. A long strip of flames stretches across the gravel driveway, making the house flicker and glow. A woman with purple hair suddenly walks into the room.

"Right," she claps her hands together, "you're all going to walk barefoot across burning hot coals!"

Jaws drop. Hands grab hands. She tells us to high five one another and believe in ourselves. There's a lot of cheers of "we can do this." Then, when the flames die down, she leads us outside and tells us to take our shoes and socks off.

"Remember," she says, "just walk straight across the coals. Don't rush it, but don't hang about. Just keep going and you'll be fine."

We all look at each other nervously. One of us, Rachel, happens to work as a nurse in a burns unit. What we're about to do goes against all her best advice. But we all line up, wiggling our bare toes, and we watch the coals glowing. I lean down and hover my hand over it. "Whoa," I call back. "That really *is* hot. You can feel it."

My amygdala is sending frantic messages to my brain, saying *Fire bad! Fire bad! This is not wise!* My body is reacting with an increased heart rate and shallow breathing.

I figure if it's the BBC telling us to do this, they've probably made sure it was safe. Or I guess we could all sue them, if I lose all my toes. Or maybe this is some massive ruse, and the cameras everywhere are part of a high-profile snuff film collective that I've foolishly signed up for. This last idea sounds surprisingly plausible when it occurs to me. The coals look *scary*, and they are very, *very* hot.

The woman with purple hair claps her hands, "Okay, let's do this!"

I step up to the coals. The floor looks like lava and I have to walk on it. We start the build-up.

She shouts, "Name?"

I shout, "Peter Laws!"

"Can you do this, Peter?"

"Yes I can!"

"Then walk!"

I stride out. There's no hesitation. A second later my body is pressing all its weight through my bare feet and into red hot coals of fire. I'm shocked by how they feel underneath. There's no real heat to speak of, or sharpness either. If anything, it feels fluffy. But as I reach the end, everybody erupts into applause, and I let out a whooping cheer for myself and the rest of us. There's no skill involved here. There's no mind over matter. It's just basic physics, really. Walking on hot coals is safe when you do it right—but the fear, and the exhilaration after it, is as real as anything. You don't get that high-five, beat-your-chest feeling from walking across carpet. You get it when you walk through fire.

CHAPTER FOUR

HIDING THE BODIES

She's lying on a silver slab, fully and comprehensively dead.

A man hitches her up while a woman shimmies the arms through some sleeves. She's overweight, technically obese I guess. I see her body quaking as they tug her around. They're yanking a deep purple jacket on her, with a white frilled hem. It's her funeral outfit. The sort Margaret Thatcher would have worn: formal and feminine. I picture her alive in the shop, trying it on, patting the sides down and catching herself in the mirror thinking: *Hey, this works . . . this is me.*

Her plump cheeks rock gently. She's probably in her sixties; although she's one of the first corpses I've ever looked at, so I'm not sure how easy it is to age the dead. Do they look older than they really are or younger?

The undertaker is next to me and I'm very silent as we watch. I hear his delicate breathing, drawing in and drifting out. He's got what I might call a sensible haircut and he fiddles with the sleeves of his formal suit. He could be an estate agent or be selling expensive radios in John Lewis, but he's not; he's *here*, dealing with the dead. He called me a month ago because he had heard I'd just started as the minister of the local Baptist church. Like any businessman he wanted to make connections with the people he would be working with. He's already given me a free, A4-sized calendar and a black leather diary with his company name on it.

Quite frankly, I'm dreading leading funerals, and the biggest fear is getting them wrong. I have dreams of blanking out in the pulpit and stumbling over words. If you get the groom's name wrong at a wedding, people snigger. Mispronounce the name of the guy in the box though, and people aren't so forgiving. A colleague opened a funeral service by remembering with thanks the death of someone who was sitting right there in the congregation. Oops. Nobody laughed.

I want to get this right. To be ready for obscure questions like: *How do I know these ashes really are my dad, and not some pic'n'mix of other people?* So when the undertaker invited me to tour his "facility," I said yes. Then I put the phone down, gazed out of the window for a bit and wondered what the heck I'd just done.

Before today, I'd only ever seen one dead body in my life. My nana.

I wasn't supposed to have seen her, because I was only ten. She was laid out in a small bedroom in her house and my mum said it'd be too much for a little kid to see, but I needed the toilet and there wasn't one downstairs. I headed up, flushed, washed my hands and turned. I couldn't stop myself. It was the same compulsion I get to touch wet paint. I had my chin down but I rolled my eyes up so I could glance across the landing at the door where I knew she was. I expected it to be closed, maybe with flowers hanging from it.

It was open. She was right there.

Nana was in a coffin with her grey-looking head crushing heavy lines into a bright white pillow. I remember a thin, almost lipless mouth.

I froze, blinked the image away, then hurried back down the stairs. I didn't tell anybody what I'd done because I'd specifically been told not to look. I didn't want to cause any more upset. Still, that image (peaceful yet ominous) flickered on the back of my eyelids for the rest of the day. It's one of those memory files that remains vivid, even when I pull it out years later.

Today, I'm seeing more bodies than I have in my entire life.

So far the undertaker and his colleagues have shown me how they log the ashes (it's a meticulous, detailed system to avoid mix-ups), and I've seen the ashes themselves. They sit on shelves in red plastic tubs which are almost the exact same colour as caterers' tomato sauce bottles. They all look identical but each has a white label. The undertaker mentions that when a baby is cremated there's sometimes barely any ash left at all, a thought which lingers in my mind for a while.

They don't actually cremate anyone here; the bodies head off to the crematorium for that. But they'll collect the ashes if the relatives can't make it and store them here for collection. It seems like a lot of people don't bother picking them up, because there's shelf upon shelf of ex-individuals up there. They tell me some tubs have sat there for weeks, months even. Undertakers can legally throw them away eventually, but not all do. There's an undertakers in Southampton who've got unclaimed ashes dating back to 1975.[1] If that's your granddad or something, then put down this book and give them a call to sort out the pick-up. It's okay, I'll wait.

When you do get the ashes back, there's a company called Andvinyly that can press them into a vinyl record for you. If you're still alive and planning ahead, they'll even record personal messages from you so that loved ones can play *you* back, whenever they like. It's the perfect, hipster, keepsake.

I'm learning a lot today. Like how you don't need permission to bury a body on private land. Philip Topham in Nottingham buried his wife Catherine in his suburban front garden. She's there, surrounded by flowers and some candles, a few feet from the front door. There's surprisingly little red tape involved in home burials, as long as you dig the hole deep enough. You need two feet from coffin to surface, and you must keep the cadaver away from water sources.[2] You should also keep the Certificate for Burial handy, too. If someone spots you sliding a body into a hole, you can always whip that out so they won't call the police. Also, bear in mind that, according to estate agents, burying a corpse in the garden is likely to knock about £50k off your house price.

I also learn that if you find a corpse with its eyes open and you want to shut them but can't, you do *not* pull them shut. You don't glue them closed either, no matter how much they're glaring at you. It damages the delicate tissue which is harder to disguise later—helpful to know if you're planning on an open casket. Find some Ray Bans, if you're that bothered. Oh, and if you see loads of bruises on the corpse don't freak out and start shouting *MOYDER!* It's often just gravity making the blood pool, now that the heart isn't whizzing it down the usual highways anymore. And the old classic, don't get shocked when the dead gasp loudly. Corpses do that, and it's just latent air, the final breaths they pulled in from the world, racing back out to where it came from.

Top tips, I think you'll agree.

Earlier in the day, I walked past a huge metal door and asked, "Is that . . . a fridge?"

The undertaker nodded. "You can look inside, if you like."

I nodded, and he slid the door back. It rattled on metal runners, and inside I saw steel shelves, this time not with pots of ash on them but fully intact human bodies. I'm not sure why, but some were covered with cloth and some weren't. I stood there for a moment thinking of my nana and realised that this was a growing up moment. The next spike in my graph of death awareness. The undertaker waited for a few moments and then slid the door shut, "This way."

Which is when he led me to this room to watch the lady in the purple jacket being prepared.

It's grim seeing a dead body, I admit; although now that I'm down here it's not quite as disturbing as I expected. My heart's definitely beating faster, but there's an unreality about the bodies that puts a strange distance between them and me. They're strangers after all. In a way, all the dead are strangers. I suddenly notice that I'm standing with my hands clasped together in front of me, all solemn, like people do in a two-minute silence.

My brain's trying its best to assemble all these images together—the woman, the pots of ash, the fridge full of people, and that old flutter of my nana in the dim upstairs room. I'm reminded of a thousand fake corpses I've pondered in horror novels, films and art. They've been my way of dealing with the real ones, because there's a backbeat to all morbid culture that says: *Life's going to end; life's going to end.* Stephen King says that death "is the trump card which all horror movies hold."[3] Macabre culture explores this topic, sometimes lingering over extreme (if simulated) detail.

So, people might think that because I'm a horror fan I'm going to be thrilled by what I see here today, like this is what *all* us horror trolls are working up to really, sights of *genuine* death. But believe me, seeking out real corpses was never on my bucket list. Yet now I'm here, I'm curious. I'm fascinated. I'm moved. There's this odd sense of awe, not only at the woman's body but at the life that has left it.

Finally, the undertakers yank the sleeve into place, and the body quakes and settles.

I feel like it'd be nice to know her name, but I don't ask for it in case it sounds too intrusive. Somewhere in this town right now, this woman's family might be thinking of her. I picture a husband staring at an open wardrobe and weeping into his fist. In a few days' time they'll all see her coffin, but I've been told it won't be an open-top (it rarely is these days). This means that most people won't see what she's wearing, but I do. I see her pretty, purple jacket, and I wonder if she wore this for weddings or parties, or even for the funerals she attended but didn't headline.

Corpses make you ponder these things.

But then something happens that I will never forget.

The two undertakers lift the dead woman's head a little, and a seam tears open in the back of her neck. Yellow fluid *gushes* out of her. It splashes down the chrome legs of the bench and covers the floor. The man quickly grabs kitchen roll and drops to his knees to mop it up, while I suck in a breath. I do it very quietly so as not to be unprofessional.

"Happens, sometimes," the undertaker says. "We minimise it though."

"Minimise it, how?"

"We block all the orifices."

I wait a moment. "With what?"

"Cotton wool and cloth. It works pretty well."

My gentle philosophising on death vanishes as I watch the man mop her up. There's a clumsiness to it. At one point he even chuckles and rubs the back of his hand across his receding brow. Then he shrugs like he's saying: *I've just gone and spilled a glass of lemonade on the floor. Doh!*

I realise in this moment how abstract and removed my experience of death is. Whereas right now, it's pure physicality.

And perhaps the reason my brain is struggling to categorise all this is because I'm the product of a society that avoids death like it's toxic. We don't talk about dying because it's the ultimate downer subject. One New Year's Eve, for example, a bunch of our friends got together at our house and we danced around the lounge to *Jools Holland's Hootenanny*, clinking glasses and swaying hips. Then as the clocks chimed midnight, we all clamped arms in a laughing huddle when one of my friends thought it would be a good time to announce, "Hey, Peter, I just remembered—"

Everybody looked at him, eager for something funny or profound, the first message of the new year.

"—I had a dream that you were going to die this year!"

Talk about a buzz kill. I wanted to slap him. Though to be fair, it's not the first time I've been involved in messing up a new year moment. I accidentally farted one year, right on the stroke of midnight, and my smiling, embracing friends frowned, wondering why this sparkling new year of opportunity smelled like a farmyard.

Anyway, I managed to survive that death prophecy and many subsequent ones after it, but who am I kidding? Another flip of the calendar is coming when that sad little prediction will come true. Death is coming. Maybe it'll be years, maybe it'll be tomorrow. Maybe it'll happen on the very day you're reading this sent—

Or maybe you and I will be hanging around for decades and decades. I read an article once in which a Nobel Prize-winning scientist in the genetics of ageing said today's humans may live till they're 150.[4] I often quote this figure to friends, especially when pub conversation slides into deep things.

"Hey, that might be me!" I usually say, genuinely hopeful.

Yet the numbers are, in the end, irrelevant. Death is on a train right now with my name on his ticket, and—sorry about this—he's got your ticket too, somewhere in his bum bag. He's getting *closer* each second. He's rarely late.

Which makes it all so weird when you look at our society, because we act as if death only shows up for other people. We're obsessed with burying the most inevitable thing in our lives.

It's a far cry from the Victorians, who were big into memento mori. These "reminders of death" included clumps of hair from significant cadavers that people would wear in lockets. Or they'd pour wax on a corpse's face and make a death souvenir. They did it for men, women and children. Just do a Google image search on Victorian death masks. It's like scrolling though spooky selfies on a centuries-old version of Facebook.

Even more than masks, Victorians also embraced the new technology of photography, taking pictures of loved ones, sometimes post-mortem. They'd sit with the corpse in group shots; sometimes it's easy to spot who the dead one is. Old cameras had slow shutter speeds, so they'd pick up the slight movements of the living, who appeared ever so slightly blurred. Whereas the unmoving dead were the perfect models. They stayed still and sharp. I've seen Victorian photographs of what look like sleeping babies—only they're not sleeping. Families would display these pictures in their house. Can you imagine having a shot of your mum's or baby brother's corpse on your mantelpiece? How about as they sometimes posed them, with the eyes still open? So, in the past, it would've been hard to live your life without seeing a corpse at some point. Mortality rates were crazy high. Disease and ropey medical care was killing people off *fast*. In 1830, the well-to-do Londoner was lucky to live to 44. Tradesmen and clerks would reach 25, and a labourer's life expectancy was a paltry 22.[5] Child mortality rates were horrendous too.

Bodies would stick around the home for a decent (moderns might say indecent) length of time. This meant that our ancestors didn't just *see* corpses, some of them physically handled them too. Instead of calling in the professionals like we would, the family or others from the immediate community would wash the body, lay it out and presumably mop up the torrents of fluids that splashed from unexpected seams. I guess they had to plug their loved ones' orifices too, which isn't exactly my idea of a fun family activity, but they did it. Imagine modern families doing this today: it's nearly unthinkable.

My nana lived in a time when even kids could get a close-up look at death. She saw her first cadaver courtesy of *her* mother, my great-grandma, Granny Katie. Katie was the go-to lady for "sorting out corpses" in Barley Mow, a north-eastern community near Birtley. She laid them out and cleaned them up, mounting them on wooden body boards that my mum said were kept in the back of the cupboard under the stairs. During the 1930s, Granny Katie was called to the house of a local man who'd hanged himself. She took my nana along, who was a teenager at the time.

When they pushed through the door, they found he'd been cut down, but he'd crashed awkwardly across a sideboard. That's when Granny Katie spotted an ideal educational moment: she told my nana that she had to wash him. Then she spun on her feet, closed the door and locked it. Nana was trapped inside with the slumped body. For ten minutes.

Ten minutes of hammering on the door to be let out while a cadaver did "the plank" on furniture designed for ornaments rather than people. When she was finally let out, my nana had done what she was told and washed the body. Afterwards, my great-grandma apparently dropped this piece of wisdom: "After today you'll know that it's not the dead that'll hurt you." If you tried that little object lesson with a kid these days, you'd expect a call from the social services, and a widespread public shaming to boot. Back then it was just an introduction to a community service—my nana helped out with other bodies after that.

In a much less dramatic way, I learned that same lesson about the dead through Nana. The young girl who rattled her fists on a door to get out grew old enough to be the first cadaver *I* ever saw. Thankfully, I wasn't locked in a room with her. Like classic moderns, my parents told me I wasn't allowed to see her because it wouldn't be appropriate. But I looked anyway and learned that it's true: the dead don't hurt you, but they might just teach you something.

In the past, the dead could be particularly instructive when it came to law and order. Up until the nineteenth century, British criminals could be executed in public and even children were encouraged to look. Bodies hung from the gallows and were left there, while the world had a good gawp. In Münster, Germany, you can visit St Lambert's Church and still see three human-sized cages hanging from the steeple. In 1536 Catholics tortured and killed three Protestant Anabaptists as revolutionaries. Their corpses were hung in these cages and left to rot there . . . for 50 years.[6] To us, this reads like hideous barbarism, but back then it made good social sense: it might shock people out of committing crime or treason.

In time the public corpse would begin its gradual retreat behind closed doors. Nineteenth-century advances in science and medicine meant that people understood the principle of contamination better. Fever hospitals were wisely shifted out of the densely populated residential areas, and death rates fell as a result. These new medical centres had more space, which meant isolation wings could be built for the infectious cases. The result? Fewer people died of infectious disease, and those who did passed away out of town, alone in specialised rooms. Even prisoner executions gradually left the public square, and began to take place behind the prison walls.

An even earlier factor in the disappearance of visible bodies from everyday life was the birth of the life insurance industry. In the late eighteenth century, life cover in the UK meant people had a bit of cash to spend on funerals. Undertakers stepped in and saw their businesses thrive. Gradually, bodies that had been washed, dressed and prepared in the parlour at home were being looked after behind the closed doors of the funeral parlour instead. Graveyards, which were formerly given space next to churches, in time appeared in the fresh, open air of the country-side—both because the town graveyards had become full and because keeping the bodies away from populated areas helped prevent the spread of disease. A side-effect was that bodies became distant—mortality was being wiped from public view.

Fast-forward to today, and we've become masters at hiding death. Our photo albums bulge with grinning selfies celebrating *life*. There are no buzzkill shots of Grandpa's corpse. If a body ever *does* appear in the community, it's usually behind closed doors. If it's not, the police have special barriers and tents to shield it from view. Ambulances routinely carry body bags, with zips to ensure coverage. At funerals, coffin lids tend to stay closed. We've become so efficient in hiding dead bodies, that it's perfectly normal for us to live our entire life without seeing one.

Now, let me be clear. I'm not actually complaining about this. Just because I like morbid, creepy things, doesn't mean this chapter is about to launch a campaign to "Get cadavers back into the community!" Our modern norms do protect us from infection and disease, not to mention the privacy issues that have become so important to us these days. Yet this lack of having death in our face does have its negative effects. Not least, because it makes the subject itself taboo.

We don't talk about it with one another. Try it over dinner tonight: *Hey, sweetie, if you die before me, I reckon I might move into a flat. What do you think?* Conversations like this seem crass and psychotic, despite their 100 per cent relevance. Some of us even skip the death talk because we think it'll jinx us. A 2016 survey by the non-profit group Dying Matters found that 15 per cent of us don't talk about death, or make plans for it, because we think that by doing so, it'll somehow bring death on.[7]

Being so inarticulate and jumpy about our mortality means we avoid tricky, yet extremely important, conversations. A 2014 Dying Matters survey found that only 21 per cent of adults have spoken to someone else about their end of life wishes.[8] Another survey by the Childhood Bereavement Network found that 46 per cent of parents have made no alternative childcare provision, should they die. One in six admitted they simply couldn't face discussing it. One in four assumed it wouldn't be needed.[9] I guess they're not aware of the grim statistic, that one in twenty young people will have a parent die by the time they're sixteen.[10] So, we skip it and pretend it's not relevant to us.

We live longer, so we've more time to get attached to life. We even feel like there's a realistic chance of living into super-old age (cue a long line of death-busting diets like the Fruitarian and Paleo Diets). And when our skin starts to die, we pay a surgeon to make it look new again. Our death-averse society might even fast-track us through grief too. For example, a year after a friend of mine lost his wife, some elderly ladies said he really should "be over it" and that it was about time he got "back to normal." It's like we can't cope with the idea of co-existing with the inevitable loss.

Yet it appears that we're wise enough to not avoid this subject completely, and this is where macabre culture opens its glowing eyes again. We've become experts at hiding the realities of mortality, but have you spotted what we do instead? We surround ourselves with *simulations*. Through crime dramas, horror films and Halloween scare attractions, we engage in only the type of memento mori we can handle. We simply replace the real bodies with fake ones. Critics might say such "make-believe mortality" is worthless, but the fact that we've developed such inventive ways to keep the cadaver on our radars tells us something about the human condition. We *could* have removed bodies from both the public square *and* from art and culture—but that's not what we chose.

If anything, the declining visibility of death over the centuries has led to the *rise* of its image in ever more elaborate expressions. Journalist Vicki Goldberg describes this, beautifully, as "the decline of death and the ascent of its image."[11] Of course, it's not like death hasn't been in art for centuries—it has—but the significant rise in fictional, idealised death came when mortality rates *fell* in the nineteenth century. Glance through many of the big works of fiction of the eighteenth and nineteenth centuries and you'll find a glut of deathbed chapters. They're as ubiquitous as the sex scene in a thriller or the "car won't start" bit of a horror movie. Today we might not stand at the foot of a gallows anymore, watching a prisoner swinging in the wind, yet if you switch on any TV crime drama, or watch late night news, you'll see death graphically described or forensically portrayed. In a way, we still keep bodies in our lounge today. It's just that we can switch them off with a remote.

But it's right to acknowledge the danger of focusing too much on fictionalised death, precisely because of its unreality. Glossy Hollywood dramas give us the impression that when we die we'll be awake and lucid, ready to pass on final words of comfort and farewell to our loves ones. The author, professor and playwright Robert Jay Kastenbaum surveyed college students about this very question. He asked them to write a detailed account of what they thought their deathbed moment would look like. Ninety-six per cent said they expected to be alert and lucid.[12] Yet we simply can't assume that these ideal goodbye moments will come. We might not even die *where* we want. Cancer charity Marie Curie Cancer Care issued a report in 2014 showing that where Britons hope to die doesn't always match reality. Sixty-three per cent want to pass away at home, yet only 20.8 per cent actually do. A mere 8 per cent actually want to die in hospital, yet 54.8 per cent do. One per cent want to die in a care home, yet 17.8 per cent actually do.[13]

Yes, death can be surprisingly peaceful, but sometimes it's loud and too painful to even think straight, never mind communicate. At least macabre culture has an honesty about it: it reminds us of the loud, untimely, sudden death. It's a bleak but helpful caution that we ought not idealise our passing. Rather we might do well to share our love with others before we reach the deathbed. *On* the deathbed, it might be messy.

All this death talk can be a bit depressing, but not everybody feels the same sinking feeling when the topic comes up. I met a woman at a paranormal conference, where I was a speaker. There was a gala dinner one night, and we sat at the same table. In passing, she mentioned a present her boyfriend had made her. I asked what it was.

"My coffin," she said.

I coughed. "Pardon?"

"He made my coffin, and now I keep it in the lounge. It's all ready for me to use when it's time."

My jaw dropped and I asked to see photos. She pulled out her phone and gladly showed me snaps of him planing the wood and finishing the edges. Then she showed me the finished coffin in her lounge, upright and open with a mannequin inside it, complete with black dress. On the top sat a stuffed raven.

"That's pretty unusual," I said. "In fact, there are some people who'd even call that *weird*."

She shrugged, smiled and slid her phone back into her bag. "Nah, I reckon you're the weird one."

"Oh, really?"

"Yes. Because death's the most natural thing in the world, so why hide away from it? You should live with it. Accept it."

She told me she was a pagan. She's in touch with soil, so the idea of her becoming part of it again seems logical. She has no desire for heaven—she said she'd live on in her children. That night I couldn't forget what she said. I envied how chilled she was, and I realised that I could never be that relaxed because, let me be straight up with you, *death scares me*. It freaks me out. My own death, but more than that, the death of the ones I love. Simulated death? Fiiiine. I give that a thumbs up. But real death? Not a fan.

You might expect me to be more laid-back about dying, being a church minister and all. I've certainly met fellow Christians who act relaxed about the subject. For example, I've sat in nursing homes holding the hands of pensioners close to the end. Some of them flick through the Biblical passages on heaven like it's a holiday brochure. They're ready to pack their flip-flops. *I can't wait!* they say. *I'm looking forward to hugging my mum. I'm gonna hit the streets of heaven and walk without a Zimmer for a change.* Not every older person does this, but many I've prayed with are filled with hope and expectation about the end of life.

I have this hope too, by the way. I genuinely suspect that death really isn't the end, just the end of the beginning. But I'm not quite ready for it, yet. My family and friends are still alive. I'm pretty healthy; I've kept all my hair. There are places I still want to go (Japan) and people I want to meet (Stephen King). Death to me isn't an escape from a crappy life, it's an interruption to the cool one God's already given me. And if it happens to the people I love, death feels like a hideous offence that clashes with my sense of eternity.

So, I struggle to be chilled out about mortality. I don't want to go bowling with Death, but that doesn't mean I'm going to ignore it completely. I've grappled with the Reaper in simulated ways—through writing novels of grisly murder. This reminds me not to be naïve: death can be messy and sudden—lonely even. Through spooky tales of ghosts, I'm reminded that there is *hope* in the face of death—it may not be the end (more on that later). Morbid culture does us a service because it keeps this subject on the table, and for me at least, it's prompted me to make sensible plans like wills and alternative child care.

We might think the memento mori-loving Victorians were weirdos for putting death on the mantelpiece, but I bet they shivered and wept about corpses as much as we do. Yet when the end did turn up for them, they were better prepared to cope with it. Today, there's a growing realisation that to ignore this subject isn't very helpful. Charities in the UK like Dying Matters are actively trying to encourage people to discuss and make plans for their passing.

Death Cafe is a great example. This non-profit organisation supports the running of volunteer discussion groups across the globe. The first was held in someone's house in September 2011. Today, there have been over 5,000 cafes worldwide. The idea is to give people a chance to meet and talk openly about mortality over cake and hot drinks. Gallows humour is clearly allowed: the website shows a pretty pink teacup with a skull on it.

What seems creepy, weird and morbid can turn out to be a surprisingly positive experience. Guests discuss their fears and grief openly, in a relaxed, non-clinical environment. People realise that they don't have to deal with this subject alone and they don't have to hide it either. They start feeling more comfortable about making concrete plans for their passing—especially with hardcore icebreaker questions like: *Cremation or burial?* Some even leave with a rare sense of positivity about death. One Death Cafe guest told a newspaper journalist: "I've heard of people saying that death can be a really special time. Imagine that—how differently we would all feel about it if that could be the case?"[14] Of course, we should recognise that not all deathbeds are ideal, but an embrace of the morbid can be strangely life-affirming.

Others are trying to capture the positive power of funerals. I spoke to Rachel J. Wallace, a photographer who offers what she calls "farewell photography."[15] Clients hire her to help remember the day when they said goodbye to a loved one. It's a way to appreciate and celebrate the life of the deceased, and it also provides a chance for those who couldn't attend the funeral to feel connected. I ask her if she has ever been asked to take photographs of the bodies. She says it happens occasionally, especially if the funeral is for a child; Wallace has also taken family portraits of grieving parents with children who have died. The "farewell" side of her photography business isn't massive, Wallace tells me—she does about one funeral a month. Yet she suspects it will start growing as more people realise it's possible.

I call the National Association of Funeral Directors to ask how prevalent the funeral photography business is. Like Wallace, they say it's small, but growing. They tell me that the biggest current growth is in the number of people getting the cremated remains of loved ones turned into jewellery, so they can be carried close.

There are even some folks trying to make corpses more noticeable at funerals. They're sitting the deceased up at tables, holding cups or cigarettes at fixed angles. I saw photos of a Puerto Rican taxi driver whose body was placed sitting in his cab, his white gloved hands curled around the wheel. [16] The mourners filed by as if he might give one of them a lift to the airport. Some will call that ghoulish; for others it's a chance to remember him as he was. Even elephants have been seen to linger around their dead companions.[17] They don't run away—they take the time to look.

Perhaps morbid culture persists because deep down we know that we *ought* to gaze on these things too. Once in a while. Not to glorify death, but to prepare for the inevitable, to appreciate others while we can.

In other words, we look on death to elevate life.

The caretakers finally dress the woman so she looks kind of normal now. Except for the face. The face of a corpse can seem unreal. It's only when my tour concludes and I step out into a sunny St Albans street that I really see why.

I see passers-by. A blonde woman is jogging in a bright pink tracksuit. She dodges a discarded Dr Pepper can. A man in sunglasses and a tie, but no jacket, is striding along, phone stuck to his ear. He's getting animated about something and smiling. In a tyre-garage opposite, I see a man wiping his hands on blue overalls, while another jabs at a button. Both of them watch a car rise on a pneumatic platform, and they're laughing. I realise just how much people *move*, especially their faces. It's astonishing. Everyone is alive and looks brighter than they did this morning. I stand for a few minutes on the pavement and think of the words of English professor Eric Wilson, writing about the work of Keats. "Why is the real rose more handsome than the porcelain?" Wilson writes. "The living one is finite, decaying, bound to die, and the mortality produces the luminousness."[18]

The thought of this scares me a little, but this morning it's making me see the world in a new way. It's like switching life from murky Betamax to full-on Ultra HD. After watching that woman's body being mopped up, it's impossible for me to ignore death. Yet it's not as terrifying or even as disturbing as I expected. Instead, it's making something unfurl in my head and heart. I want to hug my wife. Frankly, this morning I had been hoping that she'd go out tonight so I could have the TV to myself, because the box set of *Knight Rider* I bought off eBay just arrived.

Yet now my day of death is complete, I hop back in the car and set down my calendar and diary from the funeral home. They slide about in the passenger seat as I drive home, playing music loudly with the window down. Although it's cold, I want to feel the wind ruffling my hair. I spend the afternoon writing a sermon, then I cook a half-decent stir-fry for my treasured wife, who, many years ago, held a single red rose as she walked down the aisle towards me. When she finally walks in from work, I throw my arms around her, hug her for a long time and then hand her a drink.

She kicks off her shoes; I ask her about her day.

Chapter Five

ZOMBIES, EVERYWHERE

I point my shotgun at the guy in the wheelchair.

"Peter!" a voice comes from behind me. "Don't shoot him!"

I ignore the voice and keep the barrel in place. Through the darkness I can just about see the occupant of the wheelchair, about eight feet away. He's wearing a long white hospital gown and his fat hands are curled around the wheels. He might spring the chair forward at any moment. He's not like the others. Under the strands of his long, sticky black hair, I spot a breathing mask.

"This one looks really weird." I curl my finger on the trigger and take a step forward.

"Don't," the other man whispers. "It's a bad idea."

I nod, but I keep my aim. I move slowly. *Really* slowly. I can hear my own pulse drumming a rhythm in my ears. There's no light down here, but I do have a tiny orange torch that the soldiers gave me earlier. It dangles from a cord around my neck and barely lights up my hand, never mind this massive room scattered with old computers, desks and moulded plastic chairs. I've held this torch between my teeth for an hour now, so that I can cock the gun easier. My jaw aches as I glide the almost pointless beam over this lump in the wheelchair. I'm a bargain-basement action hero, firing out a fading sunbeam.

He isn't moving at all. His hands remain still. His hair glistens. I bet he wants to eat me.

The other man sees me cocking the gun. "Careful!"

"Mmm-hmm." I lock the gun into my hip, finger on the trigger.

I don't fire off a bullet for two reasons. First, the soldiers told us that some of the infected are called Screamers, and it's an extremely bad idea to shoot them. Best to stay still and tread air until they go away. Second, I'm not a trigger-happy chump. I only have a measly ten bullets, and I already wasted one on the former British Prime Minister, John Major.

I should probably explain that.

About ten minutes ago I stumbled into a pitch-black room and bumped into what I thought was a table. It was actually Mr Major, lying on a cot bed. I shone my mouth-torch on him and saw him smiling madly, staring through his glasses. I shouted "Shit!" and pulled the trigger before realising he was just a mannequin wearing a mask. I wasted a slug on the PM, and I won't do that again.

My fellow shooter is creeping away now. He's off to find other corpses to kill, but I wait because I'm really getting into this face-off moment.

The shape in the wheelchair is motionless. So am I.

Maybe I should shoot him, after all.

I'm in Kelvedon Hatch Nuclear Bunker. It's a giant hide-out in Essex, England, and it's the place that would have housed a devolved British Government had the mushroom clouds bloomed. Thirty-eight feet of dirt, steel and cement are above my head, and above *that* is a field, a dirt track and an ordinary-looking bungalow plonked in the middle of farmland. That's all you see from above ground. It's only when you walk through the front door of the bungalow that a 91-foot tunnel opens up before you. It takes you down, down and down again.

It isn't a working bunker anymore. By day, it's a Cold War museum that's easy to find. You just follow the multiple brown road signs on the nearby A-roads that say "Secret Nuclear Bunker."

My wife and I came to this bunker on a day trip once—because I'm a romantic like that. I brought her to this dingy Cold War tomb with its dusty old phones, boiler rooms and mannequins staring through gas masks. The most chilling part was seeing all the 1980s cathode ray tube TV sets, looping the "Protect and Survive" videos that the government would have broadcast in the case of a nuclear strike. With a Sergeant-Major-style narrator, they dished out miserable tips in the most dispassionate way possible, like how to efficiently bury your radioactive relatives. This place delivers plenty of creeps, even by day.

But on certain nights of the year, when the sun itself goes underground, the lights are switched off in Kelvedon Hatch and folks come down here to shoot airguns at actors dressed as zombies. Running the show are a "tactical response team." These soldiers are played by a mixture of actors and off-duty police officers.

The event is called The Last Survivors,[1] and it's just one of hundreds of zombie themed "experiences" run across the UK these days. All week I've been sent emails and digital copies of letters from fake military personnel, telling me the details of tonight's mission. There's medical research we need to retrieve from Outpost 16 and a whole bunch of dead people to kill. I was one of the earliest to arrive tonight. Eager beaver, that's me. I stopped my car on the dirt track because a sign said *WARNING— INFECTED ZONE: Please Wait IN YOUR VEHICLE Until Escorted.*

It was spooky up there in the dark, surrounded by fields, completely alone and with my headlights only partly lighting up the track ahead. I couldn't see any lights from nearby towns, just black empty farmland and bushes. I can see why the government picked this spot. Even a nuclear warhead might overlook it.

Another sign said *ROLL UP WINDOWS AND BE VIGILANT FOR INFECTED*, so I quickly rolled mine down. I leaned my head out, wondering if an actor was going to come stumbling out of the trees and grab my hair. Kind of hoped for it, to be honest.

The legal disclaimer I signed today was pretty clear. I may well get touched by a zombie, and I might get fake blood on me (with "no guarantee it would wash out"). The waiver added other hesitations to my signing too, like the fact that I may "die" or "get blinded" or be "partially or totally paralysed" down here. I had to agree that, legally speaking, such personal disasters would never, *ever* be the fault of the organisers. So I already feel the tension.

The Last Survivors is run by Antony, a graphic designer. He's expecting his first baby any day now, but he's here at the event tonight, apparently. I think he might be playing one of the zombies. I assume he'll have his mobile handy, under his zombie outfit, just in case he has to stop chewing neck, apologise, and head off to the maternity ward. Try explaining *that* to the midwife.

After ten minutes of watching the silent trees up above, another car slowly pulled up behind me. Then another. Nobody got out. Engines were switched off. Headlights too for a while. I had my most horrifying thought of the night, just then: what if this *wasn't* a zombie event after all, and was instead an elaborate cover story for dogging—the growing phenomenon of strangers meeting up in remote places to have sex with each other in cars? To be honest, Essex *is* known for that stuff. A friend even told me that a live documentary about dogging was being filmed in Essex this very weekend. For a shaky minute or two I wondered if my invite to

"Shoot the Dead in Deep Tunnels" was just a common euphemism for "Shag Lonely Housewives in a Honda Civic." Maybe I was the naïve vicar who didn't know this established lingo and was about to be surprised by a camera crew bursting through the bushes while everyone else undid their pants and laughed: *Ha! He thought this was about actual zombies! Bless.*

But then a car came hurtling behind us and skidded across the field at top speed, lurching up over the hill before vanishing. Next, a cool 4×4 with flashing emergency lights slowly pulled up and a soldier got out. He came up to my car and shone a bright orange light in my face.

"Alright, Sweetheart," he looked down at a clip board. "Name?"

"Um . . . Peter Laws."

He flicked the beam into the back seat, and saw two empty child seats. "You've come *alone*?"

"Yep. Just me."

He chuckled at this, like I was pathetic, then he shook his head and moved to the next car. After he'd ticked us all on his list, he led me and eight other guys through the bungalow and down here, where he and another "soldier" gave us guns and torches. They split us into two groups. I'm with a group of blokes on a stag do. One of them paid an extra £60 to get a night-vision camera strapped to his gun barrel. We've been instructed to search this bunker for attaché cases filled with medical evidence. While we're at it, we need to wipe out the horde.

I've shot four zombies so far (five if you count the ex-Prime Minister), and now here I am, pointing a gun at an evil hippy in a wheelchair. I lean in because I can hear one of the old printers whirring. Then I realise it's not a printer. It's him. He's making a clicking sound with his mouth. My eyes flick to his fingers, resting on the curved wheels. Did his fingers just move?

I think his fingers just—

"RAAAAAAAAAAAAAHHHHHHH!" He screams and flings the wheels forward frantically.

He's crazy fast. I stagger back and pump the shotgun.

Pop!

I've shot him in the chest.

Turns out this really *is* a bad idea after all, and my teammate was right. This one is a "Screamer," and he goes totally ape-shit.

Now the wheelchair's chasing me through the darkness and its occupant wants my brains in his belly. I fire off another bullet at him without thinking and he screams back at me. I scramble, shocked at how fast the chair is. The room's almost pitch black and I'm *sprinting* through it, smashing into plastic chairs, retro computers and huge printers. It's like the set of a *Resident Evil* game, and I scamper through it, torch in gob, totally exhilarated.

Suddenly, I spot the rest of my group in the far corner of the room. They're looking for the silver flight cases we've been ordered to find. I run at them spitting out my torch and I shout, "HE WON'T DIE!"

It's like birds scattering after a gun shot. We burst away from the wheelchair-killer, everyone running in different directions. But the Screamer keeps on at *me* and spins back on his wheels to hem me in. This guy could be a Paralympian. In fact, my tunnel-focused brain tells me he's the top Paralympian wheelchair-racer on the planet, and, as he whizzes his wheels between the tables, cracking chairs aside, I notice that I'm laughing. I'm laughing really loudly because I see my escape: there's a door behind me, and I vanish through it.

"Ha, ha! See ya!"

I slam the door shut and turn to look for the stairs.

It's a toilet block.

I stop laughing.

It's a very dark toilet block, and I'm trapped.

The Screamer's now slamming his hands against the door and scraping his nails down it. I spit out my torch again and wave it in a frantic circle at the frosted window. I shout "Help!" to my group, which sounds as pathetic as it is authentic. I don't know what else to do. I have to push my whole weight against the door because he's trying to heave himself and the wheelchair through. Behind me I see three cubicle doors, half closed. It's too dark to see if there's something in here with me. But it feels like there *might* be.

The pounding dies down eventually and I wait, panting. Then as the scrapes grow quiet, I risk it. I push the door open a touch and stick the barrel of the gun through so I can—

"RAAAAAAAAHHHHH!"

The Screamer pushes his face through the crack, forcing his cheeks through. I slam it shut again and he pulls back enraged, slamming and scraping. The heart rate monitor glows on my wrist. I'm on 130, which is way over double my usual resting rate. Then behind me, something happens that genuinely scares me. I hear the taps turn on. I can't see anybody in the room, but I can hear water gushing against porcelain. It sounds like there's another zombie in here, washing his hands before dinner.

I cock my gun again and pump the barrel (this motion, by the way, feels as brilliant and alpha as I'd hoped). I listen as fingernails scrape on the other side of the door, watching the cubicle doors, and waiting for a dead, hungry thing to come shuffling for me. There's no sign of the others, now. Just me and these zombies who, it seems, are everywhere.

But then, aren't they always, these days? Aren't zombies *everywhere*?

I met the late George A. Romero once, in Milton Keynes. He's the film director largely credited with inventing the modern zombie. I met him at the MK shopping centre (which, if you're interested, doubled as a futuristic United Nations building in *Superman 4*—the crappy one, with Nuclear Man). Romero wasn't there shopping or pottering about; he was a guest at one of those geek conventions that I sometimes go to called *Collectormania*. It's usually filled with sci-fi and fantasy celebs ready to sign bobble head toys and books and buttocks, but sometimes, when the stars align, it pulls in a few horror heroes too.

When I heard Romero was coming, I lined up eagerly. I was one of those crazy people who pay twenty English pounds just to meet another human being. I was pretty nervous, handing over my Blu-Ray of *Dawn of the Dead* to be signed. But from that five-minute moment I got a treasured selfie of us together, his signature—*To Peter and Joy, Stay Scared!*—and the memory of him beaming at me when I told him I was a church pastor, and saying: "Wow, man, that's wild." Money well spent, I'd say.

I'm pretty sure that Romero was a millionaire, but some would argue he ought to have been a multi-billionaire, because his ideas on zombies have spawned a megalithic industry. If it weren't for him, I doubt tonight's organiser Antony would be paying for his baby's nappies with zombie profits.

Romero reminds me of the guy who supposedly invented the World Wide Web: Tim Berners-Lee. Lee didn't really *invent* it, but he did implement the first communication between a client and a server via HTTP (whatever the hell that means). His breakthrough relied on previous work by a bunch of others, but *he* was the one who took that work and turned it into a modern phenomenon. Similarly, Romero didn't invent the zombie, and he never claimed to, but in 1968 he re-invented it with *Night of the Living Dead*. As we'll see in a moment, it's a film which even today offers an instantly-recognisable template for the most celebrated monster of our time.

These days the zombies have well and truly crashed through the windows of our cultural farmhouse and made themselves at home. Yet they weren't always so welcome or loved, and one of the reasons for this tentative introduction was because they came from a mysterious, complicated place.

The earliest European travellers discovered African shores in the fifteenth century. By the time Elizabeth I took the throne in 1558, the slave trade had developed, and along with it prejudices about black people as inferior to whites, and even as potentially *inhuman*. You see it in popular art well into the nineteenth century, like the work of cartoonist Robert Cruikshank. His 1820 picture "The Devil's Ball" shows white people partying in hell, while a black man with hooves and snakes for hair sits on the back of a skeleton, playing the fiddle. "There Never Were Such Times!" says a black imp with exaggerated lips, as other black demons surround and pervert the whites.[2]

The quest to "civilise" these lands was one of the ideals of the Victorian missionary movement; gallant and pious whites would interact with the strange black and brown men to educate them in the "superior" European culture and religion. This all stoked the Victorian comic imagination, and soon the image of a missionary being cooked in a pot by natives with bones through their noses became a much-used sketch in nineteenth-century comic papers and music hall productions.[3] Readers and audiences were left either laughing at the nigh-on insanity of the missionaries, or applauding their heroism. Meanwhile, the natives themselves became figures of savage threat and exotic danger.

African cultures seemed confusing and complex too, which only led to the sense of disorientation. Explorers had many unfamiliar religious and cultural practices to unravel. You get a sense of this whenever you try to pin down the origin of the word "zombie" itself. Scholars aren't sure where the word actually came from. Some say it's from the Kongo term "*nzambi*," meaning a god, fetish or spirit of a dead person. Others say it derived from the word "*zumbi*" from the Bonda language, which refers to a cadaver.[4] To find out more about the word's convoluted history, I ask Sarah J. Lauro, an English professor at the University of Tampa; one of her academic focuses is "the history of the transatlantic zombie."[5] How cool of a speciality is that?

"My own personal hunch," she tells me, "is that the word "zombie" probably comes from a combination of terms coming out of the Kikongo-speaking and modern-day Angola regions of Africa. It's a mix of the word "zumbi" which is a Kikongo fetish and a "vumbi", an Angolan ghost or a spirit of the dead—which can also enslave souls. So, the zombie concept combines the idea of the ghostly with fetish objects. Basically, it's a corpse that can somehow do work after death."

This is still just a theory. She adds, "How exactly these all became conflated into the entity we today call the zombie is a much longer story, one that has historical gaps we can only guess to fill."

Compare the complicated source of zombies to some of our more long-standing monsters. Westerners in the nineteenth and twentieth centuries, for example, found a Romanian Dracula fairly easy to compute. Yes, he was a foreigner who guzzled veins, but at least he was a white, educated aristocrat. They could handle a German Frankenstein too. He was foreign and he robbed graves and "played God" with cadaver parts, but at least he was a white, educated aristocrat. And of course, both of these monsters sprang from the pens of civilised Brits.[6] But chicken-slashing, witchdoctor natives from a confusing religious landscape that was *real* and largely uncharted? This wasn't just weird to the West, it was *scary*, and it played into an already present fear of the demonic savage.

But plenty of other whites would visit these lands too, not to convert the natives from their cultures or to enslave them, but to observe and document their fascinating ways—and to figure out the mysteries of their beliefs and culture. And it's this approach that really enabled the zombie to make its first, proper "hello" to the world.

William Seabrook was a fascinating and controversial man. He was an American soldier, sexual sadist and adventurer who loved to combine travel writing with his love for the weird and macabre. He took a hands-on approach to his research. For example, to aid his research on West African cannibalism in 1931, he decided he'd need to try it himself. He nabbed some human flesh from a Parisian hospital and cooked and ate it, just so he'd know the taste of "long pig." It was "like a good, fully developed veal," apparently.[7]

However, it is his 1929 book, *The Magic Island*, which remains his most lasting legacy, because it was *this* that really brought the foreign zombie crawling onto domestic shores.

It was 1928 when Seabrook visited Haiti, and he became fascinated by the country. He found that the majority of the population had descended from African slaves who were shipped over to work on the plantations; so Haitian culture was heavily influenced by that heritage. By the time he arrived, Haiti had become the epicentre of Caribbean voodoo. While studying the traditional local beliefs, he learned about a creepy practice. A *bokor*, or voodoo sorcerer, could put someone into a death-like state with a magic potion or powder. Then, after the family burial, the bokor would dig the body up and revive it. Only now, it had no willpower of its own, and it became a slave to the bokor master. These slaves were forced to work endless hours, and Seabrook even claimed to have met a few of these "zombies," toiling in the cane fields. This poisoning people into something that "looked like death" was common enough to have even been outlawed in the Haitian Penal Code of 1883.[8]

Seabrook eagerly brought these tales of poisoning, burying and re-awakening cadavers back to his homeland, and America loved them. *The Magic Island* was *the* smash-hit travel book of 1929. The showbiz world soon took note of this newly imported monster, and what was *especially* enticing, as writer Jamie Russell points out, was that it came copyright free.[9] Properties like Frankenstein and Dracula involved lengthy intellectual ownership negotiation. Not so with the zombie. It wasn't even the property of Seabrook because he was reporting "fact."

So, Seabrook had brought the zombie to town, but its first steps into wider culture were shaky. A 1932 stage production called *Zombie* tanked, which left it to Hollywood to really get the creatures moving. They did it that same year with the horror film *White Zombie*, in which a young American woman is enslaved in "death" by Bela Lugosi.

This was a major twist. Seabrook had already freaked people out that there were black zombies in the world, obeying their voodoo overseers. Now Hollywood was peddling an even more disturbing possibility: a *white* zombie! The dark powers of Haitian voodoo were infecting everyday Americans, which played into racist fears of cultural infestation.

The biggest shock came when this independently produced horror movie made a higher net profit than the previous big-budget horror films from Universal. Film promoters, sniffing a zombie goldmine, pushed the marketing into overdrive. According to Russell, "they played up the racial dimension in a series of startlingly crass ways."[10] He cites the American and British press books for the film, which include promo tips that would make us wince today, such as: "hiring several negroes to sit in front of your theatre and beat a steady tattoo on the tom-toms . . . and every once in a while have them cut loose with a couple of blood-curdling yells."

Or how about this great bit of "ballyhoo, that will bring actual pounds into your box office—arrange for a parade of zombies through the main streets of your city, the men following a girl in white . . . Tip off newspaper offices that "Black magic" is being practiced on the streets of your city."

The poster for *White Zombie* promised that: *Unusual Times Demand Unusual Pictures*. And indeed they *were* unusual times. Americans were in the thick of a tumbling economy and exploding unemployment. *White Zombie* debuted in 1932 which was a year that historian Frederick Lewis Allen describes as "the cruellest [year]" of the Great Depression.[11] In Haiti, the zombie had become a symbol of the fears of slavery and loss of individual freedom. Many African settlers to the island had suffered this, so could appreciate the fear. Now, millions of Americans were seeing *their* reflections in those zombies too, as they were being forced to shuffle blank-faced into the welfare queue that, as Jamie Russell writes, "reduced princes to paupers, bank managers to bums and whole families to beggars. The zombie—a dead worker resurrected as a slave into a hellish afterlife of endless toil—was the perfect monster for the age."[12]

Despite the success (and squirm-inducing tom-tom marketing) of *White Zombie*, the monster never really caught on. Not in the same way vampires and werewolves had, anyway. There was a spattering of zombie movies in the decades that followed, but few made much of a cultural impact. People found their "mindless slave-drone" metaphors in science fiction instead. Like the communist pod people of *Invasion of the Body Snatchers*. Unlike zombies, those guys still looked like they brushed their hair in the mornings. They could happily chat and easily pass as human. This is what made them so unnerving in the time of the "Red Menace."

Whereas the shambling zombies may have looked a *bit* like us but acted like lobotomies-on-legs. They were the "dead" vision of us and had, in a sense, crawled back into the grave for a bit, patiently waiting for culture's call for them to rise once more.

That call came from an unexpected place. Not Haiti or even Hollywood, but from Pittsburgh, Pennsylvania where George A. Romero was in advertising at the time. He was making commercials for beer and washing powder, when he and his colleagues decided to try something more ambitious: they would make a horror film. Romero sometimes says that he was just ripping off Richard Matheson's book *I Am Legend*, changing the vampires to zombies, but that's selling himself short. He added vital elements that continue to resonate and shape zombie culture as we know it today. That's saying something, when the film doesn't even mention the word zombies once (the creatures are called "ghouls" instead). At the time he had no idea he was about to create a massive new juggernaut of morbid culture.

Romero's undead ghouls ditched the voodoo heritage of Seabrook and Lugosi's depictions. In typical 1960s fashion, these creatures didn't obey authority either. Gone were the tragic slave-butlers of African folklore, doing whatever their bokor master told them. The only master these beasts had was their hunger, because Romero had thrown in a nifty cannibalistic urge too. They craved human flesh.

What also changed—and this is vital in understanding why zombies are so popular today—was the *scale* of the threat. For the 1930s audience, the biggest danger zombies brought was taking over your wife or kids, or even you, but you were still only dealing with maybe a handful of these creatures. In *Night of the Living Dead*, however, Romero flipped the switch to full-on apocalypse mode. Now zombies were everywhere and the threat was exponential. Anybody bitten or recently dead was going to rise too. The cynical, jaded 60s generation had lived through the Cuban

Missile Crisis; they'd been born around the time of the bombing of Hiroshima; they'd seen the Watts riots in LA. The concept of complete global disaster wasn't just scary—it was *plausible*.

Plus, the overall message of the movie (that the world was going down the toilet) made a chilling, contemporary sense, because by then, 60s flower power had all but sunk into pessimistic realism. Spoiler alert: the film famously ends on a horribly glum note. The hero of the film is black, which was a shock to white cinemagoers in itself, but in the end he's mistaken for a ghoul and gets shot in the head. We've rooted for him for 96 minutes, only to see him dragged by a hook onto a fire, while a bunch of gun-toting rednecks shoot him and throw his corpse on a fire. There are no survivors. No happy ending. It's an exercise in trying and failing, because the new system of social breakdown is going to get you in the end. Finishing on a nihilistic tone like this was bleak enough, but when Romero was driving the first print of the film to show to distributors in New York, the car radio announced that Martin Luther King Jr had been assassinated.[13] He knew then that his film was going to push even deeper buttons than he'd expected.

However, perhaps the key factor that really installed zombies into international morbid culture today wasn't the film's powerful social commentary. It was a technical, copyright error.

The film was originally called *Night of the Flesh Eaters*, but when the distributor changed the title card to *Night of the Living Dead*, they forgot to put the copyright notice on the final print. These days a lapse like that wouldn't matter much. But in 1968, if copyright notice wasn't given up front, the film automatically became public domain.[14] This is why, if you feel like it, you can go and download this movie right now for free, and you aren't doing anything illegal.

As a result, Romero and the makers barely saw any of the tens of millions the film wound up making, but their (massive) loss was scary culture's gain: the world saw the movie. More crucial than that though, the story and its dramatic framework was openly copied in hundreds of other films, over and over. And much like the producers of *White Zombie*, these imitators did it without any fear of a court case. Maybe Romero couldn't have fought them anyway, even if he *did* retain copyright. But now filmmakers didn't have to worry. Like Hollywood had discovered in the 30s, the zombie was walking again and it was copyright-free. This meant that the Romero Zombie Commandments were now public property:

1. they're cannibalistic,
2. they're global,
3. they move in groups,
4. you have to shoot them in the head,
5. you can become one of them if you're bitten,
6. they're not drugged, they're dead,
7. you need to hole up in a building and block the doors to escape them.

These commandments are seen throughout zombie culture today, even here, in this cold war nuclear bunker. It's about 50 years since *Night of the Living Dead* came out, and yet here I am, paying £90 to hide in a toilet block. I'm surrounded by the flesh-eating undead in a simulated global apocalypse. Without Seabrook and Romero, I wouldn't be trapped in this toilet—which isn't me blaming them by the way; it's me thanking them profusely.

It rather begs the question: why are zombies still speaking to us *today*? The bewitched slaves of Seabrook and Lugosi resonated with people trapped in the Depression-soaked 30s, and the rudderless, bleak hordes chimed again in Romero's cynical, paranoid 60s. But what are these dead folk, who seem to be speaking louder than ever, saying to us now?

In the decades that followed *Night of the Living Dead*, the copyright-free commandments of Romero's zombies would be replicated in a never-ending loop. The Italians became masters of the Romero-style zombie movie in the 70s and 80s; then in the 90s, the undead started chomping digital brains on games consoles, most notably with the smash hit Playstation franchise, *Resident Evil*. The new millennium saw cinema-riffs on the zombie genre with *28 Days Later* (2002) and *Shaun of the Dead* (2004); then in 2010 a TV network joined the wave with a series based on a popular zombie comic book. AMC's *The Walking Dead* became a ratings phenomenon, and after its third season it was attracting more 18–49 year olds than any other broadcast or cable TV series.[15]

When the Brad Pitt horror epic *World War Z* was released in 2013, many critics chuckled (including me). I figured a big studio like Paramount was coming way too late to the zombie party. After all, that was the same year *Midget Zombie Takeover* came out; the barrel-scraping had already started. I thought zombies were getting old hat by then, but *World War Z* grossed a healthy $202,359,711.

Today, the zombies just keep on coming and they don't seem to stop. Now they've spilled into every conceivable cultural expression. You can get zombie fitness apps and zombie-themed weddings. There are university courses in zombie biology, and even zombie-themed cruise holidays. Little kids collect zombie plush toys, and my own church converted their sanctuary into a zombie escape game for local kids. This wasn't even *my* idea—it's just that the youth worker knows that moaning corpses are a hit with teenagers these days.

Why are zombies more popular and more mainstream than ever?

One of the key reasons is that these monsters fit particularly well with modern belief systems. We aren't nearly as convinced by the supernatural as we are by science. There was a sense of this, even with Seabrook back in the 30s. He was open-minded to the spooky stuff, but he still offered rational explanations for seemingly supernatural things. But today, there's a relentless push to make our lives (and our nightmares) rational and quantifiable. Modern zombies no longer require curses, spells or meddling with a religious order. Now they're born of down and dirty stuff that everybody can understand, like germs. We've been through pandemics of HIV/AIDS, SARS and the Zika virus, so the idea of global collapse due to infection makes perfect sense.

To some people, the zombie uprising actually feels *possible*. I went to a party once of an old university friend. Conversation wound up on scary things (this often happens when I'm around), and my friend's husband mentioned that he was well-prepped for the zombie apocalypse. Turned out, he had three survival bags: one in his car, one at home and one at work. He showed me his night-vision goggles, water purification tablets and the real shotgun he has locked in a safe, along with a cellar filled with supplies. If the zombies *do* come, I suggest we go to his house.

This, I reckon, is another key reason zombies attract us today. It's not just the zombies themselves, but the entire situation they bring about. I once asked a church congregation if any of them would like to safely experience a zombie apocalypse situation. Quite a few hands went up, and so did mine. Why? I reckon it's because, while the collapse of society may well be terrifying, it speaks to our need for adventure.

In a zombie-takeover scenario, it doesn't matter if you have a driving licence, or even a car. All you need to do is pick an abandoned one in the street and get going. You don't have to go to school anymore, or work. No more studying for exams. No more end-of-year appraisals. Pensions, piano lessons, *The X-Factor* line up—it all just goes out of the window.

You can skip the gym too because you'll be running plenty (and you'll barely have any food to make you fat, anyway). I mean, yeah, the bit about having to shoot your friends in the head isn't so great. (Unless you have crappy friends, in which case, it might be the best part.) But when zombies are on the scene, life suddenly becomes a lot more epic. Scary, yes, but *epic*.

I think this appeals to a suspicion we all have: that we're hopelessly dependent on the structures of society. We want to experience adventure, but we also feel shockingly underprepared for it. I mean, can *you* make a candle from scratch? That sort of fear struck a loud bell of consciousness in the 60s and 70s, with the self-sufficiency movement. There was a global oil crisis, and coal miners were striking. Cosy moderns sat in their cold, Habitat-furnished houses with no lights or TV, and thought: *Crud. We're were way too reliant on others.* Pop culture explored this fear through sit-coms like *The Good Life* and the apocalyptic series *Survivors*, from Terry Nation.

In response, alternative communities started cropping up. Environmentally conscious middle classes left their jobs and tried to work the land. The only problem was, many of them had crappy agricultural skills. They saw their crops dying. They couldn't even fix a tractor motor, so they poured over books like *The Complete Guide to Self-Sufficiency* by John Seymour, which taught you handy stuff you didn't learn on *Blue Peter*. Like how to kill a pig. Some of them stuck with it, but most of the communities folded and people traipsed back to the Fossil-Fuel God.[16]

Fast forward to the new millennium, and we're more reliant on that god than ever. We get all the food we want; we have media content on tap. We're addicted to electricity, jacked up on Wi-Fi. If we chop off our thumb in a bizarre lawnmower accident, there's a doctor to help us. Plenty of us still face frightening problems in life, but a lot of us are pretty safe, relatively speaking—we're well looked after.

The zombie scenario wades into our cosy lives, slaps our face with a rotting hand and says: *Grow up, you little baby. How are you going to cope when society explodes?* And the thing is, we know it just might. Here's a fun fact to drop in to conversation at your next dinner party. The executive director of the United Nations World Food Program recently took up the popular saying that society is only seven meals away from anarchy.[17] That's right. If your town or city misses seven consecutive meals, the polite lines of property and law are going to vanish. Cue the neighbours kicking your door in to feed their dying baby.

Of course, we don't know for certain that will happen—but the zombie scenario is cool for us moderns, because it challenges our preparedness. Will I be able to light a fire with no matches? Do I know how to get fresh water? No wonder there's such a side industry in zombie culture of "how-to" stuff, like books on where to hide, or how to tell if a neighbour is infected, or tips like cutting your long hair—because ponytails are like cocktail sticks to zombies. The zombie scenario seems laced with opportunities to learn and grow, to be more self-sufficient.

The classic survivalist who lives in a bunker of guns and water bottles, waiting for the end of the world, can still be a figure of fun to us. Yet with devastating hurricanes, earthquakes, diseases and the threat of war hitting the headlines all the time, there are growing groups who wonder: what if they're right? Writing in 2013, the *L.A. Times* TV critic Mary McNamara noticed a surge in shows involving global cataclysm and the destruction of democracy as we know it. "Once," she writes, "we looked to the individual as the key to conflict—man versus nature, man versus man, etc.—we now worry more about society, what it will look like, how it will survive." The zombie is the ideal monster to reflect "today's zeitgeist of fear of a world-changing event."[18]

Yet zombies don't just appeal to our epic fears. They probe more personal forms of dread too. The most obvious is how they confront us with death itself. We just spent a whole chapter talking about how modern society hides its dead, while at the same time offering a glut of simulated corpses to ponder. Our culture can't seem to stop creating worlds in which corpses refuse to stay hidden. They force their way back into our houses, insisting on engagement.

The walking dead speak to other, time-bound fears too. They've been seen as metaphors for everything from the AIDS crisis to the cookie-cutter education system. And since the majority of zombie films have been made since the 11th of September 2001, they might just be a way of dealing with that most modern of global horrors: terrorism. Stephen King explores this interpretation in his non-fiction book *Danse Macabre*, when discussing the Zack Snyder remake of Romero's *Dawn of the Dead* (2004):

> By 2004, only three years downriver from 9/11, rampant consumerism was the last thing on our minds. What haunted our nightmares was the idea of suicide bombers driven by an unforgiving (and unthinking, most of us believed) ideology and religious fervour. You could beat 'em or burn 'em but they'd just keep coming, the news reports assured us. They would keep coming until we were dead or they were. The only way to stop them was a bullet in the head. Remind you of anything? . . . You can't debate with them, you can't parley with them. You can't even threaten their homes and families with reprisals. All you can do is shoot them and then steer clear of the twitchers. Remember that their bite is worse than fatal.[19]

If you think he's stretching this metaphor, look no further than the 2012 movie *Osombie: The Axis of Evil Dead*, which has the strapline *Bin Laden Will Die Again!* He's right there on the DVD cover, with staring, undead eyes. The film basically says: *Hey guys! Wouldn't it be a hoot to kill this guy a second time?*

We ought to slow down on this part and take it in. There really is a sense of glee in the dispatching of zombies. It's one of the key components of the entire genre. You can chainsaw them in half, ram pickaxes through their skull. I've seen a zombie killed with a spork. Another, with a dildo. Baseball bats are a good bet because they keep you at arm's length. Crossbows not so much. They look cool, it's true, but you need to get the damn arrow back which isn't so great when there's a crowd of them. And of course, your key asset in the zombie apocalypse is the humble gun.

Zombie culture says: *Grab as many weapons as you can, get out there and use them—on your neighbours and your work colleagues.* Had a bad day at work? Been stuck on a train packed with commuters? Take out your frustrations with an X-Box shotgun and a million pixelated victims. Where else do we get the chance to run wild through society, smashing windows, stealing cars and even bashing heads in? It's not that we desire this in real life, but in zombie world, it feels . . . liberating.

But zombies aren't just bowling pins, waiting for us to strike them down. They do subtler work too: they remind us of ourselves.

We humans today have got pretty much everything at our fingertips, yet we feel emptier than ever. We're more secure than we've ever been, but we're convinced we're going to lose it. We're way better connected with other people through technology, yet we feel like our relationships are shallow. We watch the deep, life-long friendships in sitcoms and see beautiful people hugging each other, and we sigh, because *we* don't have that. We don't have friends into whose kitchen we can just walk in and drink stuff from their fridge. 'Tis the stuff of dreams, this.

We live in an incredibly fragmented society. People keep themselves to themselves. We tell our own child off in public but wouldn't dream of doing that to a stranger's kid, in case we get put on some register. We don't know the names of our neighbours, and on trains and buses we don't strike up conversation with strangers because that feels odd, nay psychotic.

I learned that the first time I visited London. I was all Huckleberry Finn about it. Wide eyes, head cricked back and looking up at the scrapers. I hopped on a Tube train and was munching Extra Strong Mints. I turned to the guy sat next to me and said, "Do you want one?"

He looked at me like I was trying to kidnap him.

I don't offer anymore. None of us does.

Instead, we retreat into ourselves so we don't get hurt or stand out too much. We sit, staring at the private, managed little world on our phone. We laugh at the screen and live vicariously through it, but we feel sadness and guilt because, while it feels like we're part of a huge crowd, there are no real relationships there. We're obsessed with our own needs and can't control our appetites. We shuffle into stores and buy the latest product because we're always hungry. Have you noticed that about zombies? They don't eat someone's brains and say: *Hmmm. I think I'm done with eating humans. I'm gonna be a vegetarian.* Nah. They *can't* stop eating. They'll *never* stop because they are never satisfied.

And neither are we.

Both we and zombies are hopelessly addicted to consumption.

I discussed consumer culture with some monks in a monastery once. We were drinking beer around a roaring fire, and I asked them about their vow of poverty. They got no individual pay, and their possessions belonged to the entire community. I struggled with the idea of it, so I asked if they ever felt it took away their individual freedom.

"That's the big lie of rampant consumerism: that it brings you freedom," one of the monks said. "So many people think they own their things—except they don't. Their things own *them*."

I went to bed that night and thought of zombies. I thought: *Hang on a sec. What if the monks are the free ones, and I'm just a shuffling corpse, chewing on capitalism?* I thought about how much time I'd spent trawling the internet that week, trying to see what features the new iPhone was going to have. I remembered thinking how the new dual-camera on the latest model was going to make my current one a useless brick—despite my current one being perfectly fine.

Most commentary on modern zombies says the current walking dead are completely different from the old school voodoo versions, i.e. slaves who were subject to their bokor masters. But I think that the humble modern zombie has retained some of that theme. Lots of it in fact. It's just that our masters have upscaled to become multinational corporations.

Maybe that's why zombies matter to us so much at the moment. Because we sympathise with them. We see them dragging their feet through abandoned shopping malls, and we think: *Hey, I'm doing that. I'm just shuffling through life. I'm part of a crowd, but sometimes I feel horribly alone. And what if my existence could be boiled down to little more than sleeping, walking and consuming?* Maybe zombies fascinate us simply because they remind us so much of ourselves.

I make a final push against the toilet door.

The wheelchair zombie has finally gone. I hear his wheels squeaking off into the darkness, as he goes to look for a new meal.

I slip out of the toilets and start looking for more attaché cases. I shoot more zombies. One on the stairs, one in a dark corridor. I find myself whooping a lot as I run, ducking and dodging the grasping hands. Then something happens that I'm not expecting. An alarm goes off and doesn't stop, and a woman's voice is saying: "THE SELF-DESTRUCT SEQUENCE HAS BEEN ACTIVATED. ALL EMPLOYEES PROCEED TO THE EMERGENCY EXIT!"

We have three minutes to get out, before this place is overrun with the dead.

Everybody sprints for the stairs, and in the panic we all bottleneck at the final door, the one that leads to the 91-metre corridor that'll get us out of here. Everyone else pushes through, but I can't help it. I go *back in*. I wait for a while, shotgun raised. A crazy noise is coming from the other levels, so I move towards the metal stairs. I look up to where the Screamer was. There's a hideous sound of zombies coming: insane moans and wild groaning almost drowns out the alarm. I hear one of them roar. I can't even see them, but it's obvious they're getting closer. Fast.

The double doors crash open.

Time to go.

I spin on my trainers and rush after the others in my group, slamming the doors back with my shotgun cocked. They're walking fast up the corridor, but they're still just *walking*. I glance back and see black screaming shapes filling the space behind me.

"They're here!" I shout at the top of my voice, followed by a bellowing: "RUN!"

Nobody's walking anymore. I run too, but not so fast that I lose my place at the back. I want to be the last one out because every now and then I can spin round and fire off my final shots. But mostly I run, as I hear their screams behind me.

It's this moment that is the most thrilling of all. Me screaming "Run!" and sprinting up this corridor as an alarm squeals and lights flash, the undead right at my heel. I can tell you the technical term for how this situation feels right now: it's amazeballs. I've played countless hours of zombie video games—but none of them felt like this. No wonder these events are proving popular. For an experience-hungry public who want the next stage on from virtual reality, immersive simulations like this are a natural progression.

In real life, I'm a million miles away from being an action hero. You won't see me fighting baddies in alleyways; I don't kick down doors and pull triggers. But I have an imagination. So I've fully embraced the idea that for the last two hours I have been a totally bad-ass ghoul killer. And as I run, I feel like a fully alive human. This feels like *life*. And the moaning folk who have given me this wonderful feeling are dead and cold and rotting.

They're called zombies, and they're us, and I'm glad they're in my country.

CHAPTER SIX

KILLER CULTURE

I have the late Charles Manson's hair in my hands.

It's a thick, dark-grey lock curled inside a clear plastic sandwich bag. This hair comes from the head of a man who horrified the world in 1969. In August of that year, he commanded his most starry-eyed followers to butcher five people at the home of director Roman Polanski, in Benedict Canyon, near Hollywood. The "Manson Family" had killed people before, and they killed more the next night, but this was the crime that made them famous. On the 8th of August (and into the 9th), they shot or stabbed a writer, a coffee heiress, a celebrity hairdresser, a friend of the gardener, and Polanski's actress wife, Sharon Tate. She was eight months pregnant when they stabbed her sixteen times, which pretty much takes the death toll to six. Manson groupie Susan Atkins, who was later convicted for these multiple murders, used Sharon's blood to write "pig" on the door as they left.

I look at the hair in my hands. I wiggle the bag. It's just hair. But it's *his* hair. And the really whacky part is that I'm not standing in a crime lab or a climate-controlled museum, viewing exhibits with plastic gloves on. I'm in an English high-street shop, and if I wanted to, I could buy this hair and take it home. Maybe I could keep it on my mantelpiece, or Sellotape it to my head. I could leave it on someone's takeaway dinner in a tasteless prank. Or I could do what I think many buyers might do. Whip it out at dinner parties and guarantee an end to any lull in conversation.

This curled lock of Manson mane costs £40, and comes housed in a special glass vial with a photograph of him inside. There's an optional corded vial too, in case you want to wear it as a necklace.

The shop selling it is called Pandora's Box, and it's nestled in the cobbled streets of York—a pretty, antiquated English city, which ripped off most of its ancient architecture from Harry Potter sets. It sits near a health food shop, an estate-agency, and a place that sells knitting supplies. I found it easily because there's a skeleton dangling outside.

Here there are shelves packed with oddities, like animal skulls and pickled calves. It sells antique asylum records and microscope slides that hold the actual cells from aborted babies. When Heather Bowser, who owns the shop with her husband Greg, shows me these abortion slides, her voice is soft and affectionate. Reverent, actually. She doesn't like the idea of these kids being forgotten; so she collects them and keeps them in the shop's permanent museum collection. I held one to the light earlier, like a photographic negative, and looked through a child's only trace on the world. The only physical one, at least.

They sell a vintage embalmer's hair clamp from a New England mortuary. It currently has a starburst price sticker on it—the type you see in supermarkets offering 2-for-1 on hot dogs. This one says: *Used for styling the hair of the deceased.*

It's late afternoon on the 5th of November. Soon, fireworks will start popping in the sky to celebrate Guy Fawkes Night. The 31st of October has been and gone, but in here it's Halloween all year round. The taxidermy, animal skulls and vintage Parker Brothers Ouija board are fascinating enough, but it's the true crime stock that I've really come to see.

Manson is still in my hand when I turn to Heather, who has agreed to an interview. Heather is a young American and her hair, unlike Manson's, is dyed purple. Her T-shirt says *Strange and Unusual* on it. Yep.

I realise that she got this lock of Manson hair from a desk drawer, and wonder if this might be an under-the-counter item.

"Why don't you put his hair up on display, around the shop?"

"Oh, we do, but it pretty much sells as soon as it comes in. So we have to hold it back a bit." She taps her glasses up. "People often come and take pictures of the hair. Either to tell others how cool it is or how gross."

I glance at the Certificate of Authenticity that the shop produces. "And how do you know all this hair is actually his?"

"Well, if people want a DNA test then *they* can pay a grand for one, but we know whose hands it's passed through. We can't reveal the original source because they'd be cut off from the criminal, and we don't want that to happen."

"We try to keep killers' hair accessible," Heather's husband and business partner Greg says as he joins us. He's English, with a Northern accent, and he looks spookily like the Yorkshire Ripper, Peter Sutcliffe. If I was anywhere else, I'd keep that observation to myself. But here, it comes flopping out of me.

"You look like the Yorkshire Ripper!"

He smiles and nods. Then tells me his truck-driving dad was one of the many suspects in those crimes, during the 80s. He reckons this is probably what sparked his interest in murderers.

In the weeks leading up to this visit, I've been immersing myself in the "murderabilia" market, and I've found that there are true crime trinkets which go for *much* higher prices than this hair, online. That's what this is, by the way: murderabilia. A word that's as clumsy-sounding as it is unnerving. As you read this, folks are in coffee shop queues or in their offices over lunch, typing in their credit card details to buy items with a physical connection to the world's most savage killers. These items are mostly sold through websites with delightful names like Serial Killers Ink, Murder Auction, Supernaught and Dark Vomit, and there's a wild and vast array of items on offer.

All the big names in serial killing crop up, like Aileen Wuornos, who shot seven men dead and had a film made about her called *Monster* (2003). You can buy the last ever *TV Guide* she owned when on death row for $850. I guess the cover article on "Why Everybody *Still* Loves Raymond!" is a bonus.

Elsewhere, I found a cruddy-looking signed picture of a dinosaur, drawn with pen. The artwork is so ropey, you'd tell your toddler to scrunch it up and try again. But it goes for $1,200 because it's by Satanist serial killer, Richard "the Night Stalker" Ramirez. He killed thirteen people and committed 30 other crimes (including rape and torture).[1] Ted Bundy brutally raped and killed at least 30 women (including children), but a Christmas card he wrote while on death row currently goes for £5,000. Child-killer Ian Brady is nowhere near as hot right now. A two-page ranting letter he wrote in 2011 sells for a mere £300.

The late Charles Manson crops up a fair bit too; among his memorabilia is one of the weirdest items I've come across. His unfinished burrito, wrapped in foil, was nabbed during a prison visit in 2002.[2] It'll set you back $995. It's well past its sell-by date, but I wonder if the person who pays a cool grand for a half-eaten burrito might be tempted to eat a little bit of it themselves? Or at least touch their lips to where *his* lips were? Because this murderabilia thing is fuelled, partly, by a sense of connection with those who most people would call monsters. It's a quest for understanding.

To get a handle on the industry, I speak to one of its leading lights, Eric Holler. He runs one of the most prominent murderabilia sites, Serial Killers Ink. I ask him how he first got into this industry, and he says it was when the killer rapist Richard Ramirez (who can't draw dinosaurs very well, remember) asked him if there was some way Holler could become his eBay art dealer. This was back in the 1990s, when Ramirez was still in prison.

"I accepted, of course," Eric tells me, as if to decline such an offer would have been the response of a crazy person. "At that time, true crime collectibles as a hobby really didn't exist. I was one of the very first to tap into what would eventually become what it is today."

He says his customers range from university professors who want teaching aids for class, to soccer moms. He sells all around the world, but he tells me that the United States and the United Kingdom seem to be hot spots. I ask him what his top sellers are.

"Without a doubt, our most popular items would be pieces that are either directly or indirectly associated with the likes of Charles Manson, John Wayne Gacy, Ted Bundy and Jeffrey Dahmer."

That's a lot of murder and a lot of coin as a result. And here I am, in a high-street shop, surrounded by killers' hair and morticians' clamps, where people pay to get close to death and to those who bring it.

Simple question really: *What the hell is going on?*

To find some answers, I seek out Jon Kaneko-James, a London-based writer and historian who tells me that the practice of collecting death souvenirs is probably as old as death itself.

One of the most prominent historical parallels, he says, are religious relics. For thousands of years, believers were creepily eager to possess the material remains of saints and holy figures—whether it's the finger of St Pancras, a rib from St Cassian or the jawbone of St Susanna. At one point in the twelfth century, even John the Baptist's head was knocking about in Constantinople—only there were two of them to choose from. These body parts were symbols of virtue, or even vessels of miraculous power. In other words, they were highly collectable. Like an early version of Pokémon.

Even the most pious folks would go to twisted lengths to acquire these death pieces, like Bishop Hugh of Lincoln. In 1191, the monks of a Normandy abbey showed him what was reputed to be the arm of Mary Magdalene. Itching to have it, Hugh pulled out a knife and tried to cut a piece off. The blade was too blunt, so he horrified the monks by using his mouth instead. He bit two chunks from her arm. Gotta catch 'em all, I guess. Imagine if today the Archbishop of Canterbury dug up the body of Mother Theresa and chewed off parts of her leg. He'd be carted off as a swivel-eyed lunatic. The Bishop of Lincoln, by contrast, ended up being canonised.[3]

Pieces of hangman's rope—and even the executed corpses themselves—were sometimes chopped up and sold off, direct from the gallows. When Elizabeth Broadingham was burned at the stake in York in 1776, for murder, spectators scooped up her ashes as a keepsake,[4] and after Louis XVI was guillotined in 1793, Parisians pushed forward to mop up the blood-soaked earth with their handkerchiefs.[5] High-profile executions like this deserved a memento, and this was, to be fair to them, in the days before fridge magnets. One of these handkerchiefs was submitted for DNA testing in 2012 and was proven to contain Louis's blood.[6]

A vivid case of more modern murderabilia happened in the nineteenth century when a guy called William Corder shot his lover to death. The fact that he was hanged didn't stop him becoming a celeb. There were theatre productions, puppet shows and songs based on the murder. People even flocked to the crime scene, while 7,000 people turned up for his execution. For a few weeks after, you could even visit a shop in Oxford Street, London where a piece of his scalp was on display.[7] Today it has been moved to Bury St Edmunds, where it's still on show to the public.

I first noticed the desire for killer collectables when I saw the British TV reports of Ted Bundy's execution. I was fourteen at the time, and I remember the crowd outside the prison pumping homemade signs saying *Bundy BBQ* and *Tuesday is Fryday!* A young woman was interviewed on camera, and she looked like any one of his 30 victims. Only she was alive and smiling, mocking him by wearing a tin-foil cap on her head (much like the electric chair skull-cap that was about to conduct the charge into Bundy's brain). This execution had a full-on party atmosphere. But there was an image from his execution that I never really forgot. A middle-aged man with a ragged perm and cream chinos was standing against the cloudless Florida sky . . . and he was selling T-shirts. The design was a red-ink cartoon of Bundy being buzzed to death in the chair. Across the top were the words *Burn Bundy Burn*.[8] I've trawled the murderabilia sites to see if these tees come up for sale, but you can't get them anywhere. Eric Holler, the murderabilia dealer, tells me he hasn't seen one on the market in 25 years—and he lives a mere twenty miles from the very prison where Bundy was executed.

The rarity of those T-shirts intrigues me, and I wonder how many of the victims' family and friends bought them that day. Who knows? Maybe they're now folded neatly in attics, passed down through families, never to be sold. Kept by people who despise Bundy, but are keen to hold onto an object from a day that was historic and meaningful to them. Or perhaps there's another explanation for their rarity. Maybe all those T-shirt owners just burned them in disgust when they got home.

Is that what this murderabilia thing is about? Holding on to history?

That's the frequent response I'm getting from collectors and true crime aficionados. They tell me that buying handwritten letters or swatches from the shirt of a death row inmate is emphatically *not* a way of supporting the crimes. Rather, they're unflinching attempts at remembering reality.

The shop I'm standing in now makes this point explicit on its online entry for the Manson hair:

> We do not believe that the crimes Mr Manson is accused of are OK, we do not support the behaviour of his supporters. We believe that history and specifically dark history is fascinating. An interest in the darker side of history is not indicative of supporting the beliefs of those committing the crime.

When I ask Eric Holler about this, he gives a similar response. He insists the industry isn't as sick as it sounds. "It's no different from the people who collect war medals or Nazi memorabilia," he tells me.

There *is* a logic to that argument because even lofty, respectable institutions collect murderabilia too. Like the National Museum of Health and Medicine in Washington, DC, for example. They've gone to great pains to preserve three items from the autopsy of President Lincoln. They've got the bullet, some skull fragments created by the shot, and the surgeon's probe that popped the slug out. It's the full set, and nobody's saying they're a bunch of sweaty degenerates for having it. Because it's history; it's educational.

However, as we chat in his shop, Greg is happy to admit that the attraction to this stuff isn't *just* to do with logging and learning about past events. It's also about the relentless drive to own objects. "I'm a hoarder. I'm a collector, and I just love to have these things."

"So," I ask him, "what's the murderabilia item that you'd *love* to own?"

He answers instantly: "I'd like something from Ed Gein. You know, the rock star of serial killers. That's the stuff *everybody* wants."

If you're unfamiliar with Gein, you've probably heard of him from the movies. He was the inspiration for Norman Bates in *Psycho*, Leatherface in *The Texas Chainsaw Massacre* and Buffalo Bill in *The Silence of the Lambs*. This necrophiliac, grave-robbing murderer (how's that for a Tinder profile?) turned his Wisconsin farmhouse into a veritable cathedral of the macabre. And his collection included—brace yourself because this is *not* nice—human lips dangling from string on the windowsill and a soup bowl made from a hollowed-out skull. I've seen the actual crime scene photos, and it's clear he took time and care with his home. There were skulls rammed on bedposts, and skin vests and skin bracelets that he wore around the house. They found nine skin masks hanging from his wall and a belt that he'd decorated using female nipples. And on his kitchen table, police found a cup filled with four noses.[9]

When horrified officers discovered this gore show, the items weren't thrown away or burned with a flamethrower. Most were reburied in a cemetery plot, paid for by the Madison Diocese of Wisconsin.[10] Much like the murderabilia crew, Catholics see a power in macabre objects. They couldn't just be dumped or obliterated. They needed to be put to rest in a place of *remembrance*.

So, for murderabilia fans, this hobby is in part a desire to connect with history and in part the relentless desire to collect rare things, but it's also about shock too. After all, Pandora's Box sells Christmas baubles with Charles Manson's face on them. That's hardly something the National Museum of Health and Medicine does.

I talk to Heather and Greg about this aspect of murderabilia.

"We both love that shock factor. The idea of freaking people out," Heather says, and looks over at Greg. He smiles back. "It starts as a kid, when you go home with crazy-coloured hair. Then shocking people just ends up being your life."

This makes sense. Because what do you do if you have a rebellious streak *and* the distinctly uncool hobby of collecting? I think of all those people with thousands of stamps or Beanie Babies or Harry Potter wands, lined up and logged on shelves and desks. I recently read about a bloke who has a massive collection of spoons in his house. *Spoons*, for crying out loud. I think: *What if murderabilia is just an anti-establishment version of stamp collecting?*

But then I think of these true-crime collectables, and a thought clangs in my head like a rusty old bell. *Don't serial killers love collecting morbid objects too?* Only criminologists don't call those objects murderabilia. They call them trophies. And, rather than collecting for its own sake, don't murderers collect trophies to do something far more worrying: to relive the thrill of the original kill?

Ted Bundy kept mementos—keepsakes from his victims, like their necklaces, or their heads. Like various other serial killers, he took Polaroids of their used, degraded bodies. Bundy was interviewed extensively after he was caught. When asked why he took these pictures, and why he was a hardcore murderabilia collector, he gave this skin-tightening answer:

"When you work hard to do something right, you don't want to forget it."[11]

The thing about collecting anything, from vinyl records to porcelain penguins, is that it's not so much about collecting as it is about *connecting*. Old guys hunt for vintage baseball cards because when they touch these things they feel their youth. Fans collect celebrity items and autographs because they think it will help them connect with the essence of that person. In a

2011 study, Newman, Diesendruck and Bloom call this "celebrity contagion," a form of magical thinking around objects.[12]

For example, when Justin Bieber has a milkshake, some people think that his immaterial essence is transferred to the glass. Some of his uber-fans, "Beliebers," will pay £65k for one of these glasses on eBay.[13] The contagion idea also explains our disgust at murderabilia because we may fear that these objects have a kind of evil residue. By touching it, we might somehow associate ourselves with the original owner. Professor of psychology Bruce Hood demonstrated this phenomenon with a simple test. Speaking at a science festival, he pulled a blue cardigan out of a shoebox and said he'd pay anybody £10 to try it on. Most of the audience were keen to do it. Then he told them that the cardigan had belonged to the serial killer Fred West. Despite his assurance that it had been thoroughly washed and bore no trace of the original owner, enthusiasm waned. Hood says that whenever he does this test, at this point, "most hands go down . . . of the few that stay up and put it on, most people move away from them. It's a powerful emotive effect."[14]

For some murderabilia collectors, this sense of inherent, evil power in a true crime object is one of the *attractions*. Criminologist Scott Bonn suggests that some believe serial-killer items may have a "talisman effect:" that a murder-tinged object might magically protect the new owner from future tragedy.[15] I speak to a man in Scotland, who wishes to remain anonymous, who similarly sees these objects as being invested with supernatural power. Only he doesn't see them as having protective qualities. He sees that power as supernaturally evil. He collects true crime artefacts as a way of keeping their residual evil power away from others.

What about the people who collect murderabilia, not as a protective talisman, but because they simply want to connect with the killer or perhaps even *learn* from them? Might some collectors be looking for some sort of vicarious buzz?

The website darkvomit.org is selling a Paint-by-Numbers set for $60 based on the "Pogo the Clown" self-portrait by John Wayne Gacy. Gacy raped and killed 33 men and young boys, but also had a thing for painting, and this set promises that you too can "Learn to paint like a Serial Killer!" The implication being that you'd want to.

It's tongue-in-cheek, I guess, but it's an odd quirk of killer culture that I keep spotting: a quest to humanise the killer and empathise with them. To even take something from them and mould it into ourselves. Of course, human beings have a natural and noble tendency to empathise. Empathy is often cited as one of the very things serial killers lack, which is a huge part of their problem. So, it's good we have it, but, man, is it confusing when it comes to empathising with folks who eat other people. Take Eric Holler, the murderabilia magnate.[16] I've seen interviews with him in which he admits that after direct dealings with these killers, he'd class many of them as not only sources of his merchandise, but as his friends.

This "killers are pals" thing is relatively common with fans of fictional murderers. Just look at movie killers like Jason Voorhees, Michael Myers or Hannibal Lecter; when they first appear on the cultural landscape they're grotesque figures of fear. A few sequels later, however, and they've morphed into anti-heroes, venerated by fans who make and wear costumes based on these movie killers, or even have tattoos of their leering faces etched forever on their skin. But for real-life killers, this move to acceptance requires a more complex dissociation between the killer as a person, or character, and the crimes they committed. For example, on the Tumblr site Mr. Bundy, a female Bundy blogger sets out this mission statement for her page:

Everything Ted Bundy related. While I despise what he did and feel utmost sympathy for his victims, I think he was a physically beautiful man and this blog will chronicle his life and my affection for him. Feel free to message me, fellow Ted-heads![17]

Affection.

That's the sentiment that'll make most people choke on their donuts, but there it is. She's not the only "Ted Head" either. I found other blogs defending him and even T-shirts that rejected the old slogan of *Burn, Bundy, Burn!* These ones said *Bundy for President!* He even features in the "Notorious Serial Killer Top Trumps" game. With at least 30 kills under his belt, Bundy's probably a prized card. But why on earth would he ever become a prized *person*, worthy of our attention, and, even as the Mr. Bundy blogger says, our affection?

I suppose the most obvious answer is that some serial killers are naturally charismatic. They're persuasive, hypnotic even. It's one of the reasons they're so good at luring people into their cars, I guess. Heck, one of them even turned up as a contestant on American TV game show *The Dating Game* in 1978. You can find the episode on YouTube in which perky drama teacher Cheryl Bradshaw fires her questions at the three eligible bachelors before picking the handsome and witty Rodney Alcala. She, and the programme makers, had no idea that by then he'd raped and killed four women in California and New York. She hung out with Alcala backstage and felt he was a little too creepy. She called off the date. But her attraction to him in the first place was understandable: he was a charmer.

It gets way more confusing to learn that there are women who would have jumped at the chance to date Alcala, precisely *because* of his homicidal portfolio. In his book, *The Serial Killer Files*, Professor Harold Schechter calls such women "serial killer groupies," and he notes how brutal killers like John Wayne Gacy, Henry Lee Lucas and Ed Gein were no great shakes in the looks department. Yet once these three men were imprisoned, something very weird happened: it was like the world's most baffling makeover. All three started getting mail from "gushing female admirers."[18]

Why would they be drawn to these savage men? Are these arch manipulators bringing women under their spell, creating new victims, even from prison? Or, as Schechter asks, are some women "so devoid of any sense of self-worth that, on some level, they believe that only a monster could love them?"[19] This may be true in some cases, but Schechter would be the first to admit that serial killer groupies are not all weak, needy people. They are, after all, *choosing* to connect with these murderers.

Some theorists have sought to explain what these women do, by arguing that they suffer from hybristophilia.[20] Coined by psychologist John Money, "hybristophiliacs" are sexually attracted to actions that most of us find repulsive. They seek out partners who have "a predatory history of outrages perpetrated on others." According to Money, liars, cheaters, murderers and rapists naturally fit the bill. It's sometimes referred to as "Bonnie and Clyde" syndrome.[21]

Hybristophilia might explain some cases, but Katherine Ramsland, a forensic psychology professor, says there can be many other complex motives at play. For example, our media places massive amounts of attention on these killers, who, as a result, often end up as celebrities. Ramsland suggests that some women figure that by connecting with these killers personally, they may experience fame by proxy.[22] They may also realise that incarcerated killers have little else to do all day (unlike Premier League footballers or film stars). Might that mean they're some of the few world-famous figures who might actually reply to a letter? Once connected with these men, some women even find themselves becoming news stories themselves—only they don't have to kill anyone to achieve the notoriety.

If this sounds cold and self-seeking, professor Sheila Isenberg adds another angle: contact with such men may even be strangely therapeutic. After interviewing dozens of women for her book *Women Who Love Men Who Kill* she noted a fascinating pattern. Sheila tells me:

Without exception, the women I interviewed for my book had all been involved in earlier relationships that were, in different ways, abusive. Some were harmed—either sexually, physically, or psychologically— as children, by their parents or other adults. Most had been in early abusive relationships with boyfriends or husbands. Becoming involved in a relationship with a man behind bars allows this abused woman to feel more powerful, more in control, often for the first time in her life, for these reasons. *She's* making the decisions: whether to visit, whether to accept the collect phone call, how to interact with the attorney. These women have the freedom to come and go, and thus are in a position of power. It may seem counterintuitive, but becoming involved with a violent, convicted murderer feels safe for a woman who's had an abusive past. He's behind bars; she's not. He can't hurt her, and she's in the driver's seat.

Clinical psychologist Dr Stuart Fischoff makes a similar argument, suggesting that, often for a serial killer groupie, the object of love is largely irrelevant. She is connecting with a fantasy, "a dream lover, a phantom limb."[23] It's a relationship she needn't ever consummate, and she can walk away from it at any time.[24] She is the one in control.

Ramsland suggests an additional reason why women may connect with killers. They may want to help a misunderstood social outcast. Whether it comes from some maternal instinct, empathy or a desire to rescue, they believe they might be the one to tame the "wild beast."[25]

Maybe these killers attract certain women because they appear to be enigmas that others lack the stomach or compassion to solve. Humans love a good puzzle, and these murderers are like "Soduku: Extreme Edition"—a mysterious cipher to pore over and crack. These theories challenge the view that, when it comes to serial killer groupies, these women can only ever be manipulated by murderers who hold all the power. Perhaps in some cases they are. Yet for many women, the attraction to killers is that the power is in *their* hands.[26]

I was intrigued to find a combination of these motivations in the case of a 30-year-old Siberian woman called Natalya Pichushkin. In 2016, she became infamous in Russia for accepting the marriage proposal of the country's worst serial killer since Soviet days: Alexander Pichushkin.[27] Known as the "Chessboard Killer," Pichushkin was caught before fulfilling his vision of murdering one person for each of the 64 squares of a chessboard. He was convicted of killing 48 people. Natalya had been fascinated by killers since childhood, and began to write to what she calls "one time" murderers when she was in high school. But she was soon drawn to killers with multiple victims. She described them as "hotter." When she was 22, she sent a letter to the Chessboard Killer, knowing that he had "caused a stir not only in our country, but throughout the world." To her surprise, he wrote back.

At the time, she was married to an alcoholic who treated her poorly. After two years of letter writing, she realised she'd fallen in love with Pichushkin, partly because she was so impressed at how clever he'd been to evade the police for so many years. Yet she also claims to have seen beyond the monster label and found something loveable. "Every maniac lives two lives," she told the *Siberian Times* in 2016. "In one body coexist two completely opposite personalities. I managed to get rid—psychologically—of my thoughts that I was dealing with a maniac. And I loved what I see behind this." She can't remember exactly when she told him she loved him, but says: "It was me who took the first step, that's for sure." She admits that her fiancé's crimes were terrible, but she rationalises them in a peculiar way. "No-one can blame him except relatives of the victims. This is the case just between him and them. All others simply do not have the right to open their mouths."[28]

Natalya says she wants to have Alexander's baby, and has a picture of his face (hovering over a chessboard) tattooed on her forearm. Yet, unlike his victims, she retains much of the power in the relationship. She can end it at any time, and she knows it's impossible that she'll ever run into him without her explicit consent. After all, he's serving a life sentence inside the "impossible-to-escape" Polar Owl penal colony in Siberia.

For some, the quest to connect with brutal killers is to ultimately understand and reform the character, for others it might be more about a forbidden thrill, or a complex experience of power. Whatever the case, murderabilia and serial killer groupies show us that rather than run from the beast under the bed, a surprising number of people are compelled to reach out and touch it, and even to collect its hair in a jar.

For Eric Holler, the complicated psychological motivations behind murderabilia collecting are kind of irrelevant. For him, it's all about business, and business, he tells me, is good. And while the killers themselves aren't allowed to profit from their crimes,[29] he and other dealers have found themselves making a comfortable living from violent death.

For many, this idea of making money from murder prompts the biggest shudders of disgust. It's a criticism that William Harder—who runs the popular collectables site Murder Auction—grabs, packs up like a blood-soaked snowball and throws right back. In an interview in 2015, he said: "*Everybody's* making money off crime, including the judges, the lawyers, the cops, even *you* guys [the journalists] today. You're not here on your own accord; you're not here for fun. You're getting paid. Everybody's making money, but if I try to make a couple of bucks . . . God forbid I make $20 off a letter."[30]

Harder's point isn't easy to ignore. We aren't so squeaky clean ourselves. Millions of us spend an inordinate amount of time and money pondering the violent demise of real victims. We might not pay for killer collectibles, but we sure like to follow the antics of these murderers on our TV screens, particularly in recent years. In 2016, documentary filmmaker Joe Berlinger told *NME* magazine that TV networks were asking him to make films about homicide like never before. That interest has been fuelled by hit crime shows like *Making a Murderer* (which was Netflix's second most watched original programme in 2016)[31] as well as the headline-grabbing most popular podcast of all time, *Serial* from 2014, which was downloaded a staggering 80 million times.[32] In 2016, the TV network FX announced that, with 12 million viewers, their dramatization of the O.J. Simpson trial was the most-watched originally-scripted premier of any series in its history.[33]

There's such a demand for this grim content that true crime gets its own dedicated channels these days. Investigation Discovery, for example, is stuffed with real-life stories of brutal murder and depraved serial killing. By 2016, it was the only newly launched cable network to make it to the top twenty rated channels in the United States, and it had found a particularly strong audience with women—including high-profile fans like Lady Gaga, Nicki Minaj and Serena Williams.[34]

Watch the news and it's no different. For the content-hungry news channels, serial killers are the gift that keeps on giving. I spoke to serial killer expert Dr Scott Bonn about this. He's a criminologist and college professor now, but he used to be a TV executive back in the 90s. He admitted that, like it or not, murder in the news is often seen by the networks as similar to entertainment shows like *CSI* or *Criminal Minds*. Murder reports draw in large audiences and so advertisers are keen to plough money into networks that show them. Bonn told me: "It's in the best financial interests of network television producers to make their crime news stories as shocking and enticing as possible to viewers."

You see a vivid example of this with the *National Enquirer*. Back in the 1950s, the tabloid magazine saw its circulation soar when it began including extremely graphic photographs of murder and tragedy. Generoso Pope Jr was the editor at the time, and one day he witnessed how people crowded around a car crash. Inspired, he rushed back to the office and instructed his reporters to find as much grisly content as possible. They did, and the subsequent stories which ran through the late 50s and early 60s featured full photographs of real boiled babies and actual dead children crushed under the wheels of cars. The strewn remains of train-wreck victims and children decapitated by their parents appeared in full, centre-spread detail. Pope even instructed his photo-retouchers to enhance the blood and brain matter in certain shots.[35] All this horror was easily accessible on mainstream newsstands. The approach appalled some, like the Chicago Transit Authority, which banned the *Enquirer*. But the new emphasis on death had worked wonders for the magazine's popularity, and the ban didn't last long. The gore, along with photos of scantily-clad women, helped turn circulation from 17,000 a week in 1952 to 1 million a week in 1966.[36]

True murder stories, and particularly serial killer news stories, can stretch for weeks or months, even years. They offer a catalogue of murders to discuss. There's plenty of scope for the studio animators to come up with fancy graphics of crime scene reconstructions, or last seen routes of the victims. And if the killer hasn't been caught, all this ongoing "he's still out there" narrative builds a steady backbeat of fear that makes viewers keep watching through fascination (*I can't believe this is happening!*), thrill (*This is horrible but kind of exciting*), and all-out fear (*We have to watch this, to stay safe*). No wonder people tune in.

In 1989, journalist Eric Pooley wrote an influential critique of local TV news called "Grins, Gore and Videotape." In it he coined a phrase that sums up what I'm saying here: "If it bleeds it leads."[37]

It's easy to blame the media for force-feeding us all this blood, but that's like ordering linguine then berating the chef for serving us linguine. We and the media are in cahoots. They've spotted our appetite, and they're feeding it. And no amount of movies, documentaries, podcasts or TV dramas seems to satiate us. We love the adrenalin it gives, and that stuff's addictive. Very few of us are serial murderers. But millions of us are serial *consumers* of murder. And it's not fiction.

But before we give up on humanity, let's consider something else. What if this obsession with murder is not that we don't care, but rather that we care a lot? And what if we pay attention in order to keep our society sane?

Scott Bonn, the TV executive-turned-criminologist, wrote the book on why we love serial killers. He called it *Why We Love Serial Killers* and it's a fascinating, chilling read. When I asked him about this weird obsession, he gave a startling response: "Serial killers are necessary to society."

Bonn argues that these killers, reprehensible and unwelcome as they are, provide a vital service to society. They reinforce our sense of right and wrong. Every time a serial killer strikes (and the media linger on it) it's like this global klaxon announcing: *Remember folks—this is what you don't do.* In our modern world of disparate opinions on morality, it's refreshing to have everybody on the same page for a change. These crimes can therefore foster bonds between communities through our shared disgust at what the killers have done, and also through our fear. And we *are* afraid. After all, these killers don't want to stop, and, worse still, they hide in plain sight.

The odds of us being a victim are miniscule, but how do we avoid these maniacs when they really could be anybody? It's not as if they put signs on their car saying *Murderer On Board*. That's the really unsettling part, the bit that makes interviewees scratch their heads as they come to terms with the discovery of a neighbour's crimes. *But he looked so normal,* they say. *He just lived his life like the rest of us. He walked his dog, he emptied his bins. We'd never have known.* These psychotic killers are not strangers. They're average folks who blend in anywhere, even in the house next door.

This presents us with a truly shocking realisation: these killers are from *our* group and *our* tribe. Such knowledge baffles and disorientates us because the idea of killing for pleasure does *not* compute. If someone kills for money, power or love, we understand it, to some degree. We look down on the woman who poisons her husband for the insurance, but we *get* it. We're capitalists and greedy too, so we can appreciate her motivation, if not her actions. We condemn the man who pushes his boss under a train, but *we've* had arguments with our boss too, and might have fantasised about throwing hot tea in their face, or clobbering them over the head with a laptop.

Serial killers are different; they threaten our sense of self and society. They make us wonder what dark secrets our neighbours might hide, underneath the friendly façade. Can we really know—or trust—anyone? Our doctor, our kid's teacher, our pastor, or even our *spouse?*

Glum thoughts like this are not conducive to sleep or society. So, to re-establish the morality of "people like us," we do something fascinating. We distance ourselves from serial killers by constructing new identities for them. Bonn argues that we do this in two ways. The more common is that we turn them into mythical beings. News agencies that would normally avoid religious or mythological language use terms like "evil" or "monster." They dish out monikers that make the killer feel less like a human and more like a fairytale beast: Richard Trenton Chase becomes the Sacramento Vampire; Otto Stephen Wilson becomes the L.A. Ripper; and Francis LeRoy becomes the Werewolf. The more inhuman we make them, the further away they feel from our own world.

If we don't use supernatural language to distance ourselves, we might dig biological trenches instead. Murderers, we may conclude, have abnormal brains.

I noticed both these effects when I watched a documentary recently about Arthur Shawcross. He butchered eleven women, and his first two crimes were the rape, murder and mutilation of two children. I was so appalled by his crimes that I started speaking out loud at the TV, shouting un-Christian, un-vicar things like: "You sick pig," "You fat monster!" I felt genuine hate for this constantly squinting beast.

I now suspect that my shouting was probably a technique to distance myself from him. I needed to dehumanise him in my mind. And when the documentary talked about his MRI scans, the distancing intensified. Shawcross's brain showed natural abnormalities which, it was said, may have contributed to him seeing murder as acceptable.[38] Hearing this was a relief. I was able to file him away as a medical mutation who was nothing like the rest of us, because we have normal brains and therefore normal ideas of what is or isn't acceptable.

Yet this MRI scan brought me something else too, something unexpected. A creeping sense of empathy. What if Shawcross, and killers like him, might be victims too? What if they are, in some ways, at the mercy of their damaged minds? Then the documentary talked about the sexual abuse Shawcross had suffered as a kid. I sat on my sofa, confused and disturbed. I loathed him and what he did, but there I was feeling an unpleasant drip of sympathy.

Thankfully, the feeling didn't last long. The narrator suggested that Shawcross might have made up all this child abuse stuff. I breathed again. Now it was easier to slot him back in the demonic monster file, but I'm old enough to know better. I know that deep down there's something more complex at work in these killers than "pure evil," something that may be impossible to unravel. But our morbid culture contains people who feel compelled, at least, to try. To see the worst of us as still *us*.

However, for most of us, our brains struggle to cope with this level of contradiction. We prefer the labels of monster or mutant, because when we decide a murderer is one of *those*, it eases the collective psyche. The "killer next door" wasn't one of us after all. They become, in the end, someone from another tribe, another *species* even. One that we spend time trying to understand, relaxed to know that we'll never be like that.

Distance is important. Because the closer the morbid gets to our personal experience, the less fascinating it is. It just feels plain horrible. I notice this when I ask Heather and Greg if they've ever turned down an item of murderabilia because they found it distasteful.

"Somebody recently tried to sell us bricks from Sandy Hook," Heather says.

I pause. It's the Connecticut school, where twenty-year-old Adam Lanza shot and killed 27 adults and kids. "And did you take them?"

She shakes her head. "I seriously felt sick to my stomach."

"We were offered the Columbine yearbook too," Greg adds. "We didn't touch that either."

"Why's that different?" I ask them.

"Because that's something I experienced the sorrow of, first-hand," Heather says. "When Columbine happened I think I was pregnant. And Sandy Hook's near where I grew up."

"So, you're saying there's no emotional distance there?"

"Exactly. I think I feel more uncomfortable when there's less distance."

This makes sense to me, but it does raise a challenge to the murderabilia market. What about the people who have no possibility of emotional distance at all?

Like the victims' families.

The man who coined the word "murderabilia" is Andy Kahan. He's a victim's advocate in the US and he's been trying to shut the industry down since 1999 (or "back when I had hair," as he puts it). When I call him in his Houston office he tells me it was hearing about the serial killer Arthur Shawcross that first introduced him to the industry. Remember, this was the killer of children and adults who also had an abnormal MRI scan. Heather and Greg have a clump of hair ripped from him too, only not from his head. It's ripped from his forearm in a big clump. Like Charles Manson's, they sell it by the strand and, when I compared the two, it looked much more wiry than the flowing locks of Manson.

When Kahan learned that Shawcross was selling his artwork through eBay, he was furious. When he found others doing the same thing, he started keeping a daily watch over the industry. He's been doing this ever since. Posing as an avid buyer, he buys items as examples and travels around America, giving talks and interviews about his quest to bring an end to the murderabilia trade. He's lobbied government and internet companies to get it banned. It was his campaign that got eBay to stop listing murderabilia in 2001. Yet he says that Facebook and private sites are still rife with it. I mention that I've been chatting with Eric Holler, aka Eric

Gein, and Kahan's response is instant. "Holler?" he groans down the phone. "He's one of the worst."

Kahan keeps a constantly updated database of exactly which serial killers are being sold; it contains 236 serial killer names. Some I've never heard of, but I recognise a lot of them, I tell him. To which Kahan makes a simple, sobering point: "Millions of people know the names of these killers. But can you name any of the victims? *Any* of them?"

This thought sticks with me. Because while our culture's obsession with killers may well have some psychological and sociological logic to it, it's a system in which the victims end up as little more than bit players. Their role is to support and supplement the more "exciting" story of the people who killed them.

Of course, this makes a twisted sort of sense. The character of a cannibalistic, necrophiliac serial killer is clearly more novel and salacious than the student nurse he kills. *Her* previous struggles are likely to have been mundane, like paying off a student loan or getting the oven door fixed. These types of things are in our lives already, so we don't tend to watch TV shows or listen to podcasts about them. We're unlikely to buy mementos of our student loan repayments or put our bills in a scrapbook. It's the stuff that feels distant from us—the wild, scary, unique stuff—that we're drawn to.

Victims' families don't have this distance. They see the effects of these killers as they really are, up close and devastating. Kahan tells me about parents who not only have to come to terms with the death of their child, but also with the idea that someone, somewhere is making money off the person who killed them. It's too much to take for many, especially when they know that the killer is often fully aware of this culture of worship. Kahan says some of the families set up a Google Alert for the killers' names. Every time a sale item from their child's murderer crops up, they see it. They can't do anything about it of course, but they see it, and from what Andy tells me, they often reach for the whiskey.

As we chat, Kahan drops a line in so casually that it takes me a second to register what he's said: "I'm also on the Board of Parents of Murdered Children and . . ." I faze out, trying to comprehend that we live in a world where organisations like that exist. He tells me that when they hear of murderabilia "the parents feel like they're being gutted all over again."

It's a horrifying (and sobering) thought, and one that all collectors and dealers of murderabilia must acknowledge. And yet, I wonder if the victims' families might find at least a *little* comfort, knowing that the murderabilia market may not be as heartless as it sounds at first. The image of a greedy capitalist building a lucrative killer-worshipping empire on the backs of dead victims is rightly repellent. Yet from what I've seen, it's not always as base as that. Murderabilia can be a complex way for human beings to ponder (and crucially, not *forget*) the dark moments of history.

Back in Pandora's Box, I hand Charles Manson's hair back to Heather and she slips it into an envelope. He vanishes from my world, filed away. I won't miss him.

Just then, Heather and Greg's young daughter Pandora comes hurrying in to say hi. It's only now I click that the place is named after her. Pandora's Box. She loves it here. She's at ease with the skulls and funeral clamps. But the fireworks are starting soon and she wants to get going. So, we all pose for a photograph, with a skeleton in the background, before she dashes out again.

I had first heard about Heather and Greg in a piece in the *Daily Star* online, which described them as "crime-mad" and "serial killer sickos."[39] But after spending the afternoon here, that's not what I see. They're into history and they love collecting things, but searching out rare golf balls or expensive stamps just wouldn't scratch their rebel-itch and their desire to shock. They're also a young couple with a child, who have managed to keep a business going in a time when local shops struggle to survive. Yet it's clear that their unusual choice of product line is hardly a get-rich-quick scheme. Even in the popular world of morbid interest, buying serial killer hair is still pretty niche. If they wanted to make *big* money, they'd turf out all these death trinkets and open a twee coffee-shop franchise instead. They describe Pandora's Box as "a follow your dreams and love what you do" type of job, before adding, "it's not a sound financial decision."

Still though, the customers *do* come. They've bustled through the shop constantly since I arrived. Some just browse and gawp at the crucified duckling; others get selfies holding a vial of Charles Manson hair. I've lost count of how many have wandered past me whispering, "This place is so cool."

Do Heather and Greg celebrate their morbid fascinations? Clearly. Do they therefore approve of the real-life murder of humans and animals? Not that I can see. Something more complicated is going on here. Throughout my time at Pandora's Box I've heard Heather use the word "beauty." She talks about how "pretty" her line of genuine bat skeletons looks, or how "precious" those slides of an aborted foetus are—the ones that she can't bear to throw away. There's a passion here to embrace the things that everybody else tends to shun. It's a character trait that's been with both Heather and Greg since childhood.

Greg grew up in Yorkshire, England. When he was young, he used to find "little bits of dead things" which he'd try to put back together. Heather grew up in Connecticut, USA, and she'd sometimes hold funeral services for animals she found that had been killed on the road.

As my visit comes to an end, I ask her, "Why *do* you do this, Heather?"

She blinks, and looks around the room at her collection. "I want to take the horrible things of the world and make them into something ordered. Make them pretty or catalogue them. It's a way of dealing with the bad things, I guess."

I smile at her because it's the same reason *I'm* drawn to morbid culture too, and why I write scary novels. Why I watch creepy movies. It's me trying to deal with the things that disturb me, instead of just ignoring them. We hug and shake hands. Just before I head off into the street, I spot one of the shop's own-branded mugs. *Don't Fear the Weird*, it reads.

It's night now and, as I head back along the cobbled streets of York, I notice a lightness in my step. I'm smiling as I button up my coat. It's not just the fact that I held Charles Manson's hair that's making me so bouncy. It's a sense of relief that I got it over with, and that this chapter on serial killers is over.

You see, most of the morbid culture I delight in is either fictional or it's rooted in history, distant from me. Yet for this chapter, I've been researching relatively recent real-life serial killers. I've done it for a solid month now, and it's started to get under my skin. I've been listening to audiobooks about them, watching documentaries and scrolling through graphic crime scene photos. I usually write in coffee shops, but this stuff has forced me to work at home—I don't want some Starbucks barista putting me on a register because she spots me pinch-zooming hideous selfies of killers in masks.

All this grim stuff has disturbed me more than I expected. Last Sunday, after a heavy week of research, I was in church. We were singing a happy song about Harvest and God providing. Hands were clapping. Voices were raised. Suddenly, out of the blue, my mind flung up a photograph of one of Ed Gein's victims, hanging from a wooden beam in a barn. I winced, and the words I was singing lodged in my throat. What made it worse was the fact that I had *no* idea what the woman's name was.

Spending lots of time thinking about serial killers, it turns out, makes me kinda glum. So I'm not the type to buy their hair—I'll save my cash for a horror movie instead. At least in those, the victims get up and walk away—and they get paid. Yet I still don't think the murderabilia crowd are monsters because I've started to understand their motivations. I'm just glad it's time for me to swim back up to the surface, and catch some air.

I buy a chunk of bread from the bakery and chomp into it greedily as I lean on a bench and wait for my bus. It's November; it's dark. The shops are closing up, and the fireworks start to crackle overhead. Little Pandora is probably whooping with delight, and I bet Heather and Greg are *ooh*ing and *aah*ing like everybody else. As I eat and reflect, I notice the people walking past me, and specifically, their hair.

There are many types of hairstyle. Permed, bobbed, shaved with a funky slicked-over fringe. Hair that's alive and bouncing, raked behind ears, hanging in eyes. Fringes puffed up with a blast of upward breath. Hipster beards and man buns. I watch them as the colours pop in the sky.

I feel among my own tribe again, and I'm relieved that Shawcross and Manson are sealed up in their little bags and out of my world.

This chapter is done and the distance is coming back. Telling me the world is okay, when I know it often isn't. Not for some people tonight. But I'm ready for the lie again.

I fling my arms around it like an old friend.

Chapter Seven

THE BEAST WITHIN

I'm hunting a werewolf tonight. In Hull.

I never really imagined that hairy man-beasts might stalk the streets of East Yorkshire. Generally hairy people, yes. But not human-animal hybrids with reflective eyes and fang-stuffed muzzles. Yet Hull just made headlines for a six-foot wolfman that prowls a lengthy city waterway called Barmston Drain. Sometimes it's been spotted up on its hind legs, sometimes on all fours; sometimes it shapeshifts right before people's eyes. One guy managed to outrun it, but only on a motorbike. A couple even saw it eating an Alsatian on Reform Street. It escaped over a seven-foot fence, dragging the dog's carcass with it.

Local historian Mike Covell wrote an article about it in the *Hull Daily Mail*, and within days the werewolf of Hull went global. Since the story broke, Mike has led numerous media companies, reporters and film crews out on the hunt, to see where the creature has been sighted.

Tonight, he's taking me.

It's a dark November evening, and I'll meet Mike in an hour at my hotel, but before I do, I use a bit of hunting initiative. I walk the streets of the city, looking for a butcher's shop. They're all closed, so I opt for a

Sainsbury's Local instead. I hover at the fridges filled with meat, trying to work out what werewolves like to eat. Sadly, they're all out of Alsatian. I grab a packet of sausages, but they make me snigger too much—it's just the image of me and this historian, running up and down the waterside with a string of sausages dangling. I shake my head and put the sausages back. This is a serious book, I tell myself. I'll get steak instead.

I scrabble around the fridge and find only salmon, which feels too civilised to be wolf food. A member of staff wanders up next to me. He's one of those chipper types, up on his toes.

"Hey! Can I help?"

"I hope so. I need steak. Like a decent chunk of it."

He purses his lips, then asks me a question that I swear staff members don't usually ask because it sounds too nosey. But tonight, of all nights, he asks, "What's it for?"

I look him straight in the eye. "It's for a werewolf."

The man blinks slowly.

I keep my face fixed, like I'm a big game-hunter. "I'm tracking the Hull werewolf tonight, and I need something to entice it out."

There's another staff member near us. She has punk hair and a nose stud. She had been sticking markdown prices on sandwiches, but now she's paused. She looks at me, grinning. "We have peppered beef. Will that do?"

"That'd be great."

The man heads backstage to get some while I have a brainwave. I look over at the woman. "And do you have any string? I need string."

"You mean, like a ball of it?"

Darn. She thinks I mean to coax the creature out like a cat with a dangling thread. I quickly explain. "Not a ball. I just need a strip of it. I want to tie it around the steak so I can drag it up and down the streets."

"Ah, right."

She's surprisingly chilled out about this. They both are, actually. Like, at this point in Hull's history, this is a perfectly normal grocery list. She vanishes behind the counter and comes back with two long strips of white cord. "We use these to wrap the newspapers up with. Will that do?"

"Perfect."

The man turns up with the two peppered steaks in a plastic carton. They look pretty thin, but I reckon they'll work just fine. I buy them and stick them in my backpack.

I realise I've got time for a kebab before the hunt. I find a cafe, and while I stand in the queue an incredibly hairy and freaky-faced man sidles up next to me. He's all beard and greasy hair, staring at the menu and licking his lips. There's a set of eyes and nose somewhere in the bristles, and he blinks a lot. He totally stinks too. I *swear* he's recently crapped himself. He must feel me staring because he suddenly flicks his head around. *Or maybe*, I think with a start, *he's sniffed the steak in my backpack!* For a dangerous second I almost say: *Are you the wolf man?* But he looks away and I find wisdom again. I find a table, too.

I sit in a moulded plastic chair and devour my kebab when a thought occurs to me. Why should the werewolf be a foul-smelling hairy bloke, anyway? I've seen a bunch of werewolf movies, and the beast often turns out to be some civilised, clean-looking sophisticate. That's the deep attraction to the werewolf idea, the thought of upstanding citizens turning feral. I glance across the cafe, looking for a polite man or woman in posh clothes. I see teenagers grunting instead.

Ten minutes later, I head to my hotel where I meet Mike Covell in the lobby. He's a 38-year-old historian, journalist and paranormal investigator. We grab hot drinks and head out, trekking through the backstreets of Hull looking for the beast. We talk as we walk, both of us glowing orange under the streetlights.

"So, when did the sightings start?"

"The reports stretch back decades," Mike says in a lovely Hull accent. "Been about twenty eyewitnesses since then, including two ex-servicemen." He reels the rest of them off on his fingers. "Shop workers, engineers, council workers. A nurse."

"Credible people."

"Yup. Reliable witnesses. They all saw some sort of wolf-like creature out here."

We turn into a street surrounded by industrial units and Mike slows to a stop. "So that's where the couple spotted the creature eating the Alsatian."

I whip my camera out and snap every conceivable angle with an enthusiastic trigger finger. I do this for all the key witness sites, feeling like I'm Fox Mulder. In time, the pavement turns to grass under our feet, and we start our long walk along Barmston Drain. It's a stretch of dirty-looking water, with wild ferns hanging over it. At one point, I spot what looks like a bike, dumped in the black water. I don't see many people about.

We have to duck under heavy branches, while the drain-bank slopes down to our right. I'm glad I brought my torch. It's the only thing stopping me from slipping in the dark and sliding into the drink. I imagine a wolf rising from the water, as I skid into its arms. Mike tells me he led a camera crew down here recently. At one point, they saw two luminous eyes staring at them in the dark. He says the crew freaked out and ran off, and no amount of consoling would bring them back. One crew member tried to chill them out by saying that those two glowing eyes were just two ducks, looking at each other, holding very still.

This duck theory seems more unlikely than a werewolf to me.

As we walk, I'm aware of my longing to see those eyes myself. I want to witness a huge beast lunge out of the bushes, because I was a werewolf fan long before I had body hair of my own. There's something about that idea of a totally normal human suddenly contorting and changing, and letting the beast within come out to play. It's a fascinating concept, and freaky too. I want to see it.

When we get to the bridge near Sculcoates Cemetery, Mike turns to me and says, "I think it's time you got your meat out."

We both titter at this, and I drop to my haunches. I tear the plastic pack open and can smell the dead flesh. It's cold in my fingers as I fish it out.

I holler out to the bushes: "Food's ready!" Then I wave the steak in the air for a bit. I think of a beast in the bushes somewhere, pricking up its ears, twitching its nostrils. Then I tie the two white cords around each hunk of meat while Mike takes a picture of me. He's texting it to his wife, chuckling. He takes this stuff seriously by the way, but there's something about the beef on a string that's turning us into little kids for a moment.

I stand up. We take one chunk each and set off, dragging them along the ground as we walk the drain again. They're bouncing up and down as we go, gathering dirt and little stones. It's going to be a very gritty meal.

"If anyone passes us," I say, "they're going to think we're walking two dead puppies."

We walk on, and talk about how one witness saw the beast leap across the drain and over a wall. I check the distance and agree with Mike: a guy wearing a fur suit simply couldn't make that jump. So, either the witnesses are making this up or —

Crack.

I freeze. There's a sound coming from the trees.

Mike and I look at each other. The meat waits behind us.

It sounds like something tapping and scratching. Claws?

I instantly run towards the sound, barely considering that it might just be a drug dealer in the bushes, sharpening his knife to mug us. We don't hear it again. I wonder if it might be firecrackers in the distance.

After we cross the bridge near the cemetery, I see something else that makes us both stop dead.

It's the flash of green eyes.

Holy crap.

I've been sceptical until now. Of course I have. But there are two luminous eyes hovering near the cemetery, and they are not *ducks*. My heart's thumping. I hear myself breathing, and I'm about to witness a bona fide—

"Oh," Mike says, "it's a fox. A bloody big one, mind."

We watch it slink out from Sculcoates Cemetery. It pauses for a moment on the pavement. It *is* big, actually. Not sure if I'd mistake it for a hominid, but it's the biggest fox I've ever seen.

"Maybe this is what people are seeing down here," I say, "just a big fox?"

"I can't imagine *that* dragging an Alsatian over a wall. Can you?"

"Good point."

We walk some more, then we realise it's time to head home, so we dump the steaks in a litter bin by the roadside. I'm not exactly shocked that we didn't find a real werewolf. I wasn't really expecting to. Hoping, yeah. But *expecting*? Nah. Because I doubt they exist. I was *hoping* though, and I still keep a little door open to the possibility. But even if they don't exist, it doesn't diminish my fascination with the idea of a human turning into some sort of monster. This macabre idea resonates not just with me, but with millions of people across cultures. Because, as we've seen already, we all have these impulses sometimes. Urges that want to break through polite behaviour and embrace more basic, primal instincts.

About a month after my werewolf hunt, Hull hits the headlines again. Only this time it's not fun, it's tragic. A young father goes on a rampage with an axe, waving it at terrified shoppers, before being tasered and shot dead by police. Something inside him skips his usual, civilised behaviour so that he acts in what appears like animal rage instead.[1]

From the news pictures, the area looks familiar. I email Mike and he confirms it. This man is killed within a few feet of the litter bin where we left the steaks.

Even the word sounds delicious: Lycanthropy.

I first heard the term in the old Universal movie, *The Wolf Man*, from 1941. I was enthralled by that film as a kid, watching it on a small black and white portable TV in my parents' house. And I logged the exotic sounding word in my memory both because it sounded cool and because I knew it would make me sound super-intelligent if I dropped it into general conversation. Like, on the off-chance a teacher at school mentioned a werewolf legend, I'd poise myself and say: *Ah, my dear lady, of course you mean Lycanthropy, from the Greek words* lycos *(meaning wolf) and* anthropos *(meaning man).*

The concept of the werewolf has captured the imagination of us bipeds across many cultures and centuries. The ancient Greeks spoke of the evil King Lycaon, who cooked the flesh of his own baby son and tried to get the god Zeus to eat it. Fussy eater Zeus refused and cursed Lycaon to turn into a wolf, permanently.[2]

In 39 BC, the Roman poet Virgil wrote about a man called Moeris who could "change to wolf, and rush away to hide in forest deep."[3] In the fifth century, the historian Herodotus wrote about the Neuri people who turned into wolves for a few days each year. He thought this story was interesting enough to record and share with the world, although he noted in his account that he wasn't convinced that they really did change.[4]

However, there were some who believed humans really *could* transform into physical beasts, and the idea of real werewolves became linked to witches in Europe in the Middle Ages, at a time when the persecution of witches was rife. By the early fifteenth century, people accused of werewolfism could face execution. One of the most notorious cases involved a rich, middle-aged German farmer, Peter Stubbe (more commonly referred to as "Stumpp"). He was a serial killer who was rumoured to turn into a wolf before killing his victims. He murdered sixteen people, including many children. He was even reported to have devoured foetuses, torn from the wombs of his pregnant victims. Outraged, the authorities publicly tore his flesh off, and broke his arms and legs with a blunt axe. Then, before throwing his body on a fire, the executioner chopped his head off and rammed it on a spike. Stumpp's dead face was left for all to see, and under it hung the symbol of a wolf.[5]

The Stumpp case became famous across Europe, and some wondered if he may have just dressed in the hide of a wolf during his killings, but others were ready to believe that he was a genuine lycanthrope—after all, surely no *normal* man could commit such crimes? It had to be the work of some beast. The latter seemed perfectly possible to many at the time, and werewolf trials and executions continued to take place across Europe.

The belief that werewolves are real still persists in some circles today (especially for those witnesses in Hull); but let's be honest, those circles are rather small. The growth of medicine, science and psychology over the last 150 years has gradually persuaded us that, while some people do indeed turn into animals, they only do so in their minds. This medicalised approach to werewolfism is known as "clinical lycanthropy."

Dr Jan Dirk Blom is a professor of clinical psychopathology at the University of Groningen in the Netherlands. In 2014, he searched the archives for cases of clinical lycanthropy and found that, while rare, they certainly do happen. The first case he found was published in 1852, and concerned a Frenchman who insisted he was a hairy, cloven-footed wolf; he would peel back his lips and eat only rotten meat, to prove his animal nature. Blom found 56 cases of lycanthropy in all (33 men and 22 women), with thirteen of these patients specifically seeing themselves as wolves. The remaining cases were variants of the condition, which is not limited exclusively to wolves. Some claimed to be a snake, a dog, a pig or even a bee.[6] Yes, that's right. Someone thought they were a *were-bee*.

This fear of falling prey to some sort of "creature" inside of us found particular resonance in a post-Darwinian world. By 1859, Darwin had published his theory of evolution, and we were coming to grips with our animal ancestry. The cultured, civilised men of the Victorian age wanted to feel they had put a discernible distance between themselves and their simian past. But the thought of the beast within haunted them, and the fear of it found expression in morbid, spooky culture.

This fear started to shape the fiction of the time. Authors like Matthew Lewis and Ann Radcliffe played on the fears and concerns of the day, helping to give rise to the Gothic novel. They showed us depraved monks and corrupt institutions, and told us that the real monsters weren't found "out there," but within society itself.

When the nineteenth century rolled around, Darwinism made people turn their fearful focus further inward. What if the monster out there was really the beast *in here*? In 1886, Robert Louis Stevenson hammered this idea home in his classic work on the horrors of human duality, *The Strange Case of Dr Jekyll and Mr Hyde*. In 1890, Oscar Wilde explored similar ground in *The Picture of Dorian Gray*, a parable of how we tend to hide the worst of our nature from the world. H.G. Wells fused this fear into science-fiction in his 1896 novel, *The Island of Dr Moreau*; here an English gentleman is shipwrecked on an island populated with frightening, animal-human hybrids.

The fear of humans regressing into an animal or evil state wasn't just seen in fiction. Degeneration theory emerged and was widely popularised by social critic Max Simon Nordau. In part inspired by Darwin's theory of evolution, and in part by contemporary beliefs and fears about ethnic differences, degeneration theory reasoned that if human beings could evolve over time, they could potentially devolve too.

Darwin didn't believe in degeneration, but his work nonetheless hinted at the proximity of our less evolved past. He talked about the "bristling of hair" when we're frightened and the "uncovering of teeth" when we fly into a rage.[7] Both expressions, he suggested, were unsettling echoes of our ancient animal selves. This idea of reverse-evolution—fuelled by the murderous Gothic doubles of literary fiction—played on the anxieties of the late Victorians, and the fear of something unpredictable and savage lurking under our skin carried on into later generations. Just look at the way werewolves were often portrayed in twentieth-century Hollywood. Nice, civil chaps would get bitten on the moors, and end up in a cycle of raw bestiality. They'd wake once a month, bleary-eyed and guilt ridden, desperate to remove the curse of the beast within. Werewolfism may have scared men in particular, being less accustomed than women to the idea of a monthly, biological cycle beyond their control, which involves the shedding of blood, not to mention a potentially beastly mood.

There were also religious reasons why becoming a beast was undesirable, especially in America and Europe, regions so strongly shaped by Christianity. The authors of the Bible set a clear division between men and animals. In Genesis 1:26, God gives human beings dominion over "the fish of the sea and over the birds of the heavens and over the livestock and over all the earth and over every creeping thing that creeps on the earth." Despite the fact that Jesus came to demonstrate a model of leadership defined by love, care, honour and sacrifice, we humans took the word "dominion" and stripped it down to being all about hierarchy. Animals became little more than resources to use and exploit. Because we've seen animals as resources for so long, raised for meat and skins, we've historically seen them as inferior to us—"base" creatures with limited or no intelligence or capacity for emotion. Certainly not something we would wish to become.

Yet in today's culture, our relationship with beasts has taken a surprising, almost revolutionary turn. There are a growing number of people who don't see our primal selves as a curse at all—but as a welcome blessing. To embrace the creature within, they say, is to *progress*, not regress, as I discover in a hotel in Birmingham, that's filled with human animals.

It's a sunny, Saturday afternoon and I'm walking through the busy foyer of the Hilton Birmingham Metropole. Every now and again I have to step aside to let a giant wolf or dog through. They stride past me on their hind legs, and I say "Hi." Some say "Hi" back to me, in northern accents. Others just bark. A few are silent, but they wave a happy paw.

Some of them seem wary of me. I see them scurry to the other side of the corridor as we pass, jowls down. This shyness might be because I look completely human and banal, or because I have a media pass around my neck, which makes it clear I'm a member of the press. Some of them clock that and spring off, worried that I'm here to expose them as sickos. This doesn't surprise me. They may have seen the newspaper articles that are already out there, with titles like "Furring Is New Sex Craze for Perverts,"[8] or the YouTube videos called "More Proof That Furries Are Mentally Ill Perverts,"[9] or forum posts with threads like "Furries Are Sick and Should Be Hated."[10] But I'm not here today to expose an animal sex-ring. I've come to find out how the once dreaded inner beast is being embraced by this subculture.

A tall fox in a baseball cap wanders past reception and hollers out to his friend. A wolf waits in the queue by a cash machine, drumming a full, furry paw on the wall. I see one dude nuzzling a tall cat's shoulder. These aren't hallucinations of mine, by the way. They're just men and women, in full-body animal suits, at "Confuzzled," a huge convention for the furry community. It's been held annually in Birmingham since 2008 and is just one of over a hundred different furry conventions that have taken place worldwide in recent years.[11]

If you're wondering what furries are, they're people who like taking on the persona of an animal. Many are in full-on, elaborate costumes, with all of their human skin covered up by fluff, but others are in subtler attire. In the queue for a hot dog, the guy in front of me looks completely human, until I notice the long furry tail dangling from the back of his trousers. It must have a rod in it, because it bounces about, quite erect. Others are dressed in jeans and T-shirts, but with little dog ears sprouting from their hair. A few have pink furry tongues poking from between their lips.

Some of the full costumes I've seen so far include: a giant grinning bunny rabbit with huge black and white ears, a cute fox dressed in surgeon's greens, a lioness with antlers and glowing green eyes, a fluffy pink dragon in her wheelchair. The list of biological hybrids is long.

This is one of the biggest hotels in the country, and it's packed with 1,645 guests who don't dread the beast within at all. Instead they fling their arms around it with purrs of delight. At one point, I sit on the decking outside with a giant possum. He's dressed in a plush velvet jacket, with a long, hairless rat-like tail sprouting from his trousers. He calls himself Sykes and says he's a zombie possum. This makes sense because there's a gaping wound on his eye and muzzle. Animal bone is clearly visible.

"It's kind of a play on words," he says, "the whole possum playing dead thing."

"Ah," I snap my fingers, "makes sense."

We chill on a lounger, and he tells me that, for most people, the furry community is just a fun form of escapism, but he says it's a serious expression of creativity too. "That's one thing you'll notice when you walk around here. We don't copy characters from movies or TV. We make up our own."

He's right. I've seen no fluffy Darth Vaders, no fuzzy Batmen. These are people who spend time and money developing bespoke, alternative personas, which they develop both online and off. They call it the "fandom," and here they're fans of each other's creations.

One of those creations waddles up as we chat. It's a six-foot-tall fox with a squeaker in its paw. It presses this little gizmo over and over again: *Eeek, eeek, eeek.* The fox is giggling like a toddler.

"Hi!" I say.

"It'd be fun to get some footballs!" the fox says randomly.

The possum and I look at each other. This feels awkward. The fox says "bye" and waddles back into the venue, squeaking all the way.

I turn back to Sykes, and notice how impressive his zombie possum mask is. It has an elaborate hinged mouth so that he can speak to me through it. He tells me about the other suits he has back home, one of which is a gargoyle.

"What's the most you've spent on a suit?" I ask.

"Oh, about two grand."

"Wow. That's a lot of money," I say, and probe him a little more before wrapping up our interview. I just want to see if he's filthy rich, and if dropping £2K is no biggie. Turns out he's just an average guy who's willing to invest in the things he's passionate about.

He shrugs and smiles: "It *is* a great suit."

I thank Sykes for the chat and get one of the hotel staff to take a picture of him throttling me. We laugh, I shake his clawed rubber paw, and I head back into the hotel. As I roam the corridors and pass the amazingly elaborate beasts, it really starts to sink in. Spending this amount of cash to turn into an animal-human hybrid is a pretty clear indicator that the fandom is way more than just fancy dress. I'm seeing little signs of it being a crazy sex cult either. There's something deeper going on here. But what?

A team of social scientists called the International Anthropomorphic Research Project (IARP) have tried to answer this question by surveying 15,000 furries between 2006 and 2016. The results show that the majority of furries are male (72.4%), under 25 (75%), white (83.2%), and most (75%) had undertaken at least some post-secondary education.[12] The study also logged the animal identities, or "fursonas," and found 6,000 distinct animals which could be roughly grouped under 852 unique species. The most popular animal choices were hybrids (14.6%) and wolves (14.3%). The least popular fursona? Insects (0.2%).

The study also looks at people's motivations for becoming a furry, finding that "belongingness" and "escapism" were key factors for many respondents.[13]

I hear echoes of these results when I chat to one of the organisers, in the bustle of a busy corridor. He isn't wearing anything furry that I can see. No tail bobbing, no ears on the head. But around his neck he has something that *everybody* at the convention seems to wear. A badge with some artwork, stating his alternative animal persona. I ask him why he comes to furry conventions, and he's very open with me.

"I can't speak for everyone, but to be honest, some of us here, including me, aren't really good at social interaction. We spend a lot of time online but want to meet face to face too."

"So, you do it in a mask? That helps?"

"For some of us, yeah. But the mask isn't always a literal one. Coming to a convention, especially by yourself, is pretty scary, but your fursona can give you confidence." I glance down at the fursona on his badge. It looks like one of the happy dogs from the kids' cartoon *Paw Patrol*.

"It's not just about hiding behind a character, though. It's about making something new and being fluid with your identity. It's fun, but not just fun. It's pretty meaningful actually."

He trails off as a voice booms down the corridor: "The Furry Parade starts in fifteen minutes! They'll be heading through here so . . . enjoy!"

The organiser turns back to me and, before he heads off, adds, "A lot of us are in our twenties. So, we've grown up with online identities, role-playing games, cosplay, all that stuff. It's not weird for us to have alternative personas. It's what we're used to. It means we're not tied to labels, so we can become whatever we want."

He heads off and I watch the parade. At one point, a guy lets me try on his giant, fluffy, homemade elephant boots. I stomp about in them for a bit. They're heavier than they look. Then I say a cheery hello to the ocean of animals that now passes by, and to the several men who dress like women. I also see one bloke wearing a babygrow with fluffy ears and a backpack. It really does seem to be a safe space to be whatever you want to be.

You see evidence of this in the IARP study, which discovered that 27 per cent of furries class themselves as "exclusively heterosexual." Their chosen *fursonas*, however, were about 17 per cent "exclusively heterosexual." The researchers concluded that having a fursona gave some the confidence to test the waters of bisexuality. "Given that homosexuality is still stigmatized in many regions, it may be the case, for at least some of these people, that being able to say, "I am not gay, my fursona is" is a way to express this aspect of their identity while simultaneously distancing themselves from the stigma it carries."[14]

When the parade finishes, I visit the large ballroom for the "Furry Frolics" event where I watch people in dog suits pass beach balls to each other while Benny Hill-style music booms out of the PA. They do this for what feels like an hour. I leave them to it, and visit the art gallery instead.

There's an adult section, blocked off with screens. I head inside and see paintings of foxes, tigers and dogs with giant throbbing penises spurting over bashful-looking rabbit people. Yowzer.

I'm just walking around in my normal clothes, with my audio recorder and huge 70s-style headphones on. I do look kind of conspicuous, but this is *my* mask: the suit of a supposedly professional press guest. To blend in better, I have a secret weapon. I've brought an old teddy I had as a kid. It's a one-eyed lion cub called Furry Face. He pokes out of my backpack, and I reckon he's amazed at the sights back there. He seems to chill people out, anyway. I see many other teddies sprouting from bags here.

Later that day, I interview a young woman who asks me to call her Farumir. She likes to dress as a wild wolf with sharp teeth and huge eyes that glow green. She's been obsessed with werewolves her whole life. Particularly since a family holiday in Turkey when she saw a black Alsatian chained to a bench. She went to pet it, but it snapped at her, barking right in her face. The six year old was startled but not scared and she never forgot that dog. It "was more like a black wolf," she told me, and the image of that animal stuck with her.

"From being a child to a late teenager I'd always been bullied. I never knew what for . . . they just seemed to have a problem with me. So, I always had fantasies of finding a way to kill them and get away with it . . . and turning into a huge terrifying monster and ripping them to bloody pieces . . . *that* was always the first daydream that came to mind. It was the kind of freedom I always wanted in my youth. To break free from the boredom and peer pressure and just be myself fearlessly . . . and tear to shreds anybody who tried to stop me." She laughs.

Speaking to Farumir makes me think of films like *I Was a Teenage Werewolf* (1957) and *Teen Wolf* (1985). Those movies struck a deep chord with teenagers, who saw their own bodies changing while new hair grew, voices deepened and uncontrollable urges erupted. In the case of *Teen*

Wolf particularly, this turning into something animal-like ends up making Michael J. Fox the coolest guy in school.

What could have just been a daydream of childhood protection for Farumir has carried on into her adult life. Beasts really matter to her. She has spent five years perfecting her own werewolf outfit.[15] "I mean I know that I'm not a real werewolf and they don't really exist," she tells me, "but I put so much work into creating myself from an alternate universe that I can't let my mask collect dust. I take good measures to keep it in top condition for every outing, and I have to say that I am my happiest when wearing it."

One of her favourite times to pull on the suit is when she's scare acting at Halloween events. "Oh God that is the best job in the world for me! Getting paid to scare people is brilliant."

For centuries, succumbing to primal urges was assumed to be a curse. Farumir, however, sees it as a liberating confidence-boost. It makes me think of the civilised Dr Jekyll, who turns into the lip-smacking, animalistic *Mr* Hyde (notice the demotion). The Victorians saw this as a chilling literary example of degeneration. Yet, do we really think this book, and other Gothic double stories, were successful because of the clean-living Jekyll? Nah . . . It's *Hyde* that really drew the crowds. I have little doubt that many Victorians had the same thought as I did when I first read the tale. Hyde certainly was wild and scary, but wasn't he the one who got to have all the fun? Didn't we thrill at *him*, because he was living life to the extreme? When Hyde is finally defeated, and the beast is caged, what we're left with seems like a happy ending. The nice doctor can slip back into an ordered society which says conform and repress. Be civil. Wear what's in fashion. Keep your sexuality mainstream. Bury your anger. Do what's expected. Never howl at the moon, even if you want to.

Being in this hotel today, it's clear that for some people, being forced into being "normal" is the biggest cage of all. The modern, mostly-young "beasts" that roam these hotel corridors have fused their creativity, and their desire for community and belonging, with a fear that the mainstream world is forcing them into one set identity. Yet they've grown up playing multiple characters in video and role-playing games, and they live in a world in which we all present mediated identities on social networks. After all, none of us posts *every* photograph to our profile page. That selfie in which we look like we've been hit with a shovel doesn't get posted. We carefully build an image of ourselves online, just like they do. Only they do it through creating a kind of spirit animal. Giving that inner wildness a chance to breathe is a way of opening the cage. The duality of identity no longer terrifies, like it did in the past. It's the key to liberation.

But what if the beast inside wants more than just fluffy suits and creative community. What if it's thirsty? For that, we turn to the vampire, and the people today who love the taste of blood.

Legends of blood-drinking vampires have long terrified the world. They're in the folklore of Europe, Haiti, Native America and Indonesia to name a few. These predators get energised not just by *seeing* the blood of their prey, but by lapping it up and guzzling it down. And when they bite you, you might even turn into one of them. For a long time, that prospect was as repellent as becoming a werewolf. Yet the vampire would help spearhead the reassessment of the beast within. A move that would shift monsters from being repulsive vermin to objects of desire . . . savages that we might actually want to *become*. Or at least dress up as.

Up until the twentieth century, vampires were often repugnant. You see a vivid example of this in the silent movie *Nosferatu* (1922). Here Count Orlok lurches across cobbled streets with horrid rat teeth and wild eyebrows. He's spindly and ill-looking too, with a bald head and big old bat ears. Not the type of fella you'd ask for a date, put it that way. Orlok was a picture of the vampires that came before him. They were a pestilence, and to feel their bite was to be infected with a corrupting, unwelcome disease.

It was Bram Stoker's novel *Dracula* that sparked a change. Not that the Count was a hunky pin-up in the novel. When we first meet him in the book, he's a tall, thin old man. Then, as the story progresses, he drinks more blood, which causes him to magically de-age. But even as a young man he's not the greatest looker. Stoker says he's a "tall, thin man with a beaky nose." And adds, "His face was not a good face. It was hard, and cruel, and sensual, and his big white teeth, that looked all the whiter because his lips were so red, were pointed like an animal's."[16]

But when the novel was turned into a Hollywood movie in 1931 starring Bela Lugosi, the vampire received a remarkable makeover. Lugosi presented the Count as a suave, exotic stud-muffin. He was handsome and well-groomed; a charmer, permanently in a tux. The black hair was slicked back, the ears normal and rounded. The only drawback was that he slept in a coffin and drank blood—but now he even did *that* seductively: at the soft-lit neck of a sexy blonde who had fallen under his control. He didn't even have fangs in that movie, just the ability to mesmerise women with his eyes. Now, the once-repulsive vampire was suddenly something enticing.

As the century went on, Vampire 2.0: Suave Edition became the standard for vampires in much of our art, literature and film. Vampires were still scary, but also romantic, irresistible and even vulnerable. Today the *Twilight* franchise and stacks of other vampire-themed TV shows and novels continue to insist that becoming a blood-sucking beast isn't a disaster: it's a ticket to power, sophistication and sex appeal.

Against the cultural backdrop of these cool fictional vampires, *real* ones started to rise. Only now they aren't hapless victims being turned against their will. Modern vampires choose it as a lifestyle option. Today, there are hordes of men and women who would openly identify themselves as children of the night.

I spend a couple of days at the Goth festival in Whitby, a seaside town famous for its *Dracula* connections. At the end of July 1890, theatrical manager Bram Stoker had just come off a gruelling theatre tour of Scotland. He took a month off, and spent it in the Yorkshire seaside town of Whitby. He instructed his wife Florence and son Noel to join him in August; so for the first week and a half, he was alone. As he wandered the harbour, saw the old Abbey surrounded by tombstones, and strolled across cliffs being smashed by the cold North Sea, an idea started to form. This was the perfect setting for a brooding figure of horror to emerge from.[17] On the 8th of August, he visited Whitby Public Lending Library (now a fish restaurant) and read a book about European history which made reference to the name Dracula—the Wallachian word for "devil." Stoker took the name, and a dark star was born.[18]

Over a century later, Whitby still celebrates its connection to the world's most famous blood drinker, and people the world over flock to see where the legend was first formed. As I wander the cobbled streets I see vampire toys, books and ornaments in almost every store. Around me are Goths and the steampunk crowd, but also, I quickly discover, self-proclaimed vampires.

I chat with them in pubs and shops and learn that the vampire community is large, diverse and global. It ranges from those who adopt it as a lifestyle choice, to others who take things rather more seriously. The people I meet in Whitby belong to the first group. Sometimes called "lifestylers" or the "fangdom," they don't see themselves as actual vampires. They have no desire to drink blood. Yet each tells me they get a genuine sense of empowerment by seeing their own personalities through a vampire lens.

There are men dressed in black leather with heavy boots, top hats and long canes, and women in black veils and Victorian corsets so tight I worry they might cough up a lung. But they smile at me and, as they do, they flash custom-made fangs.

One or two say they've loved vampires since seeing *The Lost Boys* (1987) as a kid, but when it comes to the clearest influence on the vampire lifestylers, two films stand out: Francis Ford Coppola's version of *Dracula* (1992) and Neil Jordan's adaptation of *Interview with the Vampire* (1994). Time and again, the vampires (especially the female ones) cite these movies as key doorways into the vampire lifestyle.

"The vampires in those films were beautiful and sophisticated," one woman tells me. "They were always young, and they'd live forever. And they were incredibly sensual, too. Pretty much irresistible."

They also talk to me about an element of these films that remains one of the key influences on the vampire-lifestylers to this day: fashion.

"The vampires in those films looked so fabulous," another woman tells me, as I sit with her and her friends in Whitby Pavilion, overlooking the sea. All three are in their mid-sixties, except they're dressed like no pensioners I've ever seen before. They're wearing tight leather boots, laced up to the knee, with top hats and lacy gloves. All have squeezed themselves into corsets, and the tightness pushes their cleavage to eye-popping levels. They're dripping glamour and style, not by mimicking the fashion of today's youth but by raiding Gothic history.

"Us oldies never get a chance to dress like this," one of them says, as she leans forward. There's a sparkle in her eye. "But we can when we're here. And we love it."

I say my goodbyes and head upstairs, where I accidentally wander into a photo shoot. People are lining up in their gothic outfits and vampire teeth, to get a memento. I wander the halls and chat more. One woman in a top hat and black lace sits nursing a dead baby. It's an incredibly realistic doll, with a blueish-grey face and what looks like tiny fangs. It's her vampire child, she says, which sleeps in a cot in her room. Many women are gathering around and cooing over it.

I lose count of the people who tell me how liberating it feels to stride through the town of Dracula's arrival, looking (and feeling) like they are part of the Count's official entourage.

Later, via Facebook I connect with a young woman called Danielle. Her profile picture makes me double take. She's completely naked; every inch of skin is drenched in blood from the jaw down, and she's holding her head back so you see her fangs. When we chat, she tells me she's been obsessed with the undead since childhood.

"I love dressing and acting like a vampire," she says, "because I feel so powerful and fierce . . . and I feel extremely seductive too. I like looking as pale as possible and I own a set of fangs that I love wearing. I sometimes wear them [when I go] out too and it makes me feel so good. They make me feel like I'm a *real* vampire."

I ask her how those around her responded to her blood-soaked naked pic.

"Everyone loves it and thought I looked fierce. That I looked the part."

Clearly for many lifestylers, the style of the once-feared vampires can be a liberating tool of expression and sensuality. But "lifestyling" can be about more than just fashion. In her book, *Vampire Nation*, Arlene Russo argues that: "The vampire affects the wider existence of lifestylers, from the vacations they take to the wines they drink. These people regard vampirism as a state of mind or mode of existence rather than a desire to vampirise others by feeding on them."[19]

Russo interviews lifestylers who don't just wear temporary fangs but have permanent crowns fitted. Many even incorporate vampire elements into important life events, such as Zachary Hunt, who married his wife in a candlelit, deconsecrated Gothic church, to which they arrived in a blood red carriage pulled by two black horses.[20] Other lifestylers told Russo they keep coffins in their house, and even sleep in them sometimes—like Jenna, who says a coffin "keeps the light out so in the end you get a really good night's sleep, especially in the summer months when it is light for so long."[21]

So there *is* a deep attraction to the vampire's power, seductiveness and style, but for others, vampirism takes them to much more philosophical levels. The Temple of the Vampire became a legally-registered religion in the US in December 1989. With its own Bible, clergy and sacred rites, it promotes the idea that vampires are the next stage in human evolution, although it has strict rules against members drinking blood or engaging in criminal activity. It trains members in how to gain eternal life and feed off others through a more spiritual version of bloodsucking. They call it astral vampirism. The Temple is just one of a number of religious groups that use the vampire as their figurehead. Some, such as the Society of the Dark Sun and Order of the Vampyre, identify themselves as Satanic orders.[22]

Vampirism, then, has become an authentic subculture, with many levels of involvement—from fashion to lifestyle to religious faith. Yet the group which receives the most media attention is made up of those willing to focus on the basics: the ones who believe that their own mental, spiritual and physical health relies on drinking the blood of others. They're more numerous than you'd think, and they have a fancy name: Sanguinarians, which stems from the Latin word *sanguinarius*, meaning "bloodthirsty." These people literally drink the blood of donors, be that friends or lovers, who are sometimes known as Black Swans. Clearly, it's a dangerous practice. Sanguinarians risk not only catching a blood-borne disease like HIV, but also seriously hurting their donor or even killing them. They might even get arrested in parts of the world where it's illegal for non-medics to remove the blood of another.

The dangers don't seem to stop them, however, and there are a range of websites that give advice on how Sanguinarian vampires can obtain safe blood. Sanguinarius.org, for example, encourages blood drinkers to carefully study the diagrams in *Gray's Anatomy*, so they know which veins, tendons and muscles to avoid. The site also suggests getting signed consent forms from the donors—who should be pre-tested for diseases. It notes the lower arm as a good place to drink from, but it's best to avoid the underside. Thighs, the base of the thumb and the back of the shoulder are all ripe places too, and to get more blood from a donor, the site suggests making two razor cuts in the shape of an X (not too deep). Drinkers are cautioned not to suck too hard, to avoid leaving an unsightly red mark. The site even says that animals are a good source of blood, especially when using a syringe. Oh, and there's a recipe for blood pancakes too.[23]

Feeling queasy yet?

Another site lists virgin's blood as the best of all: "Yes, people, the legends are true," it claims. "Comparing this blood to any other kind of human blood is like comparing sirloin steak to hamburger."[24] They suggest popping blood in the microwave for five seconds because, "No matter what kind of blood, it always tastes better warm than cold."

Of course, for many people, this blood drinking malarkey will smack of dangerous psychopathy or just kinky fetish. I'm sympathetic to that reaction. But for some modern vampires, this macabre diet is more than just for kicks. Some claim that blood is the only medicine to ease their crippling medical symptoms, from headaches and fatigue to extreme stomach pains.[25] Drinking blood for medical reasons is extremely rare today, and it was rare in the past too—but that's not to say it never happened. Roman historian Pliny the Elder (23–79 AD) records how spectators would rush forward to drink the blood of gladiators. (I've stood in the Colosseum where it happened, and this practice is flagged up on the signs.) It was thought to be a cure for epilepsy.

Centuries later, in 1489, the influential Italian Renaissance scholar Marsilio Ficino tried to revive the practice. He recommended that "good doctors" should energise their elderly patients by letting them drink the blood of the young.[26] Perhaps advisers at the Vatican had read Ficino's work, or maybe they had just spotted the bit in Leviticus that says "the life of every creature is its blood,"[27] because in 1492 they tried to turn Pope Innocent VIII into a vampire. The pontiff slipped into a coma, and his medics performed what's thought to have been the first blood transfusion. Supposedly, they drained some blood from three ten-year old boys and had Pope Innocent drink it.[28] It didn't work. The boys died, and so did he.[29]

These modern bloodsuckers might say they're just carrying on a long-forgotten tradition, and are simply taking up a line in Bram Stoker's *Dracula* which claims: "The Blood is the life! The Blood is the life!"[30] They just don't talk about it much in public in case they lose their job, or have their kids taken away.

I managed to speak to a Sanguinarian, a special effects artist who asked me not to use her real name. Let's call her Anna. Anna first tasted blood as a child, before she'd even *heard* of the word vampire.

She tells me: "It was really a simple and innocent act that brought me here. A cut with blood flowing from it. The colour, the smell and even the taste . . . the way it trickled down my arm in that beautiful red colour. I seemed compelled to taste it, like a child would feel about any tasty treat. I loved it at first taste. Talking about it now makes my mouth water. I loved the metallic taste, the feel of it on my tongue. It was unlike anything else I ed had ever tasted. I was hooked."

As a child, Anna knew her taste for blood wasn't "normal." She's happy to admit that. But gradually she started to see people like her in morbid entertainment. "Vampires in black clothes and pale skin were doing what I enjoyed; these were the only role models society offered me." She doesn't claim to have the supernatural powers of a vampire—there's no immortality, for example, although she does say that blood does wonders for her skin. For her, it's the compulsion to drink the stuff that makes her use the label "vampire." For Anna, it's the only identification that makes sense.

These days, her boyfriend lets her drink his blood, and friends and family have come to terms with her taste. "They know I'm still kind, caring and a good daughter and friend."

"Are there other benefits," I ask her, "from drinking blood?"

"Definitely the spiritual highs," she says. "It's often a very euphoric feeling, an uplift. It renews my strength and chases the dark thoughts and depressions of life away. There's something unexplainable about it . . . about the life force of another coming into yourself . . . it's a powerful experience. Some people have meditation to bring balance and euphoria into their life—I have this."

In the 21st century, we're learning to love the once-feared beast. From the happy werewolves, were-bears and were-foxes of a furry convention, to the vampire lifestylers with their bespoke fangs and luminous contact lenses. Yet there's another expression of the beast within that *still* terrifies modern society. It's a form of inner wildness so frightening and disturbing that very few see any redeeming features in it. But, for a small few, there may even be benefits to this flavour of beast too.

I'm talking about the controversial world of demonic possession.

Like it or not, recent reports show that the ritual of exorcism remains a living, breathing reality of modern life. Against secular expectations, and regardless of whether or not you believe the devil exists, demonic possession cases are *growing* today. France, for example, is a possession hotspot; in a region near Paris called Île-de-France the church has performed 50 exorcisms a year for the last few years. A decade ago in the same region, it was fifteen a year. Demand across France is so high that an industry of freelancers has sprung up, offering to remove the devil, for a price.[31] It's rising in the UK too. In 2016, the Christian think-tank Theos reported an "astonishing" spike in exorcisms.[32] Over the past decade, the number of exorcist priests in the US has more than quadrupled, from twelve to 50.[33] In 2016 Rome's busiest exorcist, Father Vincenzo Taraborelli, told the press that the Italian church can barely cope with the increasing demand. He claimed that 500,000 people requested an exorcism in 2015, yet he can't find younger priests to take on the role. The problem is, he says, they're just too scared.[34]

This growth in exorcism is fraught with danger, not least because it's far too easy to misdiagnose treatable conditions such as Tourette's, schizophrenia and epilepsy. Linda Chaniotis, for example, has spent her whole life trying to come to terms with being mislabelled a demon. Since the age of two, her parents would assume the fits she was having were the results of a witch's curse, and Linda was subjected to at least four different exorcisms. As a result, she felt frightened, flawed and evil growing up. She broke away from her parents at the age of thirteen. At 30, she was diagnosed with temporal lobe epilepsy. As a child, she would hide in the bathroom to conceal her fits from her parents. She says, "I feel lucky I didn't die in the bathroom on my own from one of my seizures."[35] Anneliese Michel wasn't so "lucky." In West Germany, in 1975, the 23 year old was subjected to an exorcism that lasted eleven months. She died of starvation, and her parents and two priests received suspended sentences.[36]

Clearly then, the rise in exorcism must be handled with extreme caution, but the question remains . . . why is it rising at all? There are various theories. Some religious groups say it's obvious: secularism and the lack of Christian observance is leaving us open to a Satanic onslaught.[37] Others say the growth is driven by immigrant communities, who are often much more open to exorcism, particularly those in Pentecostal church.[38] Another theory to add to the pile, which rarely gets considered, is linked to what we've seen with the furries. Namely, that there can be benefits to thinking of ourselves as two creatures in one.

Father Cataldo Migliazzo is an 80-year-old Italian priest and veteran exorcist. His skills are in such demand these days, he runs a weekly deliverance meeting where he casts out demons en masse. Every Tuesday, folks travel hundreds of miles to attend a three-hour service during which people groan, scream and jerk in spasms on the floor, calling out threats and abuse in chilling voices and animal sounds.

In a documentary about Migliazzo's work, it's clear that he fully believes these people are possessed by Satan. However, some of the other priests in the film are openly cynical. Some victims, they suggest, *like* the thought of being possessed.[39] The psychological theatre of exorcism, they say, becomes an effective way of getting attention.[40]

There can even be psychological benefits of being labelled possessed. Sadly, our world still attaches serious stigma to issues of mental illness. Mental health experts say the fear and shame of being diagnosed by doctors is one of the most common reasons people don't seek help.[41] British psychologist Dr Chris French suggests that the opportunity to blame a demon for previous wild behaviour is both appealing and reassuring. The irrational thoughts and actions you engaged in weren't actually you— they were put there by an imposter. This concept is certainly scary, and it would be beyond terrifying if it proved permanent. Yet the appeal of an exorcism ritual is that it offers a chance to get rid of that invader completely. This is an attractive prospect to those who worry that medical labels such as "personality disorder" or "psychopath" will be with them for life. Exorcise a demon, by contrast, and you're back to new again, ready to rejoin society. French says that "once those demons have been exorcised, the repentant sinner is now welcomed back into the loving arms of his or her community."[42]

For some repressed groups, being demonically possessed might even be the only way to hold any sort of social power. In her study of multinational corporations in Malaysia, Professor Aihwa Ong explored a bizarre phenomenon. Young female factory workers were being terrorised by supernatural beings in the workplace. Some claimed to see black apparitions and monsters stalking the factory. One woman insisted she saw a were-tiger. Another went to the toilet and saw a strange tall figure with a long tongue, licking the sanitary napkins.[43] The activity soon got worse. The beastly spectres began climbing *inside* these women, making them exhibit signs of demonic possession. They'd explode into rages and would damage the products they were building. They'd scream and wail death threats on the shop floor. Factory bosses were left with the tricky phone call back to HQ, explaining to corporation bosses in the US that many work hours were being lost because of paranormal activity.[44]

Ong makes a fascinating argument about this case. She thinks this demonic invasion may have been a complex form of worker protest. In Malay society, young women are expected to be shy, deferential and obedient, but during moments of spiritual possession they suddenly felt able to express their anger and frustration at their working conditions. That's not to say that they orchestrated a hoax just to be heard—they held strong spiritual beliefs about possession. But it's possible that this awareness of possession opened a subconscious door through which to let out their rage. "What seems clear," Ong writes, "is that spirit possession provides a traditional way of rebelling against authority without punishment, since victims are not blamed for their predicament."[45]

The potential dangers of this spike in possession cases are clear and disturbing. Yet in cases like the factory workers of Malay, or the work of

Father Cataldo Migliazzo, it's possible that an exorcism ritual might "work." Whether the mechanism of that success is as an elaborate psychological placebo or a genuine spiritual cleansing depends on your belief.

The point is that even the most terrifying beast within can be a bizarrely attractive prospect for some people. Furries use their beast fursona to find liberation, community and new levels of confidence and creativity. Vampires find pleasure, sophistication and a sense of wellness from a once feared monster. Small numbers of the possessed use their snarling beast as a (hopefully temporary) outlet for their frustrations and anger, and as a catalyst for change. All have found that the acknowledgment of their inner *duality* has, ironically, become a key step in finding *wholeness*.

Despite starting research for this chapter with a werewolf hunt in Hull, it's only when I'm coming to the end that I receive a Facebook message from a real werewolf. She's a twenty-something from America, and she insists on anonymity. She first realised her condition as a teenager. "I began to shift, with no control over the wolf," she tells me. "My grandpa told me why this was happening, and why I transformed."

She tells me that hunters are everywhere so she must be secretive. "Even if we've done nothing wrong hunters will track us down and hurt or kill our family and friends." Then she adds, "Vampire clans and werewolf clans have a deep hatred of each other. They believe we're pathetic doggy creatures who can't control our hunger."

To stay safe, she meets with her pack in heavily wooded areas. Here they transform in secret, away from the eyes of humans. She says city crime scenes of frenzied attacks aren't always the work of madmen. It's often them . . . "the lycans."

"As wolves, we eat animals or humans," she says. "I eat roadkill."

Our conversation ends. Later on, I send her another message.

"Hello again! I just wondered if the next time you transform, would you be up for doing it over Skype?"

I wait for a response but it doesn't come. I'm not surprised. Soon after, I give up waiting, and I head up to bed.

I lie awake, staring at the ceiling of my bedroom. Outside a breeze is making the trees hiss and there's a fat moon hanging. Of course, I don't actually believe that the woman I've spoken to tonight is an actual werewolf. Just as I doubt there's an actual six-foot lycanthrope eating the Alsatians of Hull. But as I lie awake, staring, I know that I'm the type of guy who likes to keep a door open to possibility.

And I think of how tantalising it would be if some of the normal people of my town really *were* gathering in the woods near me right now—changing. Snapping their heads back and singing to the moon as they race across the forest floor, leaping over logs and trees, searching for dinner. Liberated from our strict societal rules. I close my eyes and try to programme a dream about it. I figure it'd be fun, just for one night, if I got to feel what it might be like to fully embrace the beast within, and run with the wolves.

My mind programming doesn't work. At least not in the way I expect. I dream about visiting Buckingham Palace, where I end up pissing all over one of the Queen's chairs. I wake up in the morning laughing. In terms of beastly behaviour, it feels close enough.

CHAPTER EIGHT

DEADTIME STORIES

On the 11th of September 2001, terrorists flew planes into buildings in New York City and the Pentagon. In the weeks and months that followed, the images of that day were everywhere. On newsstands, and TV and computer screens. Bars, coffee shops, lounges and offices filled with debate and conversation. Talk-shows and newspaper columns pored over minute details.[1] If adults wanted to think about the tragedy, they had multiple opportunities to work through their shock, pain and curiosity.

It was an event so prominent, and devastating, that it would have taken a trip to the moon to keep children away from it. They knew something was wrong. They could see the shock on the faces of parents, and many kids caught a glimpse of those burning towers in the media. Thousands of kids in New York saw them from their windows.

The children of 9/11 dealt with this horror by using the only tools they had. They used art and play. Child therapist Eliana Gil worked with the family victims of the Pentagon deaths. As she spent time with them, she noted how morbid the children's games were. They would build villages and towns, then take toy aeroplanes and crash into the buildings they'd constructed. They played "games" in which houses were engulfed by fire. They'd have firefighter figurines dig out the buried people from under rubble, to return them to their toy families.

Other professionals noticed the same reaction, and it wasn't just with those related to the victims. Some New York City teachers saw their students building towers of blocks, then smashing them down, over and over again. They drew horrible pictures too. Art therapist Helen Ellis said that after 9/11, the children she saw in therapy created traumatic and disturbing artwork. So many children were creating this sort of art that the NYU Child Study Centre began to collect it. Eventually it was published as a book, *The Day Our World Changed: Children's Art of 9/11*.[2]

Some of the pictures in the book show heroic emergency workers and fire dogs rescuing people. But many, most in fact, focus on what brought their world down. Twelve-year-old Pearl Newman painted the Twin Towers in flames, one with an aeroplane wedged into it, while tiny stickmen fall from the windows screaming *Help!* in speech bubbles. In the distance another plane heads for the left tower, and the speech bubble from the cockpit reads: *Ha ha!* Six-year-old Quinn Taylor Kelley painted a figure on a bed, with a scary thought bubble coming from the head. "This is me in bed dreaming my mother is in smoke and fire." A Godzilla-type monster smashes the Twin Towers in ten-year-old Talal Jaradat's picture, "Doomsday." In "Osama's Toys," seventeen-year-old Annie Mak paints a giant Osama bin Laden, leering over the New York city skyline. He's stuffing the World Trade Centre into his fanged mouth.

Seeing children play 9/11 "games" and draw detailed, grisly pictures of such a tragic event disturbed some parents. Especially when children were observed smashing planes into toy towers with what seemed like a complete lack of emotion.[3] They just kept doing it over and over, which could certainly appear to be disturbing, unhealthy behaviour. Some parents thought it better to distract their kids from the trauma. Some shut down all morbid play by removing toys like soldiers from the home.[4]

Yet crashing planes into Jenga towers wasn't a way to perpetuate or show disrespect for the tragedy; and the adults who allowed them to do it weren't being irresponsible. They just appreciated that while adults had myriad societal outlets through which to explore and express their terror, kids channelled theirs through what came naturally to them: art and play. Eliana Gil, the child therapist who worked with the Washington victims, is now a respected expert in what's known as "post-traumatic play" (PTP). Here children deal with their pain through what appear to be morbid, unhealthy activities.

I've seen this phenomenon myself with various people I interviewed for this book. For example, Hanilee is a successful entrepreneur who grew up in a family rocked by domestic violence. When I asked her how she coped, she told me that she used to play brutal games with her dolls. What she did with them may have been disturbing to adults at first glance. "I even had my dolls abused by Ken [Barbie doll] inappropriately," she said. "I'm not proud of that. It was just what I did as a kid in a dysfunctional environment. I'd rip their heads off and bite their toes, but it was definitely a channel for my trauma."

Gil warns that, if left unchecked, post-traumatic play can potentially become toxic, and could possibly even re-traumatise the child. Yet she believes morbid games like this also have the potential to bring profound healing to troubled children. For example, when Maria Fernanda was five years old, she witnessed a major earthquake that killed her uncle. She saw him disappear under the rubble. Haunted by the sight, she cried for months afterwards, and then her mother noticed Maria beginning a repetitive game. She'd dig small holes in the ground, then place dead bugs in them and pray for them. She played this every Thursday—the day the earthquake hit. In time, she would find live bugs and put them in the holes. Then she'd watch closely as they climbed back out again. She repeated this play over and over again.[5] This cycle of burying insects, along with the passage of time, helped her find peace about the tragedy she'd seen.

Child psychiatrist G. Maclean helps facilitate successful morbid re-enactment in a clinical setting. One of his cases involved a four-year-old boy and his father, who had been attacked by a leopard in an exotic pet shop. The boy was bitten on the neck. The shocking incident left him with frequent nightmares about "animals and monsters," and he was scared to leave his mother. Maclean gave him eight months of trauma therapy, and found that the child mostly wanted to re-enact the attack—often in great detail. Sometimes he'd simply tell the story; other times he would re-live the moment with toys: he'd build a great cage and put a rubber tiger in it—and he'd always let the tiger break out. The boy even acted like a leopard himself sometimes and pretended to attack the therapist. Maclean realised he wanted the therapist to understand what it was like to go through an attack like he had. Over the course of these sessions, the child's nightmares and other trauma symptoms reduced, and when they eventually stopped, the therapy was over. Maclean concluded: "It is felt that without the intervention of therapy the boy's development would have continued in its arrested state for a threatening period."[6]

One of the reasons these two cases worked out well was that both practitioner and parent recognised the value of morbid play. They gave the boy space, and permission, to re-enact an experience that was scary, and he wasn't rushed through it. Similarly, Maria's mother could instinctively tell that this strange, repetitive ritual of burying insects was helping to heal her daughter. In each case, concerned adults were on hand to talk and nurture the child, and to make sure the play didn't get out of hand.

However, Gil says that when some adults see children play macabre, repetitive games—especially when they're based on the precise incident that damaged them—they assume it's best to stop it. She says some parents think that if a child just ignores emotional pain, it will go away on its own. Or they think that if they *do* help their child address the pain, then talking (and not playing) must be the only healthy method of communication.[7] Yet one of the reasons why morbid re-enactment can work for some children is because it can be so hard for a child to articulate their feelings. Ask a kid why they don't want to go to a particular party or why they like hot dogs, and many struggle to give an answer beyond "I just don't want to" or "I just like them." So it's not always realistic to expect a child to fully explain their deepest fears, especially when their vocabulary is limited. Also, some kids are simply too traumatised to talk about their experiences, even if they're normally good communicators.

There's also the chance that the child may not even know how they feel deep down, and they might struggle to understand their own feelings and actions. Gil suggests that post-traumatic play can be a way to access these subconscious feelings. The repetition, ritual and sometimes lack of emotion shown by children during this type of activity can almost give the appearance of "awake sleeping." This might allow the child to "access unconscious material during a trance-like state." Once the child is in this zone, it "allows for images, sensations, feelings and cognitions to come to the surface for processing."[8]

As well as identifying and understanding deep emotions, another reason children use play and art to channel trauma is because it can give them a sense of empowerment. They take the most horrific and baffling experiences of their lives, and put them into more manageable, predictable patterns. It's why children like Maria played the same game, in the same precise way, over and over. An initially shocking event is gradually turned into a predictable routine. When this happens, it can give a sense of power over something that seemed to be chaotic before.[9] It makes me think of my own use of morbid culture as a way of managing my fears, or of Heather from Pandora's Box, collecting serial killers' hair and funeral clamps. Both of us are partly drawn to the morbid because it's a technique for organising and mastering those things that make us anxious.

Gil, and therapists like her, aren't suggesting we force morbid art or play on children. She says it only really works if it's initiated by the child, rather than the clinician.[10] She's also clear that it needs monitoring in a caring, supportive environment; otherwise it could make things worse. Yet the key point for us—in this journey to appreciate the morbid streak in humans—is that when children show an interest in the scary or macabre, it's unwise to automatically assume that it's unhealthy. Letting kids spend time playing through their fears might be an important way for them to process the world around them.

But what about the children who play out morbid scenarios without having experienced any previous trauma? For example, Lucy, a writer and ironmonger, told me that when she was little girl she'd play with her dolls house for hours. "A lot of the games involved ghosts and murders. I remember taking great pleasure in making the dolls look bloodied—I used mum's lipstick." Catherine, a biblical studies student, told me how she enjoyed pushing her dolls down the stairs as a child. Liz, a book blogger who works in Tesco, said her dolls were "permanently in car crashes or having their houses burned down." None of these people told me their grisly play was to deal with a specific pain in their life. They simply found these sorts of games interesting. This doesn't surprise me because, as we're about to see, it's not only traumatised kids who are drawn to the macabre. It's kids, in general.

If you want proof that many kids get a kick out of pretend violence and horror, just spend some time playing with them. I have. I took the lion's share of looking after our children in their early years—so I've done my time in the trenches of playdates and parent and toddler groups. They are temples of giggling, puke, gusset-crud and occasional pockets of magic—and lots (even *most*) of the play is benign. But they can also, on occasion, make parents feel extremely awkward. When kids chase each other as chomping, wild-eyed monsters and pretend to chop the heads off action figures. When they sometimes run around pointing finger pistols shouting: *I'm gonna kill you, Mummy! Ka-Pow!* I've seen urbane, polite parents mortified at this behaviour. They laugh nervously, pretending it's a one-off by saying: *What's got into you today, Tarquin? Too much sugar, I'll bet.* Then they chew their fingernails for an hour.

I chatted to a mum about this once. She was quietly despairing that her son sometimes enjoyed shooting and killing imaginary things. She thought she might be witnessing the birth of psychopathy. I had the perfect solution to put her mind at ease: I invited her to a playgroup. She turned up and witnessed other kids doing exactly the same thing. "I'm gonna chop your willy off," one of them announced, and chased his friend through the church hall, holding a plastic kitchen knife aloft. Both kids were laughing. I'm not sure if the widening of this phenomenon chilled her out or worried her even more, but at least she now knew that, every now and again, other kids said gross and creepy things, and stamped on doll-heads, too.

To get a feel for how common this phenomenon is, I talk to the headmistress of my local primary school. She confirms that she's seen this morbid streak in kids throughout her career. "Kids do enjoy horrible things. It's true. For example, let's say you want to teach the kids about the diet of an animal. One way of really engaging the children would be to bring in a skull—because then you can see the teeth. And that's the way into talking about whether it's a carnivore or a herbivore . . . but they'll be fascinated, because that's a *skeleton of a dead animal*, and they think that's just amazing. They love gory things," she goes on. "Like when we study the Plague or the Great Fire of London, they'll want to know all the details, like how many people died. *How* they died. They're fascinated."

"And what do you say to people who think a child's interest in this stuff is wrong or freakish?"

She ponders the question: "I think it's too commonplace for it not to be completely normal—that's my take on it. In over twenty-odd years of teaching, it's not that I've found a class like that and thought, my goodness, they're really strange! Sometimes you do get a few kids who *don't* want to touch the skull, but the vast majority of kids love anything that's a little bit linked to gore or death."

She clasps her hands together and leans forward. "You know, just today I had a mum tell me there was a dead bird on the path. She said we'd need to clear it up because all the children were flocking around it. They all just wanted to see."

I think of the time that happened at my junior school growing up. Only it wasn't a dead bird on the school path—it was a dog's head, dumped on the playing field. I saw them scooping it into a bin bag during one of my lessons, which was a genuinely horrible sight, but it was still the absolute buzz of the school at break time. I've never forgotten that image or the questions we had, like what had happened to the rest of the dog.

"And how do the parents respond?" I ask her. "Do they mind all the grisly stuff in class?"

"The vast majority are totally fine with it. They mostly just say: *Oh, my kid would love that!*"

So, the morbid seems to get kids' attention, and one of the reasons for that is because such things feel so novel. Pulling out a skull in the middle of class is effective, precisely because it's so darn weird. You don't really expect to see dead animals in a school—but when you do, you remember.

Scientists from the University of London scanned the brains of volunteers under an MRI scanner. They showed them new images as well as ones they were already familiar with. When the novel images were shown, the section of the brain that recognises the sense of reward tended to light up. This releases dopamine, which aids brain memory. The unexpected, in other words, is exciting and memorable. (That's why, when you revise for an exam, it's much more effective to mix up old and new facts, because the brain craves and tends to remember unusual and new information.) Dr Duzel, the lead researcher on the project, said, "We have evolved to find novelty exciting. All species are attracted—and repelled—by novelty. If you do not explore you don't progress."[11]

Since novel experiences (even the repulsive ones) stick in the memory, it's no shock to see that schools would use the macabre as a tool. After all, remembering what's been taught is a key goal of education. It's also no surprise to see that tourist attractions, which can also double as educational venues, will sometimes use the horrific too.

I saw this clearly demonstrated on a visit to the Tower of London, when a jolly Beefeater guided my and other families around. He told us when the Tower was built, and where the stone used to build it came from. I saw a few yawning people scrolling through their phones. Some of the kids were kicking a pebble between them. But then he stopped to tell us a story, and everything changed.

"Let me tell you of the *horrendous* fate of Margaret Pole, the Countess of Salisbury . . ." He cleared his throat.

People looked up.

"At 7 o'clock in the morning of the 27th of May 1541, the poor Countess was publicly executed here, but the axeman that day was sadly *inexperienced*, so it did not go well . . ."

The Beefeater smiled through his short white beard, and now every phone was off and the pebble game was over.

"The blundering youth kept missing her neck! So, ladies, gentlemen and children, do you what to know what he did?"

The hive mind formed the response. "Tell us!"

"He hacked her head and shoulders to pieces in the most pitiful manner! They say he chased her around the platform as she screamed in agony! Many of the witnesses turned away in terror. The air filled with her squeals. And finally, after many, many tries, the sloppy young scamp landed the fateful blow." At this point, the Beefeater did the classic handslice across his neck. "But don't judge the lad. I suppose we're all a little jumpy on our first day at work!"

Laughter erupted from a crowd that was smiling . . . with *disgust*. Nobody walked off to complain. Instead, every one of us wanted to be a historian, especially the children. He had our attention. Later that night I checked into his tale, and found that the execution of Margaret Pole may not have been quite so gory as the Beefeater had claimed. The tale had been embellished over the years. Which rather proves my point. If history isn't grisly enough, we'll sometimes damn well *make* it awful—because those are the stories that seem to last. It's why Scholastic, the largest publisher of children's books, calls their wildly successful "Horrible Histories" brand, the "crown jewels" of the company.[12] The covers of this massively popular series promise to deliver history "with the gory bits left in," and the books have sold more than 27 million copies worldwide, been translated into 40 languages and turned into a successful TV show.[13] There's a movie going into production too.[14]

In short, images and themes of death and gore (at appropriate levels) do that crucial task that all kids and teenagers demand: they relieve *boredom*. This is important because children crave stimulation, says Joanne Cantor, communications professor and expert on the impact of the media on children. They could, therefore, be characterised as "sensation seekers." Cantor discusses the findings of studies which measured the heart rate and skin temperature of kids when they watched media violence. Both tend to increase when morbid or violent material is consumed.[15]

Penny Peck is a youth advisor and expert on children's literature. In her guidebook for librarians, she recommends a solution for children or "tweens" who have little interest in reading. "When all your other recommendations fail," she says, "often these reluctant readers will enjoy "scary" books."[16] Peck specifically recommends the horror-for-kids "Goosebumps" series by R.L. Stine. It's one of the most successful franchises in children's publishing, having sold over 350 million copies across the globe.

The fact that the worlds of literature, entertainment and education regularly feature morbid content ought to tell us something: many children find this sort of thing interesting. It's not *all* they want to think about. They love heroism too, and relationships, cute animals and fart jokes. Yet, just like adults, kids have a *varied* palate of interests. So, we shouldn't be surprised that they can enjoy memorable and novel things, like hacked-off heads in history, dead birds on the path, and the shivering thrills of a safe scare.

It's true that scary media might give some children nightmares and, yes, some may be filled with regret for consuming it, but what's fascinating is that it doesn't take long for many kids to ask if they can look into the dark again. In a 1993 study, Orbach, Winkler and Har-Even noticed that children did something unexpected when they were told a frightening story.[17] They *were* scared, but they also voluntarily re-exposed themselves to those exact tales again.

I noticed this when I was tucking my six-year-old son into bed the other night. He said, "Sing me a scary song, Daddy." So, I warbled out a twisted little kids' tune that I know freaked my daughter out when she was little. I stood by his bed and sang, *"Ladybird, ladybird fly away home, your house is on fire, your children are all gone . . ."*

My son burst out laughing, totally unfazed. "Try harder. Sing me something *scary*."

I flipped through the files in my mind and remembered a song we all saw on the internet the other day, about Yoda walking on the beach and getting attacked by seagulls. It's not frightening—it's cute and pretty hilarious actually—but I know my son has got a theory about Yoda possibly being evil.

"Are you *sure* you want a scary song?"

He nodded.

I started singing. Used my best attempt at a Yoda voice, I did. *"Rockin' . . . rockin' and rollin' . . . down to the beach I'm strollin' . . ."*

His face crumpled in fear, "Stop it!"

I stopped instantly and hugged him. Then we talked about building a gigantic pig in Minecraft instead, and all the laughs were back. But the next day in the car, he asked me to sing the Yoda song again. Later on, he asked me *again*.

His exposure and voluntary re-exposure to scary material may sound masochistic, but to Orbach and co. it makes total sense. Firstly, kids are in a constant state of categorising the world so that they can navigate it better. They use scary stories as a way to *identify* their fears. Then, in the retelling, they seek to master the fears they've identified. I'm not suggesting we force a kid who's afraid of *Jurassic World* to watch it again until they toughen up, but if they purposefully ask to see it twice, or more, it may be unwise to refuse and shove them in front of *Teletubbies* instead. Maybe we should high-five them for their courage and sit with them, as the dinosaurs chomp and roar.

We see the "expose and re-expose" pattern in adults too. In the 1970s, a female student at the University of Wisconsin was murdered. In the week after the killing, researchers examined the attendance levels at a local cinema. The depressing real-life murder drama *In Cold Blood* was showing, but, despite the local, well-publicised murder, people weren't put off going to see it. Instead, the female audience for *In Cold Blood* rose by 89 per cent that week, while a non-violent film playing across the street saw no such rise. And, get this: the ones who were particularly keen to see it were the women from the same dorm as the victim. Other dorms were less interested. The researchers looking into these figures suggested that the women may have needed time to explore what had happened in a relatively safe environment. In other words, they were afraid, so they faced the monster as best they could.[18]

Even though a reasonable level of scary content may help the development of a child,[19] many parents will naturally want to protect their children from fear. Some might even assume that a child's life is always better if it is fear-free. You can see this in how some modern parents react to traditional fairy tales.

In 2009, a UK parenting website ran a poll of 3,000 British parents.[20] The results suggested that traditional fairy tales were losing their popularity. Some parents struggled with the language of the old tales. For example, one in ten said the word "dwarf" in "Snow White" was offensive, and should be renamed. But other parents had specific problems with the story content. They felt these tales were simply too scary.[21] For example, 20 per cent refused to read "Hansel and Gretel" to their children because, at one point, the children are abandoned in the forest. A fifth didn't want to read "The Gingerbread Man" because he gets eaten by a fox at the end.[22]

Three years later, the makers of hit US TV series *Grimm* launched their own poll. The show is a dark crime drama set in an adult fairy-tale world. Parents in this survey had similar reservations. This time, a third refused to read "The Gingerbread Man" because of its ending. A third said their children were in tears when they heard "Little Red Riding Hood." Nearly half of parents avoided "Rumpelstiltskin" because the story explores kidnapping and execution. Two-thirds said they ditched *any* tale that might potentially give their kids bad dreams.

Half of those surveyed in 2012 admitted that the traditional tales were more likely to have a strong moral message compared to modern kids' books. Yet the fear of giving children nightmares meant they were choosing unscary tales like *The Gruffalo* or *The Hungry Caterpillar* instead.[23]

These surveys met with much debate in the media. Speaking to the *Telegraph*, child development expert Sally Goddard Blythe argued that the traditional fairy tales were "crucial to children's development." She said they not only taught moral behaviour, they were also honest about humanity. By displaying a vivid contrast between thoroughly good and totally evil characters, they showcased the potential strengths and weaknesses of humans. "When you don't give these stereotypes of good and bad, you don't give them [kids] a moral code on which to start to develop their own lives."

The stories also explored difficult, but important issues, like the death of parents in "Cinderella." These dark tales can teach kids about profound concepts such as loss, heroism and tragedy, and they widen a child's emotional vocabulary. She warned that ditching hard-edged stories in favour of "nice" ones might give kids the false impression that life will always be easy. "If as parents or society we seek to protect children from all unpleasant events, we do not equip them to deal with the real world."[24] Writer Ellie Levenson agreed, adding: "If parents want children not to talk to strangers and not to wander into the forest at night, then children need frames of reference for what might happen if they do."

Stories in which witches fatten up children to eat them really are scary. Yet there's a value in letting kids meet those types of people in a fairy-tale universe. "Once upon a time" characters can't harm us, but they can help children from naïvely thinking that everyone in the world is going to be helpful and nice. Besides, as children grow up, they'll hear disturbing news stories and meet unpleasant people anyway, but if they're not prepared for the possibility, they'll be in for a shock.

For example, in 2012, the Australian TV channel ABC banned an episode of *Peppa Pig* for *not* being scary. In the episode "Spider's Web," Peppa and her gang make friends with a happy, benign spider called Mr Skinnylegs. The message was to encourage kids not to fear insects. This attempt to stamp out arachnophobia didn't go down well in a country known for having some of the world's most venomous critters.[25] Audiences complained that the overly-nice approach could put kids in danger, so the public broadcaster decided not to show it to kids ever again. Personally, I reckon they could've made the point even better if, in episode one, Peppa got bitten on the wrist by Mr Skinnylegs and was plunged into a harrowing coma for a week, only to emerge a sadder and a wiser pig in episode seven. But I accept an approach like that might be a little too hardcore for kids' TV today.

It may not have been too hardcore in the past though. If, like me, you grew up in 70s and 80s Britain, you might remember a series of public information films that warned children against the dangers of drowning, fireworks and creepy men in the park. One that has lodged into the collective memory is "The Spirit of Dark and Lonely Water" from 1973. It's remembered as one of the most chilling and memorable public information films of all time.

The idea was to warn children against being foolish around dangerous bodies of water. The filmmakers could easily have gone with a happy cartoon character, telling everybody to stay dry and safe, while some poor dope pratfalls into a lake with a giggling splash. The creators chose something else instead and ended up with a 90-second horror classic.

The ad opens with a ghostly faceless figure, wearing a long, black robe, hovering above a misty lake. It's speaking with the creepy voice of actor Donald Pleasence. "I am the spirit of dark and lonely water," it says, "ready to trap the unwary, the show-off, the fool . . ."

For the next 90 seconds, the spirit uses invisible powers to drown a couple of children in lakes and ponds. A third child is saved by some cockney kids rocking up and warning against bad water-play. "Sensible children!" the spirit groans angrily, as the robe collapses to the ground. "I have no power over *them*." Then the most chilling moment of all: a closing shot of the robe, bobbing on the water, while the spirit cries out its final, echoing threat, "I'll be back-ack-ack!"

Millions of children crapped their pants when they watched that ad. Especially since it pounced on them during normal, daytime ad breaks. Cereal commercials and cartoon trailers were suddenly punctured by a sadistic ghost, drowning kids in flares. That little film petrified me, and I never, *ever* messed around near the water.

In 2006, the BBC News website polled 25,000 of its readers, asking them what their favourite public information film was.[26] The "terrifying" "Lonely Water" came fourth. Number one was a series of cartoon films called "Charley Says," one of which features a little boy narrowly escaping being abducted by a man in the park. I remember being scared by that too, but it worked. I didn't screw around near lakes, and I knew to say "no" to strangers, even (or especially) if they offered to show me some "puppies."

Maybe those scary ads saved my life. I guess I'll never know for sure. But what's clear is that this ad hasn't been shunned by those who saw it. On YouTube it has thousands of views and comments from those who saw it as a kid . . . and longed to see it again. Many of them have grown to love and value the very thing that scared them. Morbid cultural experiences can resonate for decades, and be strangely pleasurable.

Think of all the great fictional worlds for kids that last long after childhood. *The Lord of the Rings, The Chronicles of Narnia, Star Wars, Jurassic Park, Harry Potter.* Or all those Disney films that include the obligatory scary part.[27] These thrilling adventures exist in a realm that holds not only magic, heroism and fun, but consequences too. They show a universe in which people can be scared, and actually die. Stories that embrace both light and darkness create a powerful cocktail of two things we all need as humans—escapism *and* realism. Judging by the success of these enduring stories, it's clear that kids respond to that.

Yet some parents still insist their children mustn't be afraid—not under any circumstances. A bizarre example of this cropped up in 2016 on the popular internet forum Mumsnet. A mother posted that a pre-school had banned her son from wearing a certain pair of leggings. The goggle-eyed monster design had scared another child.[28] Many forum members suggested it was best to comply with the ban, although almost all admitted the design wasn't really that scary. The mum of the boy agreed, and the leggings weren't worn again. So basically, a preschool saw a little girl's fear as an instant negative and eradicated the source of it. There was no opportunity for re-exposure. No chance to learn courage. By taking the source of fear away, they justified, and possibly reinforced, a kid's fear of something that she might have proudly overcome.

Back in 1952, children's novelist, theologian and *The Chronicles of Narnia* creator C.S. Lewis responded to critics who said children's literature ought not to be frightening. He agreed that traumatising children to the level of phobia is a terrible idea (he had his own, crippling fear of insects as a child). But he also warned that building a fear-free world is a false and unproductive form of escapism. To trick children into thinking that they live in a world without fear, violence and death would, in time, rob that child of a world of courage, adventure and life. Instead, he encouraged kids to enjoy stories of "wicked kings and beheadings, battles and dungeons . . . and let villains be soundly killed at the end. Nothing will persuade me that this causes an ordinary child any kind or degree of fear beyond what it wants, and needs, to feel. For of course, it wants to be a little frightened."[29]

Author Neil Gaiman echoed Lewis' ideas in a late-night Ted Talk he gave in Vancouver, in 2014. "In order for stories to work," he said, "for kids *and* for adults, they should scare. And you should triumph. There's no point in triumphing over evil if the evil isn't scary."[30]

When Hansel defeats the cannibal witch at the end of "Hansel and Gretel," why does the reader feel genuine relief? Because the witch was so twisted, horrible and threatening in the first place. Hansel shoves her in an oven and slams the door shut. It's a horrible ending, but it can delight children, because it tells them something they're not used to hearing: that sometimes it's the weak little children who have the power to destroy the monster.

Children live in a world that constantly reminds them of their weakness. If they want to see over the fence, they need someone to lift them. If they want to unlock the door, they have to yell for an adult. They can't drive themselves to the cinema; they can't book themselves a holiday. You can even keep a kid at bay with a single palm pressed against their head, a technique I've used on several occasions. Children live in a world which repeatedly tells them that if they want to achieve anything they have to rely on grown-ups.

The world of fantasy, by contrast, tells children that, yes, there *are* scary things, like hideous witches who eat children. But it also adds that kids might be the ones to save the day. Ideas like that can give a child a rare sense of strength and potential.

Wander through any playground and you'll see kids playing non-morbid games like football or skipping, or pretending to be teachers. But you'll also see them defeating baddies or killing monsters, often re-enacting the heroes from their favourite films and TV shows.[31] The invincibility and super powers of these characters can be a thrilling prospect for children. But there's another way that children feel power: through tools. You'll see them making magic wands, swords, light sabres, and also . . . guns.

Yes, kids enjoy playing with pretend guns. When I spoke to the headmistress she said that in all her years of teaching, she'd seen kids make guns out of anything from sticks and fingers to the current gun of choice: the school tennis rackets. I admit that when I was a kid, I could even turn my cat Tinker into a machine gun. I'd just pick her up, point her in the right direction, and *Blam, blam, blam*. She was surprisingly cool about it.[32]

Kids toting toy guns in the playground wasn't frowned upon in generations past. They were everywhere. In his book, *Savage Pastimes*, literature professor Harold Schechter makes the case that modern kids' culture is nowhere near as violent as that of his youth. He grew up in 1950s America, and much of his gun-fuelled play was informed by the popular entertainment of the day. "During the 1958–9 season—when I was ten—there were no fewer than seventeen Westerns on prime-time TV, all of them rife with gunplay." He says that at least six of those films had weapons in the title, such as *Gunsmoke*, *The Rifleman*, and *Colt. 45*. Daytime shows aimed directly at kids were also full of shooting, from *The Lone Ranger* to *Hopalong Cassidy*. Toy pistols, lasers and "spud-guns" were a staple of his childhood culture, and so it wasn't a shock to see kids having "shoot-outs" at school, for fun.[33]

These days, however, a plastic pistol in a kid's hand tends to make people very twitchy indeed. That's not to say concern about toy guns is new. It has existed since the 1930s, when mothers' groups would burn toy guns, because they felt it encouraged kids to act like the gangsters of the time. Yet those worries never grew large or powerful enough to stop the thriving market. Then in the 1970s toy guns started losing their popularity. The drop was linked to Westerns falling out of favour.[34] But it was after a tragic series of highly-publicised school shootings in the 1990s that the anti-toy gun argument gathered much more traction. The Columbine High School massacre of 1999, when two teenagers shot and killed twelve students and one teacher, particularly made adults question the wisdom of toy guns.[35]

Today many schools have a no toy-gun policy, and newspapers are rife with stories of children being sent home or even suspended for bringing them in. For example, in North Carolina in 2017, five-year-old Caitlin Miller played a game with her friends. They were the king and queen, and it was her role to guard them. She spotted a stick on the floor and grabbed it to use as a pretend gun. Being the daughter of a soldier, and living in a country with thriving gun ownership, the idea didn't seem wrong to her. The teachers, however, were horrified. They dragged a baffled Caitlin to the principal's office, where she was suspended from the kindergarten for one day. The letter home explained that she was "turning a stick into a gun and threatening to shoot and kill other students." A later statement from the county school district backed up the principal, and said that schools in the district "will not tolerate assaults, threats or harassment from any student."[36]

Guns haven't only vanished from the playground, they're also less popular in kids' entertainment too. Even Woody from *Toy Story* (1995) had something his cowboy ancestors would never have dreamed of: an *empty* holster. In 2002, Steven Spielberg had the guns in *E.T.* digitally removed for its twentieth-anniversary release.[37] Yet even though gunplay is less visible, it still keeps showing up in the playground. Teacher, researcher and author on children's learning Diane Rich has observed children across the UK, and says that gun-related play can have an "irresistible lure for children," especially boys.[38]

She says that one of the reasons this sort of play is so popular is because kids feel great after achieving tasks. Making a gun is a very quick and achievable task. Five-year-old Caitlin had simply found the right-shaped stick, and instantly solved the problem of protecting the king and queen. Makeshift guns are a naturally quick solution in power and protection games. Rich also says that kids use gunplay to learn how communication works. They observe that if they point this little stick, people react in different ways. Friends might dramatically hold up their hands and drop dead. Others might run away squealing. Others, particularly adults, might tell them off. It's a way for children to test out the conventions of communication in a very simple way. Although, clearly, Caitlin was not expecting such a serious reaction from her teachers.

Pretend weapons are a great leveller, too. Ban toy guns, swords or laser pistols from a play fight and you force every kid to be reliant on their own inherent power—how fast they can run or how strong and tall they are. Keep these weapons in play, however, and the scrawny little kid can just shout *Bang!* The big guy clutches his chest and drops to the floor, because the group have agreed to a game in which everybody is equally powerful.

As well as giving weak kids the chance to play a dominant role, gun games can also legitimise submissiveness too. Jay Mechling notes that children, particularly boys, seem to get a kick out of "pretending to die." I know this well. When I was little, my friends and I used to play elaborate games of "who died best." One kid would shoot, and the rest of us would take turns rolling down the hill in melodramatic agony. Kids might like to fake dying simply because they need a rest during gunplay. They might choose to die because it gives them a chance to make the ultimate, heroic sacrifice. But Mechling suggests that these fake deaths also give kids a chance to confront and manage their own fears—not only about guns, but about dying in general. The pretend death also gives kids a chance to observe if anybody actually cares when they die.[39]

So, kids can thoroughly enjoy the morbid activity of pretend killing, yet the fact that it can be frowned upon in public means that many young people explore gunplay at home. Often through that other controversial playground of the macabre: video games.

I've always loved video games, and I've been playing them since I was a little kid in the early 80s. Because of the Atari 2600, the ZX Spectrum 48K, the Commodore 64 and then every incarnation of the PlayStation, I've saved worlds, solved mysteries and killed a million digitised characters. It's this last part, the killing bit, that has made video games one of the prime bogeymen of child development. It's been that way for four decades.

The first time you really see games being called morbid and dangerous is back in 1976, when an arcade game called *Death Race* became a national scandal.[40] In the game, the weapon wasn't a sword, or even a gun—it was a car. To score points, players simply rammed their vehicles directly into squealing "gremlins"—which in the rudimentary graphics of the time might as well have been humans. In the late 70s, media voices like *The New York Times* and *60 Minutes* asked if *Death Race* might warp the minds of players. At the time, behavioural psychologist Gerald Driessen saw video game violence as potentially far more dangerous than TV violence because the player was an actor in the process, not just a spectator. He thought *Death Race* had the potential to encourage people to get into a real car and mow down real pedestrians.[41]

The fear that violent video games could fuel real-life crime has continued ever since, and it's easy to find journalists, parents and politicians blaming school shootings or murders on violent games. However, the actual research into this area is notoriously contradictory. There *are* rafts of studies that claim games can make kids more aggressive,[42] yet many others state the opposite.[43]

For example, in 2013, the American Psychological Association (APA) formed the Task Force on Violent Media, which consisted of seven people. They carried out a meta-analysis of the existing studies, to try to figure out if violent games really were dangerous. In 2015 they released their report, saying that there was indeed a "consistent relation" between violent video games and aggressive behaviour. It was widely quoted in press headlines.

The report was met by outrage from hundreds of researchers who called it "junk science." In an open letter, over 230 academics from Harvard, Yale and Columbia universities criticised the APA for being "misleading and alarmist," and for basing serious conclusions on poor methodology and "inconsistent or weak evidence." Here's an example: in one experiment participants were asked to play a violent video game, then complete the missing letters in words like "-ill" or "explo-e." The gamers were more likely to write "kill" or "explode" than "fill" or "explore." Flimsy studies like this, the critics said, did little to prove a causal link between games and real-world violence.[44]

Based on the current research, we can't conclusively say that violent games do, or do not, cause children to be more aggressive. Some commentators say the real clues are not to be found in the psychological research but in how society has changed over the lifespan of games. Today the global games industry is worth a staggering $108.9 billion.[45] It's now more lucrative than the music and movie industries put together.[46] In 2016, 1.8 billion people were playing video games worldwide, of whom

56 per cent were male and 44 per cent female.[47] In the late 70s, adults only had to worry about a handful of violent games, like *Death Race*. Over the last few decades, however, there have been thousands of video games that depict violence. In the past five years, more than half of all the top-ten selling games were rated for mature audiences. With developments in graphics and sound, these games are *far* more explicit than the rudimentary, black and white graphics of *Death Race*—and despite the age certificates, plenty of underage gamers play them anyway. You might think, therefore, that the massive influx of these mind-warping games would have sent crime rates spiralling out of control. But they haven't. If anything, there's been a dramatic decline in crime rates for murder and drug violence over the lifespan of the video games industry.[48]

If video games were indeed warping young minds, then you might also expect that the countries which have the most violent games would have the highest crime rates. Yet psychologists Patrick Markey and Christopher Ferguson say that the twenty world countries where video games are most popular are also among the safest.[49] Youth culture in Japan and South Korea, for example, is steeped in gory, violent video games, and yet these countries have the lowest levels of teen crime in the world.[50]

Figures like this suggest that, when children commit crime, there is something far more complex going on than just "video games turned me bad." The forensic psychologist Dr Helen Smith studied thousands of children who engaged in serious, real life violence. She said, "Not one young person in my experience has ever been made violent by media influence. Young people who are already inclined to be violent *do* feel that violent media speaks to them. A few *do* get dangerous ideas from it. But more of them find it to be a way to *deal* with their rage." The idea that violent video games might be cathartic might even help explain why youth crime has reduced over the lifespan of video games. Edwin Cook, a professor of psychiatry and paediatrics even suggests that for some children, "the right aggressive entertainment might be the best thing they could see."[51]

It may be some time before we get a definitive answer on the effects of violent media on children and young people.[52] But what's clear already is that many young people are drawn to morbid content in the playground, the classroom and the gaming console. I suspect it's how we *react* to this morbid attraction that might be the real key to kids' health.

You see, while studies on video game violence are divided, almost all psychology researchers agree that some of the most significant influencers on children are the *relationships* they have with others. The reactions and opinions of adults, parents and peers have the power to either build children up, or screw them up.[53] For example, psychology professor Robert T. Muller points out that children who commit actual murder have often experienced severe abuse or neglect at home. Others have witnessed domestic violence, or felt rejected or abandoned by a parent.[54] The 2001 US Surgeon General's report suggests that media exposure simply wasn't the key factor influencing youth violence, rather it was mental stability and the quality of home life.[55] Peers also have an enormous influence on children, and are often critical in helping a child foster positive feelings. Without strong peer connections, children can suffer significant feelings of bullying and rejection.[56]

With that in mind, think back to Caitlin Miller from North Carolina, the five year old who was suspended from kindergarten for playing a game that would have been the norm a few decades ago. According to Diane Rich, prohibitions like this (however well-meaning) may be counterproductive. Children will inevitably play morbid, sometimes shocking games, some of which might even include shooting one another or teachers. Rich warns that shutting this sort of play down will give children a strong message that what they are naturally interested in, or anxious about, is simply not valued. Even worse, the child may internalise the idea that they themselves are a threatening, frightening figure, particularly when it happens in the full sight of peers, parents and teachers (and in Caitlin Miller's case, the entire world). "When children receive this message," Rich says, "their self-esteem is likely to drop . . . Their cognitive capacity is reduced, and so is their commitment to learning, as these negative messages are likely to affect their engagement in the world of education where their interests have been marginalised right from the off."[57] Kids are looking for adults and peers to understand them, to empathise. They don't want to be dismissed; they need to be valued, and to be paid positive, not negative, attention.

It's chilling to hear the motivations that kids who actually *do* end up as killers provide. Many express a desire to *finally* be noticed, because they have felt marginalised or misunderstood growing up. A craving for attention—which often translates as a desire to be famous—is seen with a depressing regularity in juvenile killers. In 2015, *The New York Times* reported on how increasing numbers of killers are so driven by fame that they keep meticulous newspaper clippings of other recent killers. This fuels their desire to "outdo" previous killers in terms of death tolls.[58] Perhaps our celebrity obsessed culture—which says nobody really matters unless they're famous—should be scrutinised just as much as violent video games.

Isn't it better to pay those kids positive attention now? To not gasp in horror when they use a stick as a gun, or draw a picture of a severed head? Shouldn't we sit with them and talk about it? To tell them that aggressive and gory thoughts are completely normal in many people? And that play, art and games can be constructive ways of dealing with our anxieties and interests? This doesn't mean kids can really climb into cars and mow pedestrians down, *Death Race*-style. It's our job to make sure children know the distinction between fantasy and reality. But we dangerously blur that boundary when we conflate playing with a plastic toy pistol with a desire to kill people with a real gun. Instead, let's sit with a kid who's playing that game and try to understand why this pretend violence, and these morbid subjects, are so interesting to them.

And let's admit that, sometimes, this stuff fascinates *us*, too.

Throughout the journey of writing this book, I've met a great many people who share my love of the macabre, and I've literally lost count of how many first saw that interest begin as a child.

A lot of them started when they saw a scary movie on TV, usually with another family member. *I watched* Halloween *with my dad and I'd never been more terrified!* they tell me. *Me and my grandma used to watch Hammer Horror movies together. They were scary, and wonderful. I loved those times.*

Others noticed their love of the morbid blossom through their education: *I saw some grotesque art by Hieronymus Bosch on a school trip, and it disturbed me so much I bought the guide. First time I ever used my pocket money on a book!*

Others still could trace their morbid tastes to very early in their lives. Richard Freeman is a cryptozoologist. He travels the world on expeditions, seeking out strange beasts and mysterious creatures. He told me his love of monsters came at a precise moment: being terrified by a deadly doll in a 1971 *Dr Who* episode called "Terror of the Autons." This wasn't just his first scary memory, it was "my first memory of *any* kind, ever." He's been tracking down monsters ever since.

Many of us stumbled on fear as a youth, and we've been connecting with it ever since, which makes me wonder if another strand at the heart of morbid interest (especially mine) is simple nostalgia. The horror film producer Brian Yuzna once told me his theory that when we feel fear as children, it's one of the first times we truly feel alive. He thinks that many people who love horror are on a quest to touch those past thrills again. It's the first thrills, after all, that are often the most precious.

Our earliest scares have a profound attraction to us. They speak of a time when life was safe and without stress and responsibility; they come from the days of long summers when death felt distant . . . but then we heard its echo. Some of the children's shows I loved as a child tried their best to hide the reality of death from me, like the car wrecks and helicopter crashes in *The A-Team*, in which nobody got hurt. But in time, morbid culture said I was ready for wisdom. People *do* die, and bodies *are* damaged. It doesn't surprise me that the most common scary books and films that I return to are the ones from my childhood. The monsters, the castles . . . they're the ghosts of what was. They're a strange sort of comfort to me.

I would constantly draw pictures in art class of severed heads and chopped-off hands. We studied Helen Keller once, and I even painted her sitting on the back of a headless horse. It's okay. She didn't seem to notice. At another point, I took all of my Star Wars figures and melted them down so I could open their guts and stuff in little balls of tissue paper, dipped in red food colouring. Yeah, I was one of *those* kids—a bit like that skinhead boy in *Toy Story* who was (of course) presented as a psychotic baddy, because he did something that supposedly normal kids never do— give his toys a hard time. I mounted these figures in a large piece of polystyrene and proudly called it "The Chamber of Horrors." I can picture it now: Admiral Ackbar with a cocktail stick carefully prodded through his fish eye.

I showed all this to my mum one afternoon. Did she call social services or an exorcist? Nope. She laughed and said "Urgh, that's a bit grim," which was good. I wanted her to be honest. Plus, she was always so clear on me avoiding real-life danger, and never hurting anybody, that I knew she didn't approve of real-life carnage. But then she said she wanted to know how I'd managed to twist the plastic so well. I'd recently told her that I'd like to be a special-effects artist in horror movies, so the queasy look of: *Wow that's gross* also had an element of *Crikey son, that's really clever and artistic; how did you do that?*

The way my mum (and dad) reacted to my interest in horror and the macabre is probably the main reason I was never consumed by it. I was never scared that my morbid tastes would slip into reality because the people that really mattered to me, the true influencers of my life, could tell straight away that melting Han Solo's face off was completely different to wanting to melt Harrison Ford's face off. Mum made me think I was like everybody else—a kid with complicated feelings who needed safe ways of expressing them. Once expressed, I could just get on with normal life.

And I have, you know. I've been getting on with life. I might have severed Luke Skywalker's legs but I've never hurt anybody physically. I've never punched a guy in the face and I've had no desire to, either (even though I've been kicked and punched in the head a couple of times as a teenager). I'm not a very argumentative guy (talk to my wife). I don't tend to shout much—I like to talk things out. I roll Oprah Winfrey style. In life, I'm not the violent ball of aggression my interests would suggest I am. Perhaps that's because since I was a very small boy I developed a pretty ingenious method of getting the dark side of my nature out . . . through stories, art and play. I'm so thankful those channels weren't taken away from me.

Decades later I'm a grown up who's still a little scared of the world. So, what do I do? I write novels with murder and blood, and what is that if not a grown-up version of those figures in the sandbox? Like those kids crashing toy planes into buildings, like my younger self melting Han Solo, I don't belittle the horrors of life; I'm just trying, in my own way, to cope with them. And so are the many morbid souls we've met in this book.

But if my mother had looked at my chamber of horrors and said it was truly sick, or if a teacher had seen my Helen Keller picture and had me suspended for the day, I wonder if I might have begun to internalise a message that hurting real-life people *was* in my nature after all, because fantasy was somehow the same as reality. Thankfully, I got a different message, from people who knew the difference between pretend bullets and real ones.

CHAPTER NINE

THE HAUNTED

I'm exploring a large, subterranean network of corridors and tunnels that runs beneath the Royal Station Hotel in Hull. I'm with the paranormal investigator and historian Mike Covell. Earlier tonight, I met him in the beautiful hotel lobby, to interview him about those werewolf sightings in Hull. But the hotel was intriguing me too. When we finished talking about beasts, I asked him what he knew about this place. Turns out, he knew quite a bit, and he'd been underneath it before.

The Royal has been a happy, laughter-filled place since it was built in 1847. But like any vintage hotel, the rooms have hosted death on occasion. The Royal has its fair share of spooky stories. In March 1908, Henry Wilson Rippon was found in one of the rooms. He had slashed his throat with a penknife in front of the mirror and fallen onto the bed. Hotel staff found the covers "saturated with blood," the penknife still in his hand.[1] In January 1919, a barrister called Gerald W. Ackroyd Simpson was found kneeling in his room, fully dressed, suspended from the bedhead by his dressing gown cord. He had garrotted himself by tying it around his throat.[2] A couple of years later, Christian R. Kiep was found lying on the floor with his throat cut; a bloody razor lay nearby.[3]

Over tea earlier, Mike had told me that ten suspects in the Jack the Ripper case had stayed in this hotel. His victims had their throats cut too.

This pattern of throat-death plays on my mind because of a strange conversation I had, late last night. It was with an Anglican Lay Minister, Matt Arnold. He, his wife Jo and I were up into the early hours, drinking home brew, laughing hard and talking theology. (Yeah, us Christians can be pretty wild, sometimes.) A few drinks in, we discussed an idea you sometimes hear in parishes: that certain geographical areas have so-called "territorial spirits" or demons. The theory goes that each of these spirits is a specialist in one particular type of attack, and so you see a pattern of crime or vice over and over again in one place. For example, I've heard of a particular church that had numerous adultery scandals, across generations, far exceeding the norm for a church of its size. Or certain streets with domestic violence at levels that are way higher than the average. And here I am, in a hotel that specialises in wounds to the neck. Maybe it's the resident spook's speciality.

Mike and I are being led through the tunnels by Charlie. He normally works on the hotel reception, but when Mike said he knew about this place, I asked Charlie on the desk to show us around. For the last half hour, he's been our guide around the hotel and under it. He's polite, in his twenties, with a huge set of jangling keys and the perfect quiff. I swear you could ski off that thing. He looks sharp and cool in his grey suit, while Mike and I look like trainspotters, out for a wet, Monday morning hike.

I ask Charlie if the staff have ever seen anything spooky down here. He nods, instantly.

"We sometimes hear glass being smashed in one of the storerooms," he says.

"Couldn't it just be a bottle falling? Wine glasses, maybe?"

"That's just it. There shouldn't be *any* glass in there. It's just for chairs and tables. But after the smashing sounds we go in and we find broken glass on the floor. We don't know how it gets there."

"Crikey," I say. "I want to see that."

We keep moving. Some of the tunnels have smooth, clean walls with electric lights. But there are plenty of stretches that are dark and need a torch. It's here where the walls turn dirty, and manhole covers appear in the ceiling. In one of these shadowy alcoves Mike tells me "a tall, black, male figure" has been spotted. I think: *How cool would that be to see him tonight? To spot a bona fide ghost with a couple of other witnesses?* Unless, of course, he had eyes for my throat.

The tunnels stretch all the way to the railway station next door and, bizarrely, Mike says there used to be a working barbershop down here. Not only that, one of the barbers who worked there became a murderer.

"Show me."

Mike nods and leads the way, while I feel a sudden wave of nerves. Spook levels are rising.

As we walk, he tells me, "The barber down here was called Bertram Lund Holmes. In the 1970s, he and his boyfriend Allan Victor Lawrence decided they wanted to kill somebody. So, they did. They picked a friend called Geoffrey Middleton. Holmes hit him with a claw hammer, then Lawrence wrapped a shoelace around Middleton's throat. Choked him to death."

It's a grim case, and yet I can't help but notice it's another one I can add to the "neck-related death" file.

"This is it . . . this is where Holmes worked."

We stop walking.

My torch throws a perfect circle of light onto dirty, yellow wall tiles. The sinks where Holmes must have washed his clients' hair are right in front of me, close enough to touch. The reports say he'd planned this murder for months, which might be why I feel so unsettled here. I'm standing where he would have stood, blow-drying perms and planning death. Then, as Mike tells us more details, my torch light falls across the mirror.

I freeze. Scrawled in the dust are two words.

HELP ME.

"Er . . ." I call Mike and Charlie over.

The room starts flashing as Mike takes a few photographs of the words. I swing the light onto the other mirror, and there's a message written on that one too.

BOO.

I laugh at this one, a little nervously, then turn my light back to the first: *HELP ME.*

I can't take my eyes off the words, smeared by a finger. It feels a lot colder, somehow. My imagination probably . . . possibly.

Charlie frowns. "I've no idea who wrote that."

It'll only be months later—when I find a crime researcher with access to the original case file—that I learn a detail which wasn't in the papers. Even Mike doesn't know about it. There's certainly no reason why Charlie would. As Holmes' victim was slowly dying, he allegedly called out to Allan Lawrence and pleaded for his life. Just before he died, he said, "Help me, save me, Allan."[4]

I keep staring at the mirror.

Help me.

I seem more spooked by this message than the other two. They're too busy looking at a strange ring-pattern on the surface of a bench. A fat candle has been burning here—for a long time, from the looks of it.

"It was probably left here after a paranormal investigation," Mike says. "The hotel used to let groups come down here to look for ghosts, but they stopped it, in case of damage."

I lean in. "So maybe *they* wrote on the mirror."

"It's possible," says Mike. He swipes his fingers across the old, bumpy wax, then he quickly snaps his hand back.

I jump. "What's wrong?"

"Ack. There's pigeon shit on it."

The black little room fills with our chuckles, and Mike and Charlie start heading out. I'm alone now, in a killer's barbershop, and I linger for a while at the mirror. Almost instantly, a tall shadow lurches to my right. I gasp and flick the torch around. It's gone.

That'll do, I say to myself and catch up with the others. Then, as we walk we hear the dull thud of footsteps. We stop for a moment, trying to work out where they're coming from. The hotel above, perhaps. I look back at the barbershop. It's now an inky black hole of shadow. My mind throws up images of Holmes and Lawrence stepping out of the blackness, a shoe lace dangling from their hands.

I speed up.

Charlie passes by a door and points at it. "The room I was telling you about . . . the one with the glass."

I flick my camera on, "I'm ready."

With a jangle of keys, he opens it up. I lean into a small, crammed storage room with stacked banqueting chairs and a couple of tables on their side. A single glass bottle lies broken in pieces on the floor. The shards look sharp enough to cut a throat.

"See what I mean?" Charlie says. "There shouldn't *be* glass in here."

I'm a bit spooked actually. Surprisingly so. Mainly, it's the barbershop and the vibe it's left. Part of me wants to be somewhere else. Yet there's a much larger section of my brain that's getting a bona fide thrill from this. I feel my mind and emotions opening up to a novel experience. Up above me is a normal, beautiful, totally unscary hotel. In it, couples are sipping red wine and flirting in the hotel bar. That's nice. Business travellers are in their rooms, checking their itinerary for tomorrow. That's sensible. I just wonder how these guests would view what us three are doing right now. We're walking in and out of cold, dark rooms, telling each other tales of the dead. And we're even *hoping* we might get a glimpse of something unexplainable. Or at least Mike and I are. Would those guests above us say this activity was morbid, unpleasant or just plain pointless? Perhaps all three, because this really does sound like a very bizarre way for people to spend their evenings.

But if that's true, then why is looking for the dead in dark, cold rooms such a boom industry these days?

Ghost hunters and paranormal investigators certainly existed in the twentieth century, but back then it tended to be left to specialists. If you thought your house had a ghost, you'd either call a vicar or you'd track down learned groups like the SPR (Society for Psychical Research). The vicars would turn up with their holy authority and sanctified water and crosses, while the investigators rocked up with fancy video cameras and strange electronic devices (my horror movie mind always has parapsychologists in moustaches and flares, like they're fresh from the disco). Both reminded us that dealing with the headless apparition of an Edwardian nanny was above most people's paygrade. It required specialist training and bespoke equipment.

The 21st century, however, has seen the world of spooky inquiry become radically democratised. Today, anybody and everybody can be a ghost hunter. This shift has come via a combination of three main factors. First, the internet has put a stop to detailed paranormal information being held in only specialist libraries. Now even the most obscure spectral data can be accessed by anybody in the world. Second, technology has put a world of surveillance and data-gathering in our pockets. Cameras, audio recorders, motion detectors? There are apps for that on your smart-phone. The third factor, and the one that has really brought the idea of personal ghost hunting to the masses, is the success of TV shows like *Most Haunted* (UK, 2002–presenet) and *Ghost Hunters* (US, 2004–16). While horror movies and TV dramas about ghosts have always been popular, these shows had everyday, likeable folk supposedly meeting ghosts for real. It was to become the ideal morbid version of an early 2000s obsession: reality TV. Filmed in night-vision, down-to-earth people would squeal at a creaky floorboard, or get orgasmic about a floating orb on camera. All this looked a little wild to the viewer at home, but it also looked fun. Audiences loved it, and the presenters of these shows wound up as "para-celebrities."

Networks quickly started pumping out more paranormal shows, with titles that scratched even the most specific haunted itch. From ghosts and celebrities (*Dead Famous*, 2004; *Celebrity Paranormal Project*, 2006) to ghosts and children (*Psychic Kids: Children of the Paranormal*, 2008), ghostly animals (*The Haunted*, 2009) and anti-social ghosts (*When Ghosts Attack*, 2013). There was such a glut of these shows that, unsurprisingly, many became cynical when so many episodes managed to uncover a spirit presence on a weekly basis.

This boom in reality ghost shows has slowed a little in recent years, making room for more popular science and high-concept game shows. But the seed was planted. Viewers quickly realised this was a new era in which pretty much anybody could hunt ghosts. Especially since it didn't have to be deadly serious. And even if a ghost wasn't found, all those hours of night-vision TV proved that being on a ghost hunt was pretty darn exciting and seemed like thoroughly morbid fun. Plus, mooching around the local graveyard was a much more cost-effective thrill than a theme park. In a time of recession, factors like this mattered.

Inspired by the TV ghost boom, equipped with pocket-sized tech and informed by a global library of ghost tales on the internet, growing numbers started forming and joining paranormal groups. Some just wanted to replicate the thrills of the TV shows, but others were genuinely intrigued by the subject matter and wanted to investigate it seriously. Today, there are thousands of ghost-hunting groups around the world,[5] and demand is so high, many have turned into businesses.[6] Some sell themselves on the promise of both ghost hunting and scary experience.

One UK outfit is called Dusk Till Dawn Events: The Ghost Hunting Company. On one of their events, they take customers to an abandoned hospital and orphanage where shadowy figures have been spotted fleeing up the stairs and through corridors. For most people, Saturday nights are for parties or wine-fuelled slobbing with Netflix. But this website promises "a terrifying place of sorrow, fear and much emotion." The whole experience sets you back £59. Not all paranormal groups charge an entry fee, but a price tag doesn't seem to put people off. When I check, the abandoned hospital experience has completely sold out.

It's not just specialist paranormal companies who are seeing a lucrative opportunity in the modern desire for ghosts. General businesses are too. For example, Haunted Rooms is an online directory of hotels that proudly promote their resident spirits. Currently, 90 UK hotels have specifically asked to be listed as haunted sites, and five in the Republic of Ireland. Ian Taylor, the manager of the Feathers Hotel in Ludlow, says, "I would certainly recommend Haunted Rooms to any haunted establishment, if you wish to take advantage of any ghosts you may have."[7] They also offer ghost hunts and sleepover events in haunted nuclear bunkers and underground tunnels.

The US site lists well over 300 hotels, and says the business was set up "in early 2009 in response to the ever-present interest in the paranormal." They say that while "other hotel directories concentrate on the view from the room, the food, or whether there is a TV or internet connection . . . what really sets a hotel apart for the rest of us is how many ghosts it has, which room number the dark shadow can be seen in, and where the transparent girl is seen playing."

Even if the tourism industry *didn't* promote haunted sites, people would seek them out anyway. The Enfield Poltergeist case from 1970s London was already an infamous paranormal news story, but it became even more notorious after it featured in the recent hit horror movie *The Conjuring 2* (2016), spurring hundreds of visitors to this private house. I found an Enfield Poltergeist Facebook group with 439 members; it's little more than a long stream of people sharing nervous but giddy selfies outside the supposedly-haunted house. The address is shared openly, for others to join in, with a lot of comments like: *Amazing scary environment!!! I think they should sell tickets now!!!* In the US, people make similar pilgrimages to the original Amityville Horror house (where in the early 70s a family was shot dead, and a huge haunting allegedly followed). On YouTube, you'll see excited clips of friends, couples and families, driving past the house and hanging around outside. You can hear the thrill in their voices—the laughter, the gasps. This is something they've *longed* to do.[8]

Modern celebrities are candid about their own paranormal encounters, too. Whether they're making it up, or they think it's legit, they still think it's relevant enough to talk about in interviews. Like Miley Cyrus, who had a little ghost boy in her London apartment[9] or actor Matthew McConaughey, who was butt-naked when he met his ghost, Madame Blue. Now they happily share their Hollywood home together. "She's a cool ghost," he says. "Maybe being nude all the time is why we get along."[10] Not to be outdone, "TiK ToK" singer Kesha even told Jimmy Kimmel that a ghost lived in her vagina.[11] How quaint.

All this interest in ghosts doesn't automatically imply belief, of course. Some of these ghost-hunting societies consist of sceptics, out to scientifically debunk the phenomenon. Yet a sizeable amount of the population does think there's something to the world of spirits. In 2017, a BMG Research survey found that 36 per cent of people in the UK believe in ghosts.[12]

Whether people believe it or not, modern secularism cannot seem to stamp out our *fascination* with ghosts. They remain a solid fixture in popular culture. We find them interesting, fun, scary and beguiling, and the 21st century has seen growing numbers of us making them part of our leisure time. Whether we're actively looking for them in tunnels, sleeping with them in hotel rooms, gawping at them on TV or just enjoying the fictional life-coach spooks of Charles Dickens' *A Christmas Carol*, the modern ghost is in exceedingly good health, and millions of us like to have them near to us in one way or another.

Critics might say that the folk who try to seek out ghosts today are regressing to ancient thinking, but those critics are wrong. Because in the ancient world, wanting spooks around wouldn't have been seen as quirky escapism or even as scientific enquiry.

It'd be seen as psychotic.

Historical ideas about the afterlife varied from culture to culture, but most people believed that they'd wind up in *some* form of it, eventually. Yet the idea that the dead might occasionally pop back to the land of the living and say hi wasn't always seen as a fun or fascinating experience. For some cultures, it would be a frightening, pant-wetting signal that something had gone very wrong in the transition from life to after-life. Had someone screwed up the burial ritual? Were the relatives not giving enough offerings to honour the deceased? Had the ghost been murdered and was now looking for its killer? In the past, a dead person at your door may well have inspired guilty panic rather than wonder.

Compare modern ghost culture with ancient Mesopotamia, for example, where the spirits of the dead might strike the living down with disease.[13] You just don't hear that idea in ghost culture today. When Oscar-winning actress Emma Stone told David Letterman that she was haunted by the ghost of her kindly grandfather (who often left quarters for her as a sign of his love) the internet went all gooey and said it was the sweetest ghost story they'd heard. *Nobody* was thinking that Grandpa Stone had laced those coins with leprosy.

Or think about how our culture romanticises the thought of a lost loved one reaching out to a grieving partner. In the 1990 film *Ghost*, the appearance of Patrick Swayze was a profound comfort to Demi Moore. Yet compare that to ancient Egypt, where the presence of a lost partner could be a stressful, guilt-inducing experience. For example, when a widower faced misfortune, he might worry that his dead wife was watching him from the Field of Reeds, and was punishing him for some misdeed. For instance, a widower's letter, thought to be from the Twentieth Dynasty, was discovered in an ancient Egyptian tomb. In it, the man pleads with his dead wife to leave him alone, and he frantically lists his good works in an attempt to get her to back off. "What have I done to thee?" he asks. "When thou didst sicken of the illness which thou hadst, I caused a master-physician to be fetched, I wept exceedingly . . . I gave linen clothes to wrap thee . . ."[14]

A ghost at the door could often mean something had malfunctioned and had to be put right, a fact made strikingly visible in ancient India. Ghosts, which they called *bhoots*, would pop up with their feet on backward—a clear signal there had been a screw-up in the afterlife processing department. Once the unresolved issue was dealt with, the dead person could be fully acclimatised to their new spiritual home—and better still, they wouldn't keep bothering the living.[15]

The most famous ghosts in ancient China were the hungry ghosts, who were often greedy for more than they had. They could bother the living and ask for food. If refused, they might curse the person's home or family. The "Festival of the Hungry Ghost" continues to this day, in which people honour the dead—and encourage them to stay in their own realm.[16] The ancient Greeks had a similar practice; they held a public festival called Anthesteria, during which people opened their homes and invited the spirits of the dead for dinner—a sort of metaphysical *Come Dine with Me*.[17] The idea was to fill the spectres up with enough chow that they wouldn't return for a year. Screw this ritual up, and the spirits might go postal and terrorise the town.

The spectral dead were generally unattractive in Europe in the Middle Ages too, particularly because the church had linked the idea of departed spirits with the schemes of Satan. That figure of your dead child, swinging his feet over his bed at night might well have filled you with hope that your dear son had returned—but how were you to know if it wasn't a demonic simulation, sent to your home to entice and corrupt? That's not to say there were *never* benevolent experiences of spirits in history. But often the presence of a ghost was not a welcome experience.

In his book *A History of Terror*, Paul Newman (not the salad-dressing-actor guy) talks about medieval ghosts that nobody in their right mind would want to spend their Saturday nights with, much less pay for the privilege. Like Jacques Tankerlay, a former curate who returned in spirit form to gouge out the eyes of a former mistress, or the dead son of Robert of Bolterbi, whose spirit escaped from the graveyard and terrorised the local community.[18]

This notion that the dead might be dangerous helps in part to explain why our cultures have developed such elaborate and precise funeral rituals. In the Middle Ages, for example, the English decreed that suicides and the violently dead should be buried at a crossroads. If the spirit rose up, they would be so baffled by the road options they'd have no idea where to go. Presumably they'd just crawl back down again and twiddle their stiff thumbs. Like vampires, they even had a stake rammed through their heart to anchor them to the grave. Some had their heads lopped off and placed between their legs.[19] In Denmark, corpses had their toes tied together so that, if they tried to rise, they'd trip over like dead nerds.[20] These days, funeral ceremonies are our way to honour the dead and keep them in our hearts; for some of our ancestors, however, the point was to honour the dead and keep them *in their coffins.*

How did we go from avoiding ghosts like the plague, to paying good money just so we might meet them in abandoned hospitals? The answer is a surprising combination of sweeping cultural forces and the handclap of a little girl.

The Renaissance began in Italy in the fourteenth century. By the seventeenth, it had swept across Europe and sparked a massive reframing of religion, culture and philosophy, as well as a growing appreciation of science. It was the cultural stepping stone between the Middle Ages and the modern world, and it would help create a world in which we'd learn to love the ghost.

What was so radical about it was that it explored an idea that seems like second nature to us; yet to the world back then it was totally radical. They embraced the value of the individual. People started to think more for themselves, and began to scrutinise long-held beliefs. The invention of the printing press in 1440 gave people the chance to consult ancient, forgotten texts, as well as write and spread brand new ones. Minds were changing, and many educated Europeans were saying that individual reason was the key to human progress. From the Enlightenment onwards, the embrace of the scientific method stoked people's desire to make up their own minds about how the world worked, based on evidence.

So, if somebody saw what *appeared* to be a spectre, they needn't consult a higher authority as to whether or not ghosts existed. Nor indeed, whether it was a good or bad thing to see one. By the Victorian period, hundreds of years of history had given even the meekest individuals an authority to interpret the world for themselves—even in the spiritual realm. It seems fitting then that it would be a young girl, perhaps weak in the world's eyes, who would give the world permission to love ghosts.

On the 31st of March 1848, the Fox family were trying to get to sleep in their small wooden house in Rochester, New York. Sleep didn't come easily, however, as the house made noises. Bizarre knocking and tapping sounds rattled through the house, but the family couldn't figure out who or what was making it. One of the Fox daughters, Kate, was approaching adolescence. On the night of the 31st, she lay in bed listening to the knocks. She'd already decided the noises came from a ghost, which she called Mr Splitfoot (a common nickname for Satan), but that night she did something that would have a massive impact on both sides of the Atlantic.

She started a conversation with it.

Kate asked Mr Splitfoot to copy her handclaps and, to the astonishment of the family, it responded with yet more knocks. Baffled, they called the neighbours round, and were shocked to hear the ghostly conversation continue, right in front of them. In time, Kate's sister Maggie used knocks to speak to the spirit too. It knocked back for her, as well.

A century earlier, such a presence in the house would have been a worrying sign that something had gone wrong in the afterlife, and that bad things (or at least, inconvenient things) were about to be unleashed.

With the Fox sisters, however, it was the start of an amicable meeting. The family and their friends were so entrenched in Enlightenment thinking that this experience was no longer a grave danger to avoid, and it wasn't like they'd be hung as witches for doing it either. Now it was just a creepy and fascinating anomaly that ought to be pursued and even tested.

Kate and the family quickly developed a system of knocks, so that they could communicate more meaningfully with the spectre. It claimed to be Charles Rosa, a murdered peddler who used to live in their house. The way he died? Throat cutting. News spread that a ghost was in the Fox home, but the real headline which blew people's minds was that it was happy to talk.

This wasn't the first nor was it the only example of modern interaction with spirits, but the observable ghostly conversations of the Fox sisters brought the idea of communicating with the dead to the masses.[21] Especially when they took their spirit show on the road, demonstrating to a growing bank of (now paying) seekers that the dead not only survive death, but are super-chatty too. Accusations of fakery from scientists or of demonism from the church (the Fox family were Methodists)[22] did little to quell the growth of something revolutionary—everyday people were now reframing spirit communication as a desirable, enriching experience.

News of the sisters spread to the UK, where people were at the time lapping up a new book called *The Night Side of Nature*. Written by Catherine Crowe, it was a collection of ghost stories presented as real, eyewitness accounts, without embellishment. This rational approach to spectres was a sensation, and the book was reprinted in eighteen editions in the space of only six years.

Inspired by the growth of ghost accounts, Americans and Europeans tried talking to the dead themselves. They'd attempt Fox-style communications in their own homes, and some were shocked to hear the knocking sounds come back. Mediums sprang up all over the place, and—although not all of them were women—it provided a rare opportunity for female practitioners to make a living, to travel, and to gain independence, fame and respect.

Newspapers filled with stories of so-called apparitions in séances and sittings, and people were ready to witness them. The American Civil War, which ended in 1865, had littered the nation with corpses. The possibility of demonstrable evidence of an afterlife struck a powerful chord for those who had lost sons and husbands in battle.

What's more, to a world that had embraced the scientific method, ghosts made a quirky sort of sense. For too long, organised religion had asked its followers to believe in an invisible God (who many felt had been a bit quiet on the signs and wonders of late). Now a form of spirituality had emerged that could be tested in any lounge or parlour, and could be inspired and informed by developments in science and technology. For example, Professor Ruth Robbins, a Director of Research at Leeds Beckett University, suggests the "spirit-knocking" method might have been inspired by the invention of the telegraph, which also used a coded language to convey messages.[23]

The problem was, all this rapping on tables stuff and having to interpret the responses was an extremely slow way to have a conversation. It became a chore. Other methods emerged, like writing with a planchette. Here a vertical pencil was fixed to a small board on castors, so mediums could transcribe what the dead were saying. Yet this method could get messy, and notes might be almost impossible to decipher. Other new approaches were explored, until the most recognisable form of spectre-tech hit the world in the second half of the nineteenth century. It made such an impact that even today it remains a morbid rite of passage for millions of teenagers, and has become both the prime symbol of personal ghost encounter, and a bona fide pop culture icon: the Ouija board.

The "talking board" received its earliest known patent in 1854, but the music professor who filed it, Adolphus Theodore Wagner, used his as a telepathy device for *living* people. He called it a Psychograph.[24] In the spirit-hungry climate of the day, however, his talking board idea soon became a handy, easy-to-make ghost-phone.

The first time the public at large really became aware of this bit of spirit-tech was on the 28th of March 1886 when a short, unassuming article called "The New Planchette," was published on page nine of the *New York Tribune* Sunday edition.[25] The article recounts an interview with a "Western man" who talks excitedly about "a new scheme for mysterious communications." He even gives detailed instructions so readers can make their own talking device at home. They need a rectangular board, of about eighteen to twenty inches, with letters, numbers and words written on it. The paper includes a handy diagram showing where to place the letters, the numbers, the "yes" and the "no." The interview also recommends including "Good-Eve" and "Good-Night," so the ghost conversations can be polite and courteous. Users put their thumb and forefinger on the planchette—"a little table" on four legs. Then they simply ask aloud "Are there any communications?" The planchette then moves across the board and offers what the interviewee calls "remarkable conversations."

This was a far more practical way of talking to spirits and, best of all, users didn't need specialised mediumship skills to try it. People loved it so much, some were becoming addicted. The article lists at least seven Ohio cities that were experiencing a "perfect craze over the new planchette."[26] It had now "taken the place of card parties" as evening entertainment. A gentleman acquaintance of the "Western man" found his family so obsessed with "the witching thing" that the man burned it. Baffled as to where it had gone, and unable to live without it, the family got their servants to build a new one. The board dutifully told them what had happened to its predecessor. It spelled out: *Jack burned it.*

Attorney Elijah J. Bond spotted the growing demand for talking boards. He patented the device in 1891 and assigned the rights to the Kennard Novelty Company, who trademarked the word "Ouija." Some say the name came from the combination of the French and German word for yes, "oui" and "ja." So, if you want to look like you know about these sort of things, don't pronounce it "wee-jee" like everybody seems to. Say "weeja" instead. Others believe that the board named itself. Charles W. Kennard simply asked it what it wanted to be called, and it spelled out the word "Ouija" in response. The board insisted this meant "Good Luck."[27]

After some business wrangling, the Ouija eventually became the project of shop foreman and soon-to-be entrepreneur, William Fuld. The board itself told Fuld to expect good times ahead and told him to build a factory. He claimed it spelled out "Prepare for big business." It was right. By the 1920s Fuld became a millionaire through Ouija sales, and *The New York Times* said the boards were as popular as bubblegum. Some Christians denounced it as evil, and ironically some spirit mediums came out against it too. Because even in the spirit world, new tech can affect jobs. With the Ouija board, mediums were seeing their role as specialist conduits to the dead effectively cut out. It also didn't help that the twentieth century had seen a series of scandals in which individual mediums were exposed as frauds. So, the public welcomed this simple, easily tested piece of wood.

The Ouija board may have told Fuld about the good times ahead, but it didn't give him a heads up about 1927. On the 24th February that year he fell three stories from his factory roof. He managed to grab an open window but, like a scene from a horror movie, the window slammed shut and he plunged to the ground. It was thought he might survive and he was rushed to hospital, but a bump in the road en route rammed one of his broken ribs into his heart.[28] The factory that the board had specifically told him to build ended up killing him. *Insert ominous thunderclap here.*

Fuld may not have made it to 1930, but the Ouija board did, and its popularity hasn't stopped since.[29] It thrived and is still manufactured and sold today. Toy giant Hasbro recently offered an all-pink Ouija, aimed especially at young girls.[30] The board has also become an instantly recognisable icon of morbid pop culture, but it's a controversial one too. Horror films like *The Exorcist* popularised the idea that Ouija boards could be the doorway to demonic attack or even full-on possession. Christians continue to see it as a doorway to danger. Some mediums and paranormal investigators also warn that the Ouija is like a direct line to hell—although it's possible that some of them simply want to divert people from the low-cost Ouija toward their own premium-rate channels to the beyond.

Despite this potential danger (who are we kidding: probably *because* of it) the Ouija has become a morbid rite of passage for millions of teenagers across the globe, who gather at parties or school libraries to summon the dead.

I was one of them. I made a Ouija board in woodwork at school, and what it lacked in carpentry finesse, it made up for with supernatural drama. Like those nineteenth-century seekers calling out: *Are there any communications?* into their candle-lit parlours, my friends and I would start our session with that classic line: *Is there anybody there?* Only this was in my red-lit bedroom, with N.W.A. playing quietly in the background. Like a spectral chatroom, we eventually summoned a young woman. I say young, but she soon announced she'd been hanged in the Middle Ages for being a witch. I forget her name, I just remember she was nice at first. Funny even. Complimentary too. But then she started saying things about us, things we hadn't told anybody else. And when we started believing she really might be a spirit, she turned a little psycho, spelling out which of us were going to die that year, and who she might kill first.

A fortnight later, thoroughly creeped out, I took that Ouija board back into school and hacked it in half with an industrial saw. All the time I was torn. Was this legit communication from the dead, or just the result of subconscious pushing? The more time passes, the more I think the latter, but I still can't be sure. But what was beyond doubt was how it made me feel: disturbed, frightened and thrilled, all at the same time. For a teenage boy looking for proof of the afterlife, and who at the time had no connection with any organised religion, the search for ghosts seemed like the most natural and immediate way of starting a spiritual quest.

The Ouija board was the mass-market progression of what had begun with the Fox sisters, and it was also a perfect symbol of it. They introduced the world to an observable, testable mysticism which captured the imagination of millions of people. They also showed us something important about modern humans: we don't want science to completely replace spirituality. Not all of us, anyway. Ideally, we want to hold on to *both*. Organised religion may well promise an afterlife, but you might have to die first to see it. Until then, you have to trust in an invisible God. Hands-on tech like the Ouija board, however, promises proof of an afterlife, right there on your kitchen table.

I make a phone call to Alan Murdie. He's a respected barrister who specialises in intellectual property and tax law. He's written key legal text books and been involved in many cases. He's also an in-demand columnist, writer and speaker on the topic of ghosts, and the current chairman of

The Ghost Club, the world's oldest society for psychical research, which predates even the SPR (of which he's also a member).

He says, "I think what we're currently seeing in the popular world of ghost hunting is, in my view, more of a revival of nineteenth-century spiritualism. Some people can go on ghost hunts, wielding bits of equipment, but frankly some of them might as well be using ritual objects. It's more spiritual evocation than hard science. We've lost the sense of meaning that earlier generations took as read. They had a worldview of faith and religion and knew their place in it. It's not that people have lost their supernatural beliefs these days, it's just that back then it was part of a clearer framework."

Sociology professor Erich Goode makes a similar point. He challenges the common rhetoric that "science is replacing religion." Goode argues that for many people it's actually "paranormalism" that is replacing religion. Indeed, people often use science (or in some cases, the illusion of it) to confirm their paranormal worldview.[31] For example, a 1980 study by Bainbridge and Stark found that paranormal beliefs increase in areas where traditional Christianity is in decline.[32]

I press Alan on why so many people are drawn to ghosts today. What he tells me is as simple as it is spooky.

"Since the Enlightenment, we've had a very anti-religious, anti-spiritual, anti-supernatural view. But nonetheless people *are* having these strange and anomalous experiences."

I think of the pensioner who walks her dog past my house each day, the twenty-something barista with purple hair who poured my Earl Grey in my local Costa, and the policeman I once sat next to at a curry night in our town. When I chatted to them about ghosts, they all admitted something, with lowered voices. None of them had made any attempt to track down a ghost, but all three had run into one anyway: a glowing ball of light slipping under the pews of an empty church; a man in a cloak and top hat sitting on the edge of the bed; a lone dog that vanished into thin air.

So far, I've had a simplistic theory that ghost hunters seek out paranormal experience because they want thrills or proof of the supernatural, but Alan's suggestion is that for some the interest starts because they've already *had* a paranormal experience, perhaps an uninvited one, and they simply want to understand what it was. Maybe ghosts are big right now because they're showing up more.

"So, do you genuinely believe these things are happening today?" I ask Alan. "You think people are really running into ghosts and poltergeists?"

"Oh, yes. In fact, if we used the same standards of evidence as we would in a criminal trial, then these things *do* sometimes happen—at least to an evidential standard you could send someone to life in prison for. But when they happen, there can be an attitude of denial, incomprehension or fear, because mainstream culture doesn't have a place for it. These things are still going on and people are experiencing them in the wider world regardless of what's said in academia, and so on."

After a moment of silence he adds, "You know, people who look into these areas, like you are . . . They quite often report coincidences or synchronicities . . . I think that comes down to the fact that we easily forget we're part of a much bigger, deeper reality."

Coincidences. I think of the odd repetition of throat-cutting that keeps cropping up as I research ghosts. I shrug it off and ponder the wider point: that paranormal belief continues to persist, even when many in academia seem to disregard it.

Erich Goode explores this idea when he compares the way the paranormal is discussed across mainstream media, like tabloids and TV shows, with the more upmarket press, like *The New York Times* or *National Geographic*. He says that, in general, the more mainstream media "tends to be uncritical in their presentation of paranormal claims." For example, a tabloid will run a story on a haunted house case because the chance that it's real is precisely what makes it news. They'll even play up that possibility in their coverage, to keep it interesting. A haunted house that can quickly be debunked, however, is hardly worth reporting.[33]

Similarly, popular horror films and supernatural TV dramas tend to favour a paranormal explanation of events, rather than a more mundane, scientific one. Would *The X-Files* have been as successful if Mulder and Scully had thoroughly debunked each case at the end of each show? Would the paranormal reality shows like *Most Haunted* have been such massive hits if they ended each episode with a clear, sober disclaimer that hauntings were just folk-tales, parlour tricks and proved hoaxes? Probably not, because the majority of tabloids, studios and networks actively encourages belief in the supernatural. Why? Because people seem to find it more enjoyable. Goode says, "Clearly the public hunger to confront and verify paranormal claims is huge, while the desire to refute their validity is precisely the opposite. In other words, paranormalism is news, no paranormalism is not."[34]

Sceptical programming does have an audience in mainstream media, but, as Goode points out, it tends to feature in the more prestigious media institutions such as broadsheet newspapers. This can make people feel like scepticism is the establishment position. And if there's one thing that people like, it's proving the establishment wrong.

You see this in horror movies all the time, like the family in the movie *Poltergeist* (1982), for example, who start to think that their house is haunted. They're confused and embarrassed at first, but when their kid is snatched by the ghosts, they have no choice but to call it legit. The authorities would think they're crazy—so instead they call in the kooky paranormal investigators who believe them. We side with these paranormal underdogs and feel vindicated at the end of the film because the entire town—police and all—gets to witness the house collapsing into a spectral void. The establishment view hasn't just been questioned, it has been obliterated. The everyday folk were right all along.

The Fox family's spectral talk-show had begun on the night before April Fools': a fact that still makes sceptics chuckle. Today's evangelical Christians—still jumpy about ghosts being potential demons—might point out that the conversation started with Mr Splitfoot, a codename for the devil. Some say it was just a childish hoax that got out of hand. Others, like Spiritualists, see it as the welcome opening of a door to the other side. Yet, whatever happened in the Fox house that night, we are still feeling the effects of that little girl's handclap today. In ancient times, generally speaking, we kept dead spirits *away* from us. Yet as the modern age developed, we invented tools and measurable methods to beckon those spirits *towards* us.

And we still call out to those spirits today, in the 21st century. We call to them through paranormal TV shows and haunted house movies and ghost hunting groups. We call to them through city ghost walks and spooky novels and Ouija boards sessions with our mates in the park. Sometimes we don't even call them, because they make the first move and call us, in unexpected encounters. For some people, these spirits are nothing more than a fun but silly hangover from a superstitious age. For others, they're a fascinating form of entertainment. For others still, ghosts are as terrifying as ever, and to be avoided at all costs. Yet for many people, ghosts provide a custom-made spirituality for our evidence-hungry, instant-results culture. It appeals to a culture that sees the dwindling of religion, yet still asks the question:

Is there anybody there?

Mike Covell and I have left both the Royal Station Hotel, and Charlie, behind. I'll be back later to get some sleep, but now Mike is showing me another haunted site in Hull.

We're standing in Sculcoates Lane Cemetery, which is bathed in orange from the street lights. Industrial buildings are all around us, but we're in a crop of overgrown grass and wild ivy. The headstones poke up through it, looking haphazard. Tree branches creak in the night wind.

"It's a strange cemetery, this," Mike says, as we walk in a little further. "A lot of the vaults were unearthed to make way for the estates round here. Bodies were exhumed. There was talk of Satanic rituals happening. Me and my wife saw the apparition of a robed monk, walking among these graves. A black-eyed child's been seen round here too."

"Wow," I say. "Busy place." It's difficult, but I resist adding that it must be the dead-centre of Hull. *Haw Haw.*

Mike tells me about an even more eye-popping sighting. He had brought a dozen people here on a 2016 ghost tour, and they heard a commotion near a grave. They peered over to see two porn actors hard at work, and two men filming it. Jaws dropped as fast as pants shot up. Mike said they were "going at it like knives in among the ivy." This "graveyard porn-shoot" made the papers.[35]

I hear no moans tonight. Ghostly or otherwise. The cemetery is very close to the road, and every now and then cars pass behind us. It sounds like we're by the shore of a small sea.

"Look down," Mike nods to the ground we're standing on. "Parts of the path are made up of old gravestones."

I squint and can see part of a date under my heel: *1887.*

Mike's looking across the cemetery, deep in thought.

I shift my feet on someone's headstone, and think for a moment. While I got spooked earlier in the tunnels, I've yet to see a ghost tonight. I wonder if some people are more receptive to them, so I ask Mike: "You seem to see a lot of activity. Are you really sensitive to these things?"

"Nah," he shrugs. "I'm not psychic or anything like that, but I *do* see things. I think a lot of it's because I'm just so relaxed. I can go into a haunted building fine, and I've slept in funeral parlours overnight to see if anything happened and I've been okay. I've been in old Victorian Warehouses and—"

"Hang on," I lift up my hand. "You *slept* in a funeral parlour?"

He nods. "One of them closed down and was empty, so I got in touch with the owners and got the keys. I spent the night there."

My eyes widen. "Where did you sleep?"

"Well, for a short while I slept on the mortuary slab."

For some reason that makes me laugh. It's not mockery. It's fascination. "Wow, Mike . . . you are *definitely* featuring in my book."

We laugh at the strangeness of this, then move on, but in the weeks that follow, I keep this image in my head: of Mike, this absolutely lovely, knowledgeable, kind-hearted dad and husband, who wanted to sleep on a mortuary slab, alone in a funeral home. I ask him more about this later, and he tells me about being diagnosed with a critical heart condition in 2007.

"I needed something to take my mind off everything," he says. "So I spent many hours reading about the paranormal. I began to really study the afterlife, reincarnation, and of course ghosts. It really helped me through a bad period and even with a still-existing heart condition—you know yourself—I'm fearless and can very happily spend many hours in the field, chasing mythical creatures, ancient animals, and spectral visitors. I know now, having spent many hours in locked-off locations on my own, that there *is* something after death. It's helped me deal with my predicament but I also now help others too."

I think about this a lot, about how the ghosts give him hope. It's one of the key reasons *I* find them interesting too. They scare me, but death without an afterlife? That scares me much more. One of the most treasured gifts my Christian faith has given me is the hope that we go on.

Mike and I say our goodbyes at the train station, then I head back to my hotel. The bar is still open, so I order a Jack Daniels with ice. I sit, swilling it, like an old-fashioned gentleman would a huge glass of brandy. I'm thinking about the tunnels beneath the lobby, and the barbershop somewhere under my feet. I try to ignore those thoughts and watch a few internet videos on my phone, of people slipping on ice or puking at weddings. There are a few ghost videos that the silent algorithms keep recommending, but unusually I skip them, because now I'm back here alone, I don't feel like thinking about ghosts any more.

It's getting late, so I head up to bed. I creak across the old corridor floorboards and decide I'd rather stay somewhere else tonight. My mind is spinning with the old stories of death, spirits and slashed throats. Earlier, when Mike, Charlie and I were poking around in this hotel, it *was* spooky but it was fun too. Alone, it's *just* spooky, and I'm surprised at how much I don't like the feeling. I know it's not the hotel. I like the place. It's just how I've programmed my mind tonight, I guess.

Finally, I turn onto my corridor and instantly remember a door that Mike and Charlie showed me earlier. There were unconfirmed reports that a woman had run a bath in her room late at night, and killed herself. No prizes for guessing how: she slit her own throat. I find my room and slip my keycard in.

I realise then, with a quiet little gasp, that the room she died in is directly above mine.

I let out a long breath. It's an instructive night for me.

I learn that I feel a sense of adventure and bravery when I'm with others, but sometimes, when it comes to ghosts, I don't like being alone. It's almost like when I'm with friends I have the modern mindset: *Let's actively seek ghosts out! Let's look for clues! Let's see them as potentially friendly.* But as midnight strikes, and I'm here by myself, I'm getting a hangover from the ancients. Suddenly, I *fear* the dead, like they did. I start worrying. What if I *do* see something in this hotel tonight? In this room. Without anybody else to verify it, I won't be able to tell if it's legit, or if I'm simply losing my mind. The thought unsettles me more than I expected, and for the first time in this entire book, I feel a shiver of unwelcome fear.

I'm surprised at myself, embarrassed actually, but I leave the lights on. I don't even take off my clothes to sleep because that cold feeling of dread has come back, the foreboding that leapt on me earlier in the tunnels. I even thumb the shape of a cross into the condensation on the window pane, but as I do it I wonder if there's a spectral thumb doing the same thing on the mirror in the dilapidated barbershop below. Unless of course that spirit's here with me now. From some angles, the cross I just drew *does* look like the start of a messy letter H.

Help me.

My fiction-writing mind is going into overdrive, throwing up scary little stories about this scenario. Like, what if the door were to swing open in the night and that tall shadowy figure Mike mentioned just walked in, passed me a little penknife, and guided me to the mirror? Or maybe he'd bring a shard of the glass that had materialised on the store-room floor, especially for me. Maybe that centuries-old witch my friends and I met on the Ouija board would finally, after all these years, come to answer my call. That would make a spooky little tale, I think; only I'm in this situation now. I'm more creeped-out than I have been in a very, very long time.

I realise then that I'm simply not as brave as Mike is. Maybe that's because I'm not quite as desperate for proof of an afterlife, not yet anyway. *I* don't have a heart condition. Or maybe (and this really might be the case), I'm just a wuss.

Or maybe there *is* a presence in the room and I'm sensing it oppressing me. Because I'm not kidding—I really do feel oppressed right now. I think of my car. It broke down this morning on the way here. The mechanic said it was strange since there was nothing technically wrong with it. It simply refused to drive. I got to this hotel on the back of a recovery truck, which means my little escape pod on wheels is in a local garage overnight. I can't even drive away from here until the garage opens in the morning.

I'm here for the night.

I laugh at how silly I'm being, but I keep thinking of the woman who cut her throat in the bath. I lie in bed, looking at the ceiling, scanning it for old brown water stains.

And that's when I hear it, just as I consider her suicide. Someone starts running a bath in the room right above me. It's just after midnight. I wonder who keeps sloshing in the water.

I can't remember when I fall asleep. I just know that it takes a while.

Chapter Ten

SISTER

I've brought my wife and two small kids to see some dead bodies today. A *lot* of dead bodies, actually. We're about to see 3,700 corpses resting in the cool air of an underground crypt. We're in Rome, and we're rather glad of the drop in temperature. Up above us, tourists are melting into the pavement, but down here the sweat on our backs is turning refreshingly cold.

This is the Capuchin Crypt, and it sits beneath the church and friary on Via Veneto. It's under the care of a Catholic order of friars, the Capuchins, whose brown-hooded robes and pale heads are said to have inspired the cappuccino coffee. The Capuchins buried their dead brothers on this site from 1631–1870, having started the practice at their previous building near the Trevi Fountain. Which, coincidentally, is where we've just come from. We strolled up the streets taking selfies and buying fidget-spinners. When the brothers followed that same route, Father Michael of Bergamo brought 300 cartloads of dead friars with him. In the coming centuries, any monk who died would be added, so that the number of brothers in the crypt reached the thousands.[1]

Having that many skeletons in such a confined space meant they had to develop a grave rota system. When a new man died, they would dig up the longest buried skeleton to make room. It was during the mid-1700s that the idea came to arrange the old bones in a new way. It saved on space, but it also became a vivid opportunity for holy funerary art. The result is this astonishing corridor of chambers, each with an in-your-face name like "The Crypt of the Pelvises," "The Crypt of the Leg Bones and Thigh Bones," or "The Crypt of the Skulls."

We creak down two steep steps and find ourselves at the start of the 30-foot corridor which houses all the bones. I notice something straight off: the sound has changed. The buzz of chatter from us and the other tourists—the requests for ice-cream and toilet breaks, the shoving and giggling—that's all vanished now. It has mostly turned to silence, with the occasional hiss of a whisper. There are six chambers off this corridor which we can't yet see. I've read that five of them are filled with skeletons.

We all step forward.

My six-year-old son slips his hand into mine, "Daddy," he gasps. "Look at *that*."

We're staring, open-mouthed, at the first, heavily decorated chamber, where four monks are ready to greet us. They've been dead for centuries. The folds in their brown robes have gradually pooled with dust. I guess that's what happens to people when they never, ever move. Two look like classic, but dirty, skeletons, but the other two have faces covered by stretched, mummified skin. They're lying back, holding crosses. I spot a rosary resting under a set of skinny fingers. They're creepily long, these fingers. It makes me think of the Grinch wriggling out a wave. I can see where the fingernails used to be. The other two monks are standing at the back, pinned to the wall inside little archways. They're bent forward so it looks like they're either praying, or about to leap off the wall at us.

My daughter moves closer to the low, wrought-iron railings that stop us getting too close. "What's all the stuff on the walls . . ." She trails off when she realises for herself.

The skeletons aren't the only human remains in here. The walls are filled with shapes—spirals and stars—*all* made up of bones. Large arches and floral motifs are actually ribs, vertebrae and knee-caps. Above us, the chandeliers are made of what look like femurs and arm bones. The back wall has a whopping pile of pelvises, meticulously stacked to support the skeletons of three children, who lie on top.

An American tour guide brings his group up behind us and we hang around to eavesdrop. He says the skeletons of these kids are to symbolise that death can come at any age. And, as an added kicker, I see two hour-glasses pinned next to them, also made of bones. The hourglasses each have a set of wings, fashioned from the shoulder blades of the dead monks. The joke, if it *is* a joke, is that *time flies*.

I notice that my wife is looking up. I follow her gaze and see another skeleton of a child, pinned to the ceiling with nails and wire. The guide says this is thought to be the remains of an infant princess called Anna Barberini. Anna holds scales in her left hand. I'd say it's two skull caps hanging by three finger bones. And in her right hand is a scythe, the symbol of death.

As if we needed any more hints, I spot a sign with this message:

What you are now, we once were; what we are now, you shall be.

Sheesh. These monks are an absolute riot. Yet as I pause to think about what's going on here, a faint smile grows. I hear the dead friars whispering, through the endless rows of tightly packed jawbones that arch above my head: *Hey, you. Yeah, you with the kids and the slack-jaw. It's okay to be fascinated by our remains. To feel a thrill down here, because sometimes spooky, even disturbing, places can be holy ground.*

It's starting to stir a deep theme in me, this, and it's related to something I haven't really looked at in this journey yet. It's about the question I get asked the most. See, people tend to ask me: *How can you like morbid, scary things?* But more often they phrase it like this: *How can you be a Christian and like that stuff? That makes zero sense to me.*

Here with the friars, I feel like they're saying: *We hear you, bro. We get it, because we were Christians* and *students of the macabre too.* But perhaps you're reading this and it still feels unclear. So, as we bring this book to shore, let me explain.

Come closer.

It's an odd story I suppose, but then spiritual walks are often slippery, unpredictable things. Brought up in a non-churchgoing family, I was a huge fan of horror and the paranormal, and I was very open about my interest. I was also openly antagonistic towards Christians too. At one point I was in a band called Creatures of the Night, and I wrote a song called "Diablo." It was a jolly country and western toe-tapper, all in a major key. But the lyrics weren't exactly Dolly Parton.

Dust off that altar, and upturn that cross!

You better burn your Bible, on God you must goss! (Goss was slang for spit, by the way.)

Screw all you Christians, cos I'm the anti-Christ.

God and Christianity? I couldn't give a shite!

You get the idea. Pretty catchy.

I gave my R.E. teacher a hard time because she was a Christian. I remember mocking her once in front of the whole class, because she said sex should be saved for marriage. "Yeah but Miss, how are you going to know if *your* bits are going to fit *her* bits without trying it out? I mean it's just physics, isn't it?" Sniggers from the class—me feeling superior. I used to do things like grabbing the class bibles and, when she wasn't looking, I'd circle the word "Satan" as many times as I could.

It's weird, because I was actually a really well-behaved, polite guy at school. But if there was a Christian in the room, it was like . . . instant idiot. As a teenager, I even tracked down a local bible-study group. I just turned up at the door one night, drunk, and they let me in. I sat on their sofa challenging their faith as they politely listened and let me talk. When I was done I stuffed a hand-written message down the side of the sofa, a melodramatic letter about a dark, Satanic conspiracy that was brewing in our town against Christians. It said stuff like: *We are watching you. Your time is coming.* Of course, I just made all that stuff up, but it sounded spooky and epic, and I thought it might freak them out. Basically, I could be a complete dick when Christians were around. Although, to be fair, I had drunk a lot of cooking sherry with my friends that night.

I also got really twitchy about the trendy young Jesus-lovers the school invited in from time to time. They came from Christian youth organisations, and I'd watch them sit with their feet on the desk looking finger-pistol cool, telling us how Jesus was "Super Awesome." I tended to write it all off as a loveless campaign to strap me into an ideological straightjacket.

I look on those people with affection now, and some guilt. They were amazingly patient with me. When I became a Christian, I even wrote a letter to my R.E. teacher, apologising. It took me ages to track her down. But in my teenage years I unfairly assumed that all Christians were crusaders on a spiritual scalp-hunt. I thought they were saying that God only spoke through antiquated bibles and guitar-based folk music but, worse than that, I saw the anti-horror movie rhetoric of some believers too. A few even said my "weird and gothic" interests disqualified me from any chance of a divine encounter. Christian-ordained entertainment was apparently the key to unlock my soul.

The God they painted seemed so house-trained and palatable it was like he'd never seen a film above a PG certificate. A deity who hadn't cried at *The Godfather Part 2* or clutched a cushion during *Psycho* seemed inconceivable to me. I vividly remember thinking that maybe on my deathbed I'd reconsider the God question, but at the time I set him aside because I got the impression that he and I simply wouldn't click.

It was surprising then, in the years that followed, when I started to hear him whispering in unexpected places—mostly as I sat in the shadows of my lounge, crunched up on the sofa in the flickering light of a horror film. All those scary tales did something I wasn't expecting. They asked: *What if those religious folks you keep trolling have a point?*

It's predictable, but the film that really opened the door to God's existence for me was William Friedkin's notorious horror, *The Exorcist* (1973). It's about the grisly and foul-mouthed demonic possession of a young girl. I'd *ached* to see this film growing up, but after a patchy cinema release and subsequent ban on home video, it was very tricky to find. Until one sunny, Saturday afternoon, when I was leafing through videotapes on a market stall in my home town. I was in my early teens, and I pulled out a blank plastic VHS case, with a £5 sticker in the corner. When I cracked it open to see what it was, the air started to crackle. Inside was a bootleg copy of the most talked-about horror movie I'd never seen.

Holding it in my hands, I felt like the tape might unleash a supernatural power, the type you couldn't rewind. I set it back in the pile, and walked quickly in the other direction. If Christians had been present they'd have probably high-fived me for my resistance. But why was I so bothered? Surely it was just a film, right? I'd seen hundreds of horror films by then. I would have to test it. I hurried back to the stall. *If it isn't right to buy it, it'll be gone*, I told myself. But there it was, waiting for me. I had to smuggle it under my jacket into my house, because I knew if my mum saw me with this particular film, she'd flip.

I waited for a night when everybody was out and I finally sat down to watch it in the dark. As the titles rolled, my heart galloped and my skin prickled. Something inside kept saying: *This is more than just a movie; this is a moment.* By the end of the two hours I wasn't quite as terrified as I thought I might be—but then, the expectation of our personal mythologies often out-punches the reality. Yet the effect of the film turned out to be far more powerful than I ever expected.

The Exorcist, like many other horror films I loved, took the supernatural seriously. It presented a world in which devils and demons weren't metaphors—they were a stark, terrifying reality. Plus, it suggested another whacky idea: that God might be the only truly effective answer to evil. The priests in this film weren't the usual sweaty perverts or sappy figures of fun, so common in our media. They were intelligent, complicated, brave and—shock horror—*heroic*. This film, and the thousands I watched after it, forced me to consider an utterly subversive notion: that God might be real and the church might sometimes be filed under "solution," not "problem." As a dedicated Christian-basher, this was revelatory.

So, I went to university, and when the Christian Union offered me God, horror movies and morbid culture had flexed my faith muscle just enough for me to consider it properly. I stopped judging Christianity based on Christians and looked at Jesus instead. I was shocked at how progressive and subversive he was, and also that he loved even those people who wrote songs about spitting on him. I avoided stereotyping church-goers, I listened to their arguments and, after a long road of thought, I took the step that changed my life: I became a Christian. This obviously shocked people in my home town. "Huh? I thought you were a devil worshipper," was how one guy put it.

I changed. However, it turns out that when you invite God into your life, he² doesn't reach through a crack in space and hit "delete" on your personality, which meant my love of the macabre remained. Some of the folks in the university's Christian Union said that would never do. I would "obviously" have to drop horror.

I tried, and kept it up for nearly a decade. I stopped watching scary movies and sold or destroyed my horror books and rare vinyl soundtracks. I'd stand in video shops (remember them?) itching to watch *The Blair Witch Project*, but instead I'd trudge to the counter with *Chicken Run* because Jesus would probably rent that. I'd leave the shop thinking that technically I'd achieved some sort of spiritual triumph. But I felt deflated and hollow. I loved being a Christian, I really did, but when it came to what I watched and read, I simply didn't feel like *me* anymore. So, I sat at home watching plasticine poultry with stoopid grins. It's an okay film and all but, man . . . it felt like the *real* party was going on back on the shelf, with the woods and the witches and the shaky-cam screams. I just wasn't invited to that crowd anymore.

I waited for my old spooky attraction to shrivel up in the same way some of my other iffy habits already had—like the inability to commit to one girl, or the desire to try every drug I'd heard of. That stuff had miraculously sorted itself out, but how I missed my monsters. I'd grown up with them, and they'd nurtured me. They taught me what was scary, and after exposing and re-exposing myself to them, they helped me learn courage. They filled my mind with fascinating concepts, even religious ones, but now we no longer played together, because people said that God had new screen-friends for me, made of plasticine and thumbprints.

Maybe my new vanilla life would have continued forever, if I hadn't stumbled on a piece of pub-quiz trivia that for me, represents the paradigm shift in my thinking.

So here it is . . . the hinge of my morbid awakening . . . it's this single little fact:

The Exorcist was banned in Tunisia.

Maybe you think that's no surprise—after all, it was effectively banned in the UK for many years. Billy Graham reportedly said that evil existed in the "very celluloid of the film itself," and thousands of religious groups campaigned for its withdrawal.[3] Yet, Tunisia's banning was very different. On the 24th of February 1975, Tunisia banned *The Exorcist* not on the grounds of blasphemy, but because it presented "unjustified" pro-paganda in favour of Christianity.[4] This might be little more than an interesting factoid for most people, but it blew my tiny mind. Around the same time, I also read that a former Church of Satan member, Nikolas Schreck, had described the film as blatantly pro-Christian: "a big-budget bible-thumper" is what he called it.[5]

This macabre, blasphemous horror film was suddenly accused of being a signpost to the very faith it was supposedly trying to dismantle. It made me wonder: *What if there were other metaphysical edges to morbid culture, and what if God might be cool with me being into it?*

I started researching this idea, and gradually found a spirituality in scary things. God didn't abandon me for doing it. I simply felt his hand slip into mine. We sat in the dark and when faith danced with fright, we watched together.

I saw Dracula cowering at a symbol that much of society found irrel-evant: the cross. I saw vampires drinking blood to gain eternal life, then noticed a very similar exchange at our communion service at church, where we symbolically drank Jesus' blood. That blood gave eternal life too. I watched zombies shuffle through cities, working on pure hunger and instinct, and it made me wonder what it was they lacked which made them subhuman. It wasn't a brain because you could put a bullet in that.

Was it something else, something old fashioned and out of vogue—a soul? These movies, I realised, were parables.

I watched men and women turn into beasts and monsters in a way that was both terrifying and freeing. It made me think about my own destructive instincts, and how I wanted to master them. Yet I also saw how these beasts were liberated from all those polite expectations that society forced on them. I loved the rebellion of it and realised that my *own* revolution was at its most subversive, most wild, when I did crazy things that I knew other twenty-somethings would mock—like admitting that I loved and needed God.

Horror seemed to be celebrating inherently religious ideas in a world that laughed at and derided them. For a start, they took the supernatural seriously. The protagonists in paranormal horror movies usually start out cynical. (*Pah! There's no life after death, so let's move into this spooky old house!*) Yet by the end they encounter ghosts and become full-on believers. (*There* is *life after death, and not all of it's friendly.*) What other genre preaches that message so consistently? Plus, horror kept pounding a seemingly outmoded concept into my postmodern brain: maybe objective good and evil actually exist.

Ironically, these were all similar messages to what the Christians with their rainbow-strap guitars had told me as a kid, but when horror movies came out with the same messages, I was scared enough to care.

I'm an oddball, I know that, because seeing morbid culture as potentially transcendent is a minority view in the Christian world today. I mean, some Christians rail against the Satanic traps of *Harry Potter*, so they can totally freak out when they see me watching *Curse of the Demon* (1957) or *Twitch of the Death Nerve* (1971). To help make their case, these detractors often quote Philippians 4:8 to me, which says we must think only on that which is "true, noble, pure and lovely." But does that mean Christians must never watch the news? Or only think of kittens in wicker baskets? Of course not. Any reasonable believer agrees that sometimes we have to acknowledge the un-lovely elements of life. The Bible says that God is love,[6] but in that same worldview the supernatural is real, evil exists, and death and suffering come for us all. If we never explore these subjects through debate, study, theology and art, we would only be thinking in half-truths.

The Bible certainly refuses to think in half-truths. It thoroughly explores the macabre.[7] Graphic deaths in scripture include tent pegs to the head, teenagers mauled by bears, dismembered corpses and stabbings that cause the bowels to discharge.[8] There are plenty of other repulsive deaths in the Good Book. These details don't always feel necessary either, like when the gospels tell us that Judas Iscariot hangs himself, after betraying Jesus. Okay, that's handy to know. But then the book of Acts adds a repulsive extra portion: "With the payment he received for his wickedness, Judas bought a field; there he fell headlong, his body burst open and all his intestines spilled out."[9] Mentioning the exploding guts of Judas seems like a gratuitous detail. Yet God seems to have looked down at the original writers and said: *Nah. Leave that bit in.*

When the Bible uses morbid material, it does so with purpose. It acknowledges and ponders the dark side because it directly reflects the world we live in. A world filled with cruelty, fear and depravity. Through these dark stories, the Bible introduces radical, subversive and ultimately positive new ideas. For example, the crucifixion of Jesus is a brutal display of violence, and the gospels take time to explore it. Jesus uses that cruel, morbid moment to model subversive behaviours like forgiving the very people who are hammering him to a crucifix. God provides the sacrifice instead of us, so the horror is transformed into hope. The resurrection of Jesus on Sunday makes little sense without the grim execution on Friday. Both are needed, and anyone who wears a cross around their neck, a symbol of execution, shows us that the morbid can be a conduit for something good.

Jesus even used dark stories in his teaching, too. Some of his parables end with folk thrown into fiery furnaces and being bound hand and foot and cast out into darkness.[10] In one parable, Jesus talks about people being broken up and crushed.[11] He didn't *have* to use this sort of imagery, but he chose to because he knew that it would speak to us. It gets our attention, and makes for a thrilling story. But the ultimate message of those grim parables is that in the real world, we strive to do good, not evil. These cautionary tales use morbid elements in order to resonate, but the dark stuff allows us to see the light.

I believe that this is what binds many morbid fans together. The horror fanatics, the vampire-lifestylers, the ghost hunters, even the mur-derabilia collectors, they certainly *do* drive down dark and frightening roads, but, for all the ones I've met, it's ultimately a quest for something good. Why do we love to ponder monsters, ghosts, death and gore? It's because we find those subjects to be exciting, thought-provoking, myste-rious and, not least, *interesting*. These are all admirable goals. I love and enjoy horror films not because they're all about death, but because the element of death turns them into such high-stakes adventures. I suspect that there are very few people who love the morbid for purely negative reasons. Most love it because it brings something positive into their lives.

There were times, especially in my early days of Christianity, when I wondered if something might be wrong with me. Was I obsessed with darkness? I learned this wasn't the case when my wife and I explored a subterranean cave. We were at a UK tourist spot called Wookey Hole and, as we crouched through the sloping, dripping cavern, I was loving the creepy atmosphere. When the guide asked if he could switch all the lights off, I was the loudest "Yeah!" in the cave.

At first, the pure pitch black was fun and freaky, and, of course, I let out a few blood-curdling moans to freak my wife out. But pretty soon I noticed something rather profound. The complete absence of light meant I couldn't make sense of anything, and after a while I realised that *total* darkness gets . . . well . . . it gets kind of boring.

The guide switched the dim, coloured lights back on, and I saw how they cast long shadows across the cave walls. It was fun and spooky again. An odd little epiphany struck me in that cave. I wasn't drawn to creepy, scary things because I was obsessed with total darkness. I was also too realistic to be obsessed with total light. It was the *combination* of light and dark that made me feel alive. The stars at night are a beautiful, awe-inspiring sight, but only once the darkness has brought them out. The light and dark are intertwined. They make sense of each other.

It would be easy to dismiss the lovers of the morbid as having fallen in love with total darkness. I've met some fans of the morbid who think of themselves that way, too. But I'm not convinced. Throughout this book I've met people who use darkness as a way of finding adventure, thrills and mystery. Who value companionship with others, as they gather in a cinema to grab each other in fear, shock, then ultimately laughter.

In many ways, the Bible has become my model for how to engage with morbid culture. It addresses both the very good and very bad sides of humanity, sometimes in extreme detail. So, I figure it's okay for me to do that too, through art and culture. The Bible also shows that it's possible to explore these topics without supporting them. For example, the Bible takes time to depict what it calls blasphemies, from the Golden Calf[12] to the self-mutilation of the prophets of Baal.[13] It expends creative legwork describing the very things it may not agree with. In the same way, when I write a murder-packed crime novel, or blast a zombie brain in a video game, I'm exploring themes of death, adventure, heroism and mystery. None of it means I condone headshots in real life.

With commandments like "Do not murder," the Bible also shows me when morbid interest goes too far. The serial killer hair I've held in my hand did something similar. The locks of Charles Manson were like an object lesson in those who embrace total darkness . . . something I (and almost all fans of the morbid) have no desire to do.

But when the Bible talks of crucifixion, it also teaches me the most profound lesson of all—something I learned when the movie I was warned against, *The Exorcist*, became the megaphone God used to break my prejudice about him and, especially, his followers: that sometimes even the most offensive, blasphemous, creepy, sick, violent and freaky experience can become an unexpected route to the light.

My family and I work our way along the corridor of the Capuchin Crypt, looking at two friezes of leg and arm bones. Nearby we see circles of flowers made from ribs and foot bones.

Long before we came here, other feet stood in this corridor, gazing at these remains. Some found the experience repellent, like the nineteenth-century American author Nathaniel Hawthorne. He wrote: "There is no possibility of describing how ugly and grotesque is the effect, combined with a certain artistic merit, nor how much perverted ingenuity has been shown in this queer way."[14]

"Perverted ingenuity." Nice phrase, that. It may have been *just* the kind of assessment that would have tickled the Marquis de Sade, who came here in 1775. Unlike Hawthorne, he wasn't disgusted by the place, he was entranced. "Never have I seen anything more impressive," he wrote, before encouraging guests to come by night to get a spookier atmosphere by lamplight.[15] I'd have liked that too, so I guess de Sade and I are on the same wavelength. My family and I are visiting in the daytime, however, so what we lack in atmospheric shadow is made up for in stark, high-definition detail: like the visible decay in the hundred collarbones above my head, or the calcification of a femur against the wall.

It would be easy to call a site like this barbaric and unhealthy, the product of unhinged minds. It's an accusation that could be hurled at many of the folk we've met on this journey together. Yet what I've been trying to point out in this book is that being curious or interested in the macabre doesn't make you a degenerate: it's just a sign of being human. We've seen how men, women and children have been drawn to the morbid throughout history. People can shake their heads at this all they want, but the idea that our species *wouldn't* be interested in that which affects every one of us (danger, decay, injury, death) strikes me as absurd.

The Capuchins based their teachings on the works of Saint Francis, who had a surprising way of referring to death. In the moments before he died, he referred to death as a *sister*. "Sister Death" was a completely natural part of existence, and her arrival didn't mark the end of life, only the end of the beginning.[16]

You see this idea with the very early Christians, some of whom requested that the dates of their death be written on their funerary inscriptions not as *dies mortis*, the day of death, but as *dies natalis*, the day of birth. I heard the exact same idea from a shopkeeper and Pagan believer in Whitby. During the Goth festival we chatted in his shop, surrounded by black candles, pentagrams and many, many skulls (only his were fake). I asked him why people are drawn to a subject that seems so repellent.

He just chuckled: "Death's only repellent if you think it's the end . . . but what if it's the *start*? If that's the case, then death is birth." He waved his hand around at the dangling plastic skeletons and fake tombstones. "Which means all these so-called morbid things are actually signs of birth . . . and people have no problem getting excited about that."

I smiled: "You're right. People dish out cigars when people are born."

"*Exactly.*"

I pondered what that shopkeeper said, late into the night, as I stood on the shore where Dracula first arrived. I looked up and gasped. Clouds glided across a moon that hung over the black, crashing sea. The sight of that moon, and the glowing clouds was a perfect cocktail of darkness and light. The result of that balance, was *beauty*.

The idea comes back to me now as I stand in a centuries-old crypt that sees little wisdom in denying the dark. It confronts and frames it as part of a new story, and in so doing, takes away some of its sting. We pass into the last chamber: The Crypt of the Resurrection. On the far wall is an impressive arch made of skulls and pelvises, which surrounds a large painting of another tomb, and another tomb gazer. It's Jesus ready to raise Lazarus from the grave. From death, a rebirth; from the darkness, light.

I can sense the bleakness of death in this crypt, and despite my faith— let me be honest with you—I still fear that moment when death finally comes calling for me. Who knows, maybe when it comes knocking, every ounce of macabre interest will vanish from my brain. Maybe I'll demand to watch *Chicken Run* in a desperate holler! Ha!

But I doubt it.

Even as the worst shadow of all looms over me, I wouldn't be surprised if I were still morbidly curious, even then. If, while I raged against the dying of *my* light, part of me might still wonder: *What happens when the light goes out, and the new one ignites?*

There's a line that I love from the wonderful H.P. Lovecraft, the cosmic horror writer from the 1920s and 30s. It's often quoted as a chilling description of indifferent deities who will reign long after we're dust. For me though, it's always been a line of hope. In fact, I'd be glad if someone says it at my funeral because I suspect that it's true. Not for some freaky old tentacled god rising from the depths (as cool as that sounds). For me it touches on the hope-fuelled-by-horror that I still have for my loved ones, for me, and for you reading this book, and the ones you love too. Heck, I reckon it even applies to these brittle old monks, gazing forever at the floor:

"That is not dead which can eternal lie, and with strange aeons even death may die."[17]

So, it's here that the crypt tour ends—with a painting of hope in the Chapel of the Resurrection. It's an image that only makes sense after a walk through the macabre subject of death, and all its related paraphernalia. This hopeful edge might not be in many people's heads, and—who knows—maybe I'm wrong about it all. It's possible. But for me, this final chamber offers something tantalising: the potential death of death. It says that these bones (and all bones) may somehow live again—like the coolest zombie movie you ever saw.

So, forgive us—me, and the army of shadow-watchers who make up this book. Because despite how it looks, we're just like everybody else. We love and adore life. We laugh. We care. It doesn't matter whether we're into faith or not. Many of us *aren't*, actually. Yet we still detest real-life violence and know the difference between real and fake blood.

But most of all, we are the people who have a Sister. A Sister who has scared the living crap out of us since we were little kids. And as we've grown older we've seen Sister Death do baffling things. Awful things. Sometimes she acts in ways that are so cruel and heartless that we long to drop her from the family for good, but we know we can't.

We *could* ignore her. That's an option many people take. But we're not the type to turn away. Instead, we've come up with a genius plan. We've invented ways to play with her. We take a deep breath and we dive right in. We turn down the lights and tell tales of monsters, ghosts, death and gore. It helps us organise our fears, our hopes, our curiosities, and what we're left with is fun and adventure. And sometimes Sister Death even drops strange little hints sometimes. That maybe hers won't be the last face we'll see after all. Which gives us chills . . . but maybe even hope. For now though, she plays best in the shadows. And so we play too.

We are human, no more no less.

And we are the frightened.

We are the frighteners.

NOTES

CHAPTER ONE: THE SINISTER MINISTER

1. Crane, Jonathan Lake. *Terror and Everyday Life*. California: Sage Publications, 1994. p18.
2. Plunkett, John. "John Whittingdale, The Horror Fan Putting the Frighteners On The BBC." *Guardian*. 18th May 2015. Accessed 3rd July 2017. https://www .theguardian.com/politics/2015/may/18/john-whittingdale-culture-secretary -bbc-rupert-murdoch.
3. Butler, Sarah. "British Retailers Spooked by Halloween Frenzy." *Guardian*. 30th October 2015. Accessed 29th September 2017. https://www.theguardian.com /business/2015/oct/30/british-retailers-spooked-halloween-frenzy-shopping.
4. Boyce, Lee. "Halloween Overtakes Valentine's Day." *This Is Money*. 24th October 2015. Accessed 13th August 2017. http://www.thisismoney.co.uk /money/news/article-3286170/Halloween-overtakes-Valentine-s-Day-biggest -retail-event.html.
5. Rose, Steve. "How Post-Horror Movies Are Taking Over Cinema." *Guardian*. 6th July 2017. Accessed 6th July 2017. https://www.theguardian.com/film/2017 /jul/06/post-horror-films-scary-movies-ghost-story-it-comes-at-night.
6. Mallows, Lucy. *Transylvania*. Chalfont St Peter: Bradt Travel Guides Ltd, 2013. p16.
7. Reuters. "Christmas Horror Movie Offends Religious Groups." *Hollywood Reporter*. 16th Dec 2012. Accessed 3rd July 2017. http://www.hollywoodreporter .com/news/christmas-horror-movie-offends-religious-146720.
8. Bates, Daniel and Helen Pow. "Lanza's Descent Into Madness and Murder." *Daily Mail*. 1st December 2013. Accessed 2nd July 2017. http://www.dailymail .co.uk/news/article-2516427/Sandy-Hook-shooter-Adam-Lanza-83k-online -kills-massacre.html.

9. Duke, David. "The 20 Schoolkids At Sandy Hook: Murdered by Hollywood, Not Guns!" DavidDuke.com. 18th December, 2012. Accessed 2nd July 2017. http://davidduke.com/the-20-schoolkids-at-sandy-hook-murdered-by -hollywood-not-guns/.
10. Berger, Joseph and Marc Santora. "Chilling Look at Newtown Killer, but No Why." *The New York Times*. 25th November 2013. Accessed 4th July 2013. http://www.nytimes.com/2013/11/26/nyregion/sandy-hook-shooting -investigation-ends-with-motive-still-unknown.html.
11. Coleman, Reed. "Adam Lanza's "Shocked Beyond Belief" Posts." schoolshooters.info. 16th December 2014. Accessed 1st July 2017. https:// schoolshooters.info/adam-lanzas-shocked-beyond-belief-posts.

CHAPTER TWO: THEATRE OF BLOOD
1. Phelan, Laurence. "Film Censorship: How Moral Panic Led to a Mass Ban of 'Video Nasties.' " *Independent*. 12th July 2014. Accessed 13th October 2017. http://www.independent.co.uk/arts-entertainment/films/features/film -censorship-how-moral-panic-led-to-a-mass-ban-of-video-nasties-9600998.html.
2. Personal correspondence with the Head of Communications at the British Board of Film Classification (BBFC). Anderson, Catherine. "Re: Press/Book Enquiry." 30th September 2015. Email.
3. Prager, Dennis. "The World Is Getting Worse, But This Time America Won't Save It." DennisPrager.com. 8th March 2016. http://www.dennisprager.com /the-world-is-getting-worse-but-this-time-america-wont-save-it.
4. TED Talk, filmed in March 2007 at TED. https://www.ted.com/talks/steven _pinker_on_the_myth_of_violence.
5. Of course, there are dips and spikes in violence statistics. As I write, here in the UK the Office for National Statistics are reporting that the "near-continual decline" in police recorded crime between 2004 and 2014, has started a "smaller but genuine increase" in homicide (up 21%) and knife crime (up 14%). However, the ONS admitted that the increases reflected "changes in recording processes and practices rather than crime."
6. Norberg, Johan. "Why Can't We See That We're Living in a Golden Age." *Spectator*. 20th August 2016. Accessed 2nd October 2017. https://www.spectator .co.uk/2016/08/why-cant-we-see-that-were-living-in-a-golden-age/.
7. Jenkins, Aric. "Read Barack Obama's Speech Bashing the GOP's "50th or 60th" Attempt to Repeal Obamacare." *Time*. 20th September 2017. Accessed 2nd October 2017. http://time.com/4950410/barack-obama-speech-bill-melinda -gates-goalkeepers.
8. McGlynn, Sean. "Violence and Law in Medieval England." *History Today*. 4th April 2008. Accessed 1st October, 2017. http://www.historytoday.com/sean -mcglynn/violence-and-law-medieval-england.
9. Ibid.
10. Figures 80 and 19 rounded up from 79.8 and 18.6. Truman, Jennifer L. and Rachel E. Morgan (Bureau of Justice Statisticians). "Criminal Victimization,

2015." Bureau of Justice Statistics. NCJ 250180, October 2016. https://www.bjs
.gov/content/pub/pdf/cv15.pdf

11. "Are Domestic Violence Rates Dropping?" Domestic Shelters. 20th April, 2015.
Accessed 22nd November 2017. https://www.domesticshelters.org/domestic
-violence-articles-information/are-domestic-violence-rates-dropping#
.WhWFi7SFg_U. Based on figures from a 2014 report: Truman, Jennifer L. and
Rachel E. Morgan. "Nonfatal Domestic Violence, 2003–2012." Bureau of Justice
Statistics. NCJ 244697, 2014.

12. Van Tuerenhout, Dirk R. *The Aztecs: New Perspectives*. Santa Barbara: ABC-
CLIO, 2005. p188.

13. Goldstein, Jeffrey H. (ed.). "The Appeal of Violent Sports." In *Why We Watch*.
New York: Oxford University Press, 1998. p12.

14. Ricard, Matthieu. *A Plea For The Animals*. Colorado: Shambhala Publications,
Inc, 2016. p200.

15. Sheed, F.J. *The Confessions of Saint Augustine, Book Six*. London: Sheed & Ward,
1999. Chapter 8, p91.

16. Self, Will. "The Revelation of St. John the Divine" in Byng, J. (ed.). *Revelations:
Personal Responses to the Books of the Bible*. Edinburgh: Canongate, 2005. p381.

17. Williams, J. *Life in the Middle Ages*. Cambridge: Cambridge University Press,
1954. p138.

18. Piperno, Roberto. "Torture and Death in the Churches of Rome." *Rome in the
Footsteps of an XVIIIth Century Traveller*. Accessed 13th January 2018. https://
www.romeartlover.it/Torture.html.

19. Homer. *The Iliad* 16:345–50. Translated by A.S. Kline © Copyright 2009. All
Rights Reserved. http://www.poetryintranslation.com/PITBR/Greek/Iliad16
.htm#anchor_Toc239246129.

20. Fiedler, Leslie. *What Was Literature? Class Culture and Mass Society*. New York:
Simon and Schuster, 1982. p50.

21. Schechter, Harold. *Savage Pastimes*. New York: St. Martin's Press, 2005. p85.

CHAPTER THREE: WIRED FOR FRIGHT

1. Bryner, Jeanna. "Woman With No Fear Intrigues Scientists." *Live Science*. 16th
December 2010. Accessed 12th January 2017. http://www.livescience.com/9125
-woman-fear-intrigues-scientists.html.

2. Ledoux, Joseph. *The Emotional Brain*. New York: Simon & Schuster Paperbacks,
1996. p170.

3. Davies, Madlen. "The Woman Unable to Feel FEAR." *Daily Mail*. 21st January
2015. Accessed 12th January 2017. http://www.dailymail.co.uk/health/article
-2919771/The-woman-unable-feel-FEAR-Mother-44-held-gunpoint-beaten
-approached-poisonous-snakes-unfazed-rare-genetic-condition.html.

4. Statistically speaking, Australians are more likely to be killed by a bee sting than
a spider bite. Death from arachnid bites is extremely rare in that country. In 2016
a 22-year-old man died after he was bitten by a redback spider on a bush walk. It
was said to be the first Australian fatality in almost 40 years. Still though, it

seems logical for them to be wary—especially when some of their spiders are horror-movie massive. viz Pearlman, Jonathan. "Young man is first to die from spider bite in Australia for 37 years." *Telegraph*. 12th April 2016. Accessed 3rd October 2017. http://www.telegraph.co.uk/news/2016/04/12/young-man-dies -after-spider-bite-during-australian-bushwalk/.

5. Mcintyre, Sophie. "Fear of spiders became part of our DNA during evolution, say scientists." *Independent*. 5th April 2015. Accessed 8th July 2017. http://www .independent.co.uk/news/science/fear-of-spiders-became-part-of-our-dna -during-evolution-say-scientists-10156573.html.

6. Darwin, Charles. *The Expression of the Emotions in Man and Animals*. New York: Oxford University Press, 1998. pp43–4.

7. Adams, Tim. "The Stephen King Interview, uncut and unpublished." *Guardian*. 14th Sept 2000. Accessed 16th Jan 2017. https://www.theguardian.com/books /2000/sep/14/stephenking.fiction.

8. Pelley, Virginia. "The People Who Get Off To Crush Porn." *Vice*. 7th May 2015. Accessed 16th January 2017. http://motherboard.vice.com/read/the -people-who-get-off-to-animals-being-trampled.

9. Webb, Jonathan. "Murder Comes Naturally to Chimpanzees." *BBC News*. 18th Sept 2014. Accessed 18th January 2017. http://www.bbc.co.uk/news/science -environment-29237276.

10. Nell, Victor. "Cruelty's Rewards: The Gratifications of Perpetrators and Spectators." *Behavioural and Brain Sciences*, 29 (2006). pp211–57.

11. Kottler, Jeffrey A. *The Lust for Blood*. New York: Prometheus Books, 2011. p181.

12. Ghose, Thia. "Why Pain Can Feel Good." *Live Science*. 26th February 2013. Accessed 8th July 2017. https://www.livescience.com/27462-relief-makes-pain -feel-good.html.

13. Kottler, Jeffrey A. *The Lust for Blood*. New York: Prometheus Books, 2011. p107.

14. Ginsberg, Benjamin. "Why Violence Works." *The Chronicle of Higher Education*. 12th August 2013. Accessed 3rd October 2017. http://www.chronicle.com /article/Why-Violence-Works/140951

15. Knauft, Bruce M. "Reconsidering Violence in Simple Human Societies: Homicide Among the Gebusi of New Guinea." In *Current Anthropology*, Vol 28, No. 4 (Aug–Oct. 1987) pp457–500. Chicago: University of Chicago Press.

16. Kottler, Jeffrey A. *The Lust for Blood*. New York: Prometheus Books, 2011. p215–16.

17. Jung, Carl. "Good and Evil in Analytical Psychology." In *Civilization in Transition, The Collected Works*, vol. 10. London: Routledge & Kegan Paul, 1964. p463.

18. Reynolds, Matt. "Machine Learning Reveals Lack of Female Screen Time in Top Films." *New Scientist*. 8th March 2017. Accessed 4th October 2017. https://www .newscientist.com/article/2123926-machine-learning-reveals-lack-of-female -screen-time-in-top-films/.

19. Gonzalez, Sandra. "Reese Witherspoon on Hollywood's Limiting Roles for Women: Things Have To Change." *CNN Entertainment*. 14th January 2017.

Accessed 4th October 2017. http://edition.cnn.com/2017/01/14/entertainment/big-little-lies-women-on-film-hbo/index.html

20. Cunningham, Todd. "Box Office: How Horror Films Like *The Conjuring* Win by Scaring Up Young Women." *The Wrap*. 22nd July 2013. Accessed 4th October 2017. http://www.thewrap.com/box-office-how-horror-films-conjuring-win-scaring-young-women-104901/.

21. Gilbert, Sophie. "Why Men Pretend to Be Women to Sell Thrillers." *The Atlantic*. 3rd August 2017. Accessed 4th October 2017. https://www.theatlantic.com/entertainment/archive/2017/08/men-are-pretending-to-be-women-to-write-books/535671/.

22. McGrath, Melanie. "Women's Appetite for Explicit Crime Fiction is No Mystery." *Guardian*. 30th June, 2014. Accessed 4th October 2017. https://www.theguardian.com/books/booksblog/2014/jun/30/women-crime-fiction-real-anxieties-metaphorical

23. Firestone, David. "While Barbie Talks Tough, G. I. Joe Goes Shopping." *The New York Times*. 31st December 1993. Accessed 19th October 2017. http://www.nytimes.com/1993/12/31/us/while-barbie-talks-tough-g-i-joe-goes-shopping.html.

24. Kottler, Jeffrey A. *The Lust for Blood*. New York: Prometheus Books, 2011. p83.

CHAPTER FOUR: HIDING THE BODIES

1. de Castella, Tom. "The Puzzle of Uncollected Ashes." *BBC News Magazine*. 20th August 2014. Accessed 4th October 2017. http://www.bbc.co.uk/news/magazine-28852698.

2. Gye, Hugo. "Would You Bury Your Loved One In Your Garden?" *Daily Mail*. 12th December 2013. Accessed 4th July 2017. http://www.dailymail.co.uk/news/article-2522613/Would-bury-loved-garden.html.

3. King, Stephen. *Danse Macabre*. New York: Simon and Schuster, 2010. p205.

4. Evans-Pritchard, Ambrose. "Nobel Scientist Tells Us We Can Live to 150." *Telegraph*. 20th January 2016. Accessed 4th October 2017. http://www.telegraph.co.uk/finance/financetopics/davos/12111287/Nobel-scientist-tells-us-we-can-live-to-150.html.

5. Goldstein, Jeffrey H. (ed.). "Death Takes a Holiday, Sort Of." In *Why We Watch*. New York: Oxford University Press, 1998. p32.

6. ChurchPop Editor. "Why Cages Have Been Hanging from This Old German Church for 500 Years." *Church Pop*. 17th January 2017. Accessed 22nd November 2017. https://churchpop.com/2017/01/17/why-cages-have-been-hanging-from-this-old-german-church-for-500-years/.

7. Dying Matters Coalition Report. "Public Opinion On Death And Dying." April 2016. Accessed 6th October 2017. http://www.dyingmatters.org/sites/default/files/files/NCPC_Public%20polling%2016_Headline%20findings_1904.pdf.

8. "Millions Leaving it Too Late to Discuss Dying Wishes." Dyingmatters.org. 12th May 2014. Accessed 5th October 2017. http://www.dyingmatters.org/news/millions-leaving-it-too-late-discuss-dying-wishes.

9. "Too Few Parents Make Plans in Case They Die Early." Dyingmatters.org. 7th October 2014. Accessed 5th October 2017. http://www.dyingmatters.org/news /too-few-parents-make-plans-case-they-die-early.

10. Ibid.

11. Goldberg, V. "Death Takes a Holiday, Sort Of." In *Why We Watch: The Attractions of Violent Entertainment*, Jeffrey H. Goldstein (ed.). New York: Oxford University Press, 1998. p27.

12. Kastenbaum, R. *The Psychology of Death*. New York: Springer Publishing Company, 1992. p31.

13. Marie Curie Report, 2014. Accessed 6th October 2017. https://www.mariecurie .org.uk/globalassets/archive/www2/pdf/patient-choice-v-cost_graphics.pdf.

14. Tucker, Eleanor. "What On Earth is a Death Café?" *Guardian*. 22nd March 2014. Accessed October 6th, 2017. https://www.theguardian.com/lifeandstyle/2014 /mar/22/death-cafe-talk-about-dying.

15. www.racheljwallace.com. Accessed 15th January 2018.

16. The Associated Press. "Puerto Rican taxi driver put behind the wheel of his cab one last time." nydailynews.com. 26th May 2015. Accessed 27th June 2017. http://www.nydailynews.com/news/world/puerto-rican-taxi-driver-body -propped-cab-funeral-article-1.2236489.

17. Wilson, E.G. *Everyone Loves A Good Train Wreck*. New York: Sarah Crichton Books, 2012. p22.

18. Ibid. p.143.

CHAPTER FIVE: ZOMBIES, EVERYWHERE

1. thelastsurvivors.co.uk.

2. Representing Blackness. The National Archives Black Presence Exhibition. http://www.nationalarchives.gov.uk/pathways/blackhistory/culture /representing.htm.

3. Cox, Jeffrey. *The British Missionary Enterprise Since 1700*. Routledge: New York, 2008. p.4.

4. Davis, Wade. *Passage of Darkness: The Ethnobiology of the Haitian Zombie*. North Carolina: University of North Carolina Press, 1988. p57.

5. If you're keen to find out more, check out Sarah's book: Lauro, Sarah Juliet. *The Transatlantic Zombie: Slavery, Rebellion and Living Death*. New Jersey: Rutgers University Press, 2015.

6. Bram Stoker was Irish, but as Ireland was at that time still part of Great Britain, I've taken this small liberty in labelling him a Brit.

7. Seabrook, William B. *Jungle Ways*. Edinburgh: Riverside Press Lt., 1931. p172.

8. Bavis, Barbara. "Does Haitian Criminal Code Outlaw Making Zombies?" Library of Congress. 31st October 2014. Accessed 20th November 2016. https:// blogs.loc.gov/law/2014/10/does-the-haitian-criminal-code-outlaw-making -zombies/.

9. Russell, Jamie. *Book of the Dead*. Surrey: FAB Press, 2007. p19.

10. Ibid. p25.

11. Rhodes, Garry D. *White Zombie—Anatomy of a Horror Film*. North Carolina: McFarland & Company, 2001. p119.
12. Russell, Jamie. *Book of the Dead*. Surrey: FAB Press, 2007. p23.
13. Abrams, Simon. "As Night of the Living Dead Gets Restored, George Romero Looks Back." *Village Voice*. 4th November 2016. Accessed 8th November 2016. http://www.villagevoice.com/film/as-night-of-the-living-dead-gets-restored -george-romero-looks-back-9305776.
14. Bailey, Jonathan. "How A Copyright Mistake Created the Modern Zombie." *Plagiarism Today*. 10th October 2011. Accessed 21st November 2016. https:// www.plagiarismtoday.com/2011/10/10/how-a-copyright-mistake-created-the -modern-zombie/.
15. Rothkopf, Joshua. "From Romero to *Walking Dead*: A Brief History of Zombies in Pop Culture." *Rolling Stone*. 19th August 2015. Accessed 21st November 2016. http://www.rollingstone.com/movies/news/from-romero-to-walking-dead-a -brief-history-of-pop-culture-zombies-20150819.
16. Bates, Claire. "What happened to the self-sufficient people of the 1970s?" *BBC News Magazine*. 12th April 2016. Accessed 9th October 2017. http://www.bbc .co.uk/news/magazine-35945417.
17. Josette Sheeran was quoted in an article by Joshua Zumbrum: "Feed the World. Let It Trade." *Forbes*. 6th May 2008. Accessed 21st November 2017. http://www .forbes.com/2008/05/06/food-trade-sheeran-biz-beltway-cx_jz_0506food .html.
18. McNamara, Mary. "Survivalist themes in TV shows, movies tap into fear of the big fall." *Los Angeles Times*. 15th December 2012. Accessed 9th October 2017. http://articles.latimes.com/2012/dec/15/entertainment/la-et-st-tv-film -revolution-hunger-games-fear-20121216.
19. King, Stephen. *Danse Macabre*. New York: Simon and Schuster, 2010. ppxx–xi.

CHAPTER SIX: KILLER CULTURE

1. Newton, Michael. *Criminal Investigations—Serial Killers*. New York: Chelsea House Publishers, 2008. p37.
2. Poster. "Charles Manson Unfinished Burrito From Prison Visit." Supernaught True Crime Collectables. Accessed 16th November 2016. https://supernaught .com/products/charles-manson-unfinished-burrito-from-prison-visit.
3. Bartlett, Robert. *Why Can The Dead Do Such Great Things?* Oxfordshire: Princeton University Press, 2013. p243.
4. Quigley, Christine. *The Corpse: A History*. Jefferson, NC: McFarland & Company, 1996. p250.
5. Wade, Stephen. *Yorkshire's Murderous Women*. Barnsley: Wharncliffe Books, 2007. p29.
6. Blair, David. "Louis XVI Blood Mystery "Solved"." *Telegraph*. 31st December 2012. Accessed 12th November 2016. http://www.telegraph.co.uk/news /worldnews/europe/france/9773174/Louis-XVI-blood-mystery-solved.html.

7. Bond, Michael. "Why Are We Eternally Fascinated by Serial Killers?" *BBC*. 31st March 2016. Accessed 17th November 2016. http://www.bbc.com/future/story /20160331-why-are-we-eternally-fascinated-by-serial-killers.

8. Eddy, Cheryl. "The Day a Serial Killer Died, A Morbidly Festive Atmosphere Reigned." *Gizmodo*. 17th June 2016. Accessed 19th November 2016. http:// gizmodo.com/when-a-hated-serial-killer-died-a-morbidly-festive-atm -1712060010.

9. Quigley, Christine. *The Corpse: A History*. Jefferson, NC: McFarland & Company, 1996. p249.

10. Ibid. p250.

11. Rippo, Dr Bonnie. *The Professional Serial Killer and the Career of Ted Bundy: An Investigation*. Lincoln: iUniverse, 2007.

12. Newman, George E., Gil Diesendruck and Paul Bloom. "Celebrity Contagion and the Value of Objects." *The Journal of Consumer Research* Vol. 38, Issue 2. 1st August 2011. pp215–28. https://doi.org/10.1086/658999.

13. Powell, Emma. "Justin Bieber's Used Milk Glass on Sale for £65,000 on eBay." *Standard*. 17th October 2016. Accessed 17th October 2017. https://www .standard.co.uk/showbiz/celebrity-news/justin-biebers-used-milk-glass-on -sale-for-65000-on-ebay-a3371486.html.

14. Leadbeater, Elli. "Woolly Ruse Incites Irrationality." *BBC News*. 4th September 2006. Accessed 23rd November 2017. http://news.bbc.co.uk/1/hi/sci/tech /5314164.stm.

15. Bonn, Scott. A., "The Macabre Hobby of Collecting 'Murderabilia.' " *Psychology Today*. 24th January 2014. Accessed 23rd November 2017. https://www .psychologytoday.com/blog/wicked-deeds/201401/the-macabre-hobby -collecting-murderabilia.

16. Eric Holler used to refer to himself as Eric *Gein*, after Ed Gein. I asked Eric why he took on the surname of a necrophiliac serial killer who kept a cup of noses on his kitchen table. He said that he had decided to use it in 2008 as his "entertainment name" because it seemed to fit in with his murderabilia business. In 2013 he switched back to his real surname, after he often found himself on TV shows and in news articles. "If I had to do it all over again," he told me, "I would have of course used my real name from the start but . . . I had no idea the interest that would eventually occur in regard to the website and myself."

17. http://tedbundyssocks.tumblr.com. Accessed 23rd November 2017.

18. Schechter, Harold. *The Serial Killer Files*. New York: Ballantine Books, 2003. p400.

19. Ibid p401.

20. "Hybris" refers to a psychological blindness, coupled with "philia" meaning attraction. It has similarities with sufferers of Stockholm syndrome (kidnap victims who fall in love with their captors), but hybristophiliacs differ in that they are not forced into these situations. They deliberately seek them out.

21. Money, John. *Lovemaps: Clinical Concepts of Sexual/Erotic Health and Pathology*. Prometheus Books, 1986. p56.

22. Wong, Brittany. "Why Some Women Are Attracted to Serial Killers Like Charles Manson." *Huffington Post*. 21st November 2017. Accessed 24th November 2017. http://www.huffingtonpost.co.uk/entry/women-attracted -serial-killers-hybristophilia_us_5a131cf7e4b0bfa88c1c051e.
23. Mina, Denise. "Why Are Women Drawn To Men Behind Bars?" *Guardian*. 13th January 2003. Accessed 24th November 2017.
24. Obviously, there are also cases of men being attracted to female killers, but it's far less common and not as well-documented.
25. Wong, Brittany. "Why Some Women Are Attracted to Serial Killers Like Charles Manson." *Huffington Post*. 21st November 2017. Accessed 24th November 2017. http://www.huffingtonpost.co.uk/entry/women-attracted -serial-killers-hybristophilia_us_5a131cf7e4b0bfa88c1c051e.
26. I think we see a similar dynamic in the *Fifty Shades of Grey* franchise, which has faced repeated accusations that its main character, Christian Grey, demeans and subjugates women. Yet legions of enthusiastic defenders of the books, argue it's more complex than that. They admire, pity and even fear Grey, all at the same time, and crucially they feel like the female character Anastasia is the only woman who can reform Grey by entering his world. Along the way she gets the bonus experience of safe, controlled danger. She is not, as critics argue, a victim.
27. She has taken on his surname in anticipation.
28. "Why I Want To Marry Serial Killer Who Butchered 49 Victims . . . and Have His Baby." *Siberian Times*. 22nd June 2016. Accessed 25th November 2017. http:// siberiantimes.com/other/others/features/f0235-why-i-want-to-marry-serial -killer-who-butchered-49-victims-and-have-his-baby/.
29. The "Son of Sam" laws in the US are there to stop criminals making money off their misdeeds; they came about in 1977 to stop serial killer David Berkowitz (now a remorseful evangelical Christian) from selling the media rights to his story. This means that the Chessboard Killer, for example, isn't likely to pocket a cheque if Disney were ever to make a musical of his life. However, murderabilia dealers do sometimes send gifts of money and supplies to their incarcerated contacts; so they can potentially earn money, indirectly.
30. Bott, Michael and KXTV. "Murderabilia" collector defends hobby website in spite of criticism by victims' families." *ABC10*. 3rd April 2015. Accessed 26th January 2018. http://www.abc10.com/news/investigations/murderabilia -collector-defends-hobby-website-in-spite-of-criticism-by-victims-families /183407206.
31. Shepherd, Jack. "Netflix's Most Popular Original Programme Revealed." *Independent*. 22nd June 2016. Accessed 24th November 2017. http://www .independent.co.uk/arts-entertainment/music/news/netflixs-most-popular -original-programme-revealed-and-its-not-making-a-murderer-house-of-cards -or-a7095506.html.
32. Hesse, Monica. "Serial" takes the stand: How a podcast became a character in its own narrative." *Washington Post*. 8th February 2016. Accessed 17th October 2017. https://www.washingtonpost.com/lifestyle/when-a-post-conviction -hearing-feels-like-a-sequel-the-weirdness-of-serial-back-on-the-stand/2016

/02/08/b3782c60-2a49-48f7-9480-a34dd9e07ab6_story.html?utm_term
=.35e9efd245ea.

33. Sorren, Martha. "How 2016 Kicked Off A True Crime TV Phenomenon That
Shows No Signs of Stopping." *Bustle.* 29th December 2016. Accessed 24th
November 2017. https://www.bustle.com/articles/198758-how-2016-kicked-off
-a-true-crime-tv-phenomenon-that-shows-no-signs-of-stopping.

34. Battaglio, Stephen. "Investigation Discovery Becomes Top Cable Channel For
Women With True Crime All The Time." *Los Angeles Times.* 5th January 2016.
Accessed 24th November 2017. http://www.latimes.com/entertainment
/envelope/cotown/la-et-ct-investigation-discovery-20160105-story.html.

35. Burns, Ric (dir.). *Enquiring Minds: The Untold Story of the Man Behind the
National Enquirer.* Steeplechase Films, 2014. This documentary is available on
Netflix UK, and you can find discussion of circulation figures at around 39mins
40secs.

36. "Enquirer/ Star Group, Inc. Company History." *Funding Universe.* Accessed 12th
January 2018. http://www.fundinguniverse.com/company-histories/enquirer
-star-group-inc-history/.

37. Pooley, Eric. "Grins, Gore and Videotape—The Trouble with Local TV News."
New York Magazine, Vol 22, No 40. 9th October 1989. p37.

38. Martin, Christopher (dir.). *Interview With a Serial Killer.* Netflix UK, 2008. See at
23mins.

39. Waddell, Lily. "Serial Killer Sickos." *Daily Star.* 25th July 2016. Accessed 15th
November 2016. http://www.dailystar.co.uk/news/latest-news/530069
/Murderabilia-UK-Britain-serial-killer-Myra-Hindley-Peter-Sutcliffe.

CHAPTER SEVEN: THE BEAST WITHIN

1. Perraudin, Frances. "Man Wielding Axe in Hull Dies After Being Shot by
Police." *Guardian.* 29th November 2016. Accessed 14th January 2018. https://
www.theguardian.com/uk-news/2016/nov/29/man-wielding-axe-in-hull-street
-shot-injured-by-police.

2. Mills, Alice. *Mythology: Myths, Legends and Fantasies.* Australia: Global Book
Publishing, 2006. p31.

3. Virgil. *The Bucolics, Or Eclogues of Virgil*, Ecologue VIII. Written 37BC.
Translated by R.M. Millington. London: Longmans, Green, Reader and Dyer,
1870. p103.

4. Herodotus. *The Histories.* Translated by A.D. Godley. Cambridge: Harvard
University Press, 1920. http://www.perseus.tufts.edu/hopper/text?doc
=Perseus:abo:tlg,0016,001:4:105. You can also read more about the story in
Mittman and Dendle (eds). *The Ashgate Research Companion to Monsters and the
Monstrous.* Abingdon: Routledge, 2016.

5. The story comes from a pamphlet, "The Damnable Life and Death of Stubbes
Peeter," translated into English from Dutch in 1590 by George Bores. You can
find this and other werewolf legends on the site of Professor D.L. Ashliman.
Accessed 11th January 2018. http://www.pitt.edu/~dash/werewolf.html.

6. Gholipour, Bahar. "Real-Life Werewolves: Psychiatry Re-Examines Rare Delusion." *Live Science*. 16th April 2015. Accessed 25th November 2017. https://www.livescience.com/44875-werewolves-in-psychiatry.html.

7. Darwin, Charles. *The Expression of the Emotions in Man and Animals*. New York: Oxford University Press, 1998. p19.

8. '"Furring" Is New Sex Craze for Perverts." *Metro*. 27th June 2007. Accessed 25th November 2017. http://metro.co.uk/2007/06/27/furring-is-new-sex-craze-for-perverts-477540/.

9. Accessed 26th January 2018. https://www.youtube.com/results?search_query=proof+furries+perverts+4.

10. Accessed 26th January 2018. http://www.ign.com/boards/threads/furries-are-sick-and-should-be-hated.200242910/.

11. Accessed 26th January 2018. http://en.wikifur.com/wiki/List_of_conventions_by_attendance#Ongoing_events.

12. Plante, Reysen, Roberts and Gerbasi. *FurScience: A Summary of Five Years of Research from the International Anthropomorphic Research Project*. Waterloo, Ontario: FurScience, 2016. Note: some specific percentages were not listed in the *Furscience* report, and were confirmed to me by Dr Courtney "Nuka" Plante, lead data analyst for *Furscience* via email on 28th November 2017.

13. The study assessed answers on a seven-point scale (1—Strongly Disagree, to 7—Strongly Agree). If you go with people who picked the midpoint or above on the scale, 80.3 per cent of furries indicated that "belongingness" played a motivational role in their fandom involvement. 84.6 per cent said "escapism" was a key factor.

14. Accessed 26th January 2018. http://furscience.com/wp-content/uploads/2017/10/Fur-Science-Final-pdf-for-Website_2017_10_18.pdf.

15. She now makes werewolf masks to order, and they're pretty spectacular. If you fancy one, then check out Farumir's website, Farumir Works: http://farumir.deviantart.com

16. Stoker, Bram. *Dracula*. London: Capuchin Classics, 2008. p207.

17. Barnett, David. "Dracula's Birthplace: How Whitby Is Celebrating the Count's Anniversary." *Guardian*. 28th July 2015. Accessed 26th November 2017. https://www.theguardian.com/culture/2015/jul/28/draculas-birthplace-how-whitby-is-celebrating-the-counts-anniversary.

18. Thompson, Ian. *Dracula's Whitby*. Gloucestershire: Amberley, 2012. p21.

19. Russo, Arlene. *Vampire Nation*. London: John Blake Publishing, 2005. p141.

20. Ibid. p149.

21. Ibid. p143.

22. Perlmutter, D. "Vampire Culture." In. G. Laderman and L. Leon (eds). *Religion and American Cultures: An Encyclopaedia of Traditions, Diversity and Popular Expressions, Volume 1*. Santa Barbara: ABC CLIO. pp281–2.

23. "Handbook: Safe Bloodletting and Feeding." *Sanguinarius*. 14th February 2015. Accessed 29th May 2017. http://www.sanguinarius.org/support/blood-matters/safe-feeding/.

24. "Getting Blood Made Easy." Vampire Website. Accessed 29th May 2017. http://www.vampirewebsite.net/gettingblood.html.

25. Robson, David. "The People Who Drink Human Blood." *BBC*. 21st October 2015. Accessed 29th May 2017. http://www.bbc.com/future/story/20151021-the-people-who-drink-human-blood.

26. Ficino, Marsilio. *Book of Life*. Translated by Charles Boer. Spring Publications, 1983. p44.

27. Leviticus 17:14.

28. It's thought this story could easily be a wild rumour, spread by anti-Catholics of the time. In some versions of the tale, the three young boys are Jewish.

29. Cooper, Christopher. *Blood: A Very Short Introduction*. Oxford: Oxford University Press, 2016. p104.

30. Spoken by Dracula's mad assistant, Renfield, this line (from Chapter 11 of Stoker's novel) has links with the Old Testament book Leviticus 17:11–12. The original verse—along with Genesis 9:4—is a actually a prohibition *against* drinking, or as some translations put it, "eating," blood.

31. "Exorcism Industry "Booming" in France, Italy and UK." *The Week*. 3rd August 2017. Accessed 26th November 2017. http://www.theweek.co.uk/87467/exorcism-industry-booming-in-france-italy-and-uk.

32. Rudgard, Olivia. "Astonishing Rise in Demand for Exorcisms Putting Mental Health at Risk, Report Finds." *Telegraph*. 4th July 2017. Accessed 26th November 2017. http://www.telegraph.co.uk/news/2017/07/04/astonishing-rise-demand-exorcisms-putting-mental-health-risk/.

33. Ray, Rachel. "Leading US Exorcists Explain Huge Increase in Demand for the Rite." *Telegraph*. 26th September 2016. Accessed 25th November 2017. http://www.telegraph.co.uk/news/2016/09/26/leading-us-exorcists-explain-huge-increase-in-demand-for-the-rit/.

34. Summers, Chris. "Italy's Catholic Church Cannot Keep up with Demand for Exorcists as More Than 500,000 People Call on Help to Rid Themselves of Demons in One Year." *Mail Online*. 13th October 2016. Accessed 26th January 2018. http://www.dailymail.co.uk/news/article-3836549/Italy-s-Catholic-Church-demand-EXORCISTS-500-000-people-call-help-rid-demons-one-year.html.

35. Chaniotis, Linda. "I Was Subjected to Exorcisms as a Child to Treat My Epilepsy." *Guardian*. 21st September 2016. Accessed 28th November 2017. https://www.theguardian.com/commentisfree/2016/sep/21/i-was-subjected-to-exorcisms-as-a-child-to-treat-my-epilepsy.

36. French, Chris. "Pope Francis and the Psychology of Exorcism and Possession." *Guardian*. 9th July 2014. Accessed 28th November 2017. https://www.theguardian.com/science/2014/jul/09/pope-francis-psychology-exorcism-possession.

37. Burnell, Paul. "Exorcisms on the Rise." *National Catholic Register*. 4–10th June 2000.

38. Rudgard, Olivia. "Astonishing Rise in Demand for Exorcisms Putting Mental Health at Risk, Report Finds." *Telegraph*. 4th July 2017. Accessed 26th November 2017.

39. Di Giacomo, Frederica (dir.). *Liberas Nos*. London: Network, 2017. DVD.

40. I suspect that this argument is true in some cases, although I'm doubtful that many people *consciously* use possession as a simple look-at-me tactic. Many possessed people seem genuinely open to their affliction being potentially real.

41. Susman, David. "8 Reasons Why People Don't Get Treatment for Mental Illness." David Susman Blog. 11th June 2015. Accessed 26th November 2017. http://davidsusman.com/2015/06/11/8-reasons-why-people-dont-get-mental -health-treatment/.

42. French, Chris. "Pope Francis and the Psychology of Exorcism and Possession." *Guardian*. 9th July 2014. Accessed 28th November 2017. https://www .theguardian.com/science/2014/jul/09/pope-francis-psychology-exorcism -possession.

43. Lim, Linda. "Women Workers in Multinational Corporations: The Case of the Electronics Industry in Malaysia and Singapore." *Michigan Occasional Papers in Feminist Studies*, No. 9. 2008. p44.

44. Ibid. p33.

45. Ong, Aihwa. "The Production of Possession: Spirits and the Multinational Corporation in Malaysia." In M. Lock and J. Farquhar (eds). *Beyond the Body Proper: Reading the Anthropology of Material Life*. Durham & London: Duke University Press, 2007. p518.

CHAPTER EIGHT: DEADTIME STORIES

1. Such as the *Guardian* article that came out less than a year later, which listed "9/11 in Numbers," including the facts that 291 intact bodies were retrieved that day and 19,500 body parts were collected. Templeton, Tom and Tom Lumley. "9/11 in Numbers." *Guardian*. 18th August 2002. Accessed 15th February 2017. https://www.theguardian.com/world/2002/aug/18/usa.terrorism.

2. Goodman, Robin F. and Andrea Henderson Fahnestock. *The Day Our World Changed: Children's Art of 9/11*. New York: Harry N. Abrams, 2002.

3. Connor, Kevin J.O. and Charles E. Schaever. *Handbook of Play Therapy*. New Jersey: John Wiley and Sons, 2016. p423.

4. Jones, Gerard. *Killing Monsters: Why Children Need Fantasy, Super Heroes and Make-Believe Violence*. New York: Perseus Books Group, 2002. pp11–12.

5. Gil, Eliana. *Posttraumatic Play in Children: What Clinicians Need to Know*. New York: Guilford Press, 2017. p17.

6. Maclean, G. "Psychic Trauma and Traumatic Neurosis: Play Therapy with a Four-Year-Old-Boy." *Canadian Psychiatric Association Journal* Vol 22 (1977). Accessed 30th November 2017. http://journals.sagepub.com/doi/pdf/ 10.1177/070674377702200204.

7. Gil, Eliana. *Posttraumatic Play in Children: What Clinicians Need to Know*. New York: Guilford Press, 2017. pp17–18.

8. Ibid. p9.
9. Brooke, Stephanie. L. *The Use of the Creative Therapies with Sexual Abuse Survivors*. Springfield: Charles C. Thomas Publisher, 2006. p132
10. In time, the children's artwork of 9/11 was widely accepted as an authentic expression of trauma. Yet in 2012 it sparked shocked anger when a Texan teacher asked the class to draw pictures of the 9/11 attacks. One mother, Ivie Gremillion, said the kids, who hadn't been alive in 2001, found the exercise confusing and scary. One pupil worried if it meant the terror attacks would happen on that date every year. It chimes with Gil's warning that authentic trauma *does* require expression, but it can be counterproductive if you push it onto kids who are not trying to process it already. Accessed 26th January 2018. http://www.nydailynews.com/news/national/elementary-school-students-forced-draw-9-11-attacks-world-trade-center-showing-planes-flying-twin-towers-mother-claims-article-1.1158918.
11. "New Experiences "Improve Memory"." *BBC News*. 2nd August 2006. Accessed 30th November 2017. http://news.bbc.co.uk/1/hi/health/5240058.stm.
12. Preston, Richard. "*Horrible Histories*: 20 years of entertaining children." *Telegraph*. 21st February 2013. Accessed 13th October 2017. http://www.telegraph.co.uk/culture/tvandradio/9857326/Horrible-Histories-20-years-of-entertaining-children.html.
13. Doward, Jamie. "Horrible Histories: The Movie Is Coming Soon, Says Creator Terry Deary." *Guardian*. 27th March 2016. Accessed 6th December 2017. https://www.theguardian.com/culture/2016/mar/27/horrible-histories-author-lets-rip-at-museums-national-trust-terry-deary.
14. Grater, Tom. "*Horrible Histories: The Movie* is in the Works with Altitude." *Screen Daily*. 12th October 2017. Accessed 6th December 2017. https://www.screendaily.com/news/horrible-histories-the-movie-in-the-works-with-altitude-exclusive/5123209.article.
15. Goldstein, Jeffrey H. "Children's Attraction to Violent Television Programming." In *Why We Watch*, New York: Oxford University Press, 1998. p97.
16. Peck, Penny. *Reader's Advisory for Children and Tweens*. California: ABC-CLIO. 2010. p131.
17. Goldstein, Jeffrey H. "Children's Attraction to Violent Television Programming." In *Why We Watch*. New York: Oxford University Press, 1998. p105.
18. Sanders, M and M. B. Oliver. "The Appeal of Horror and Suspense." In *The Horror Film*. Stephen Price (ed.). New Brunswick: Rutger University Press, 2004. p249.
19. I'm not advocating kids watch *anything* they like. One of the most noble elements of the films certification system is that it tries to protect very young minds from levels of brutality that are simply too intense to comprehend at that age, never mind deal with. So, I'm not suggesting we let toddlers watch *Silence of the Lambs* (although the pre-schooler I saw dressed as Hannibal Lecter—complete with

face muzzle, straight jacket and trolley harness—was one of the most amusing World Book Day outfits ever).

20. Paton, Graeme. "Parents Who Shun Fairytales 'Miss Chance to Teach Children Morality.' " *Telegraph*. 14th March 2011. Accessed 30th November 2017. http://www.telegraph.co.uk/education/educationnews/8378975/Parents-who-shun -fairytales-miss-chance-to-teach-children-morality.html.

21. Some of the earlier versions of these fairy tales are far more brutal. Early tellings of Cinderella have the ugly sisters hacking pieces of their feet off, just to fit into the glass slipper. Then they get their eyes pecked out by birds. Charming.

22. Paton, Graeme. "Traditional Fairytales Not PC Enough." *Telegraph*. 5th January 2009. Accessed 30th November 2017. http://www.telegraph.co.uk/culture /books/4125664/Traditional-fairytales-not-PC-enough-for-parents.html.

23. "Fairytales too scary for modern children, say parents." *Telegraph*. 12th February 2012. Accessed 18th October 2017. http://www.telegraph.co.uk/news /newstopics/howaboutthat/9078489/Fairytales-too-scary-for-modern-children -say-parents.html.

24. Paton, Graeme. "Parents Who Shun Fairytales 'Miss Chance to Teach Children Morality.' " *Telegraph*, 14th March 2011. Accessed 30th November 2017. http://www.telegraph.co.uk/education/educationnews/8378975/Parents-who-shun -fairytales-miss-chance-to-teach-children-morality.html.

25. Pearlman, Jonathan. "Australian broadcaster bans "unsuitable" Peppa Pig episode featuring a friendly spider." *Telegraph*. 13th February 2015. Accessed 13th August 2017. http://www.telegraph.co.uk/news/worldnews /australiaandthepacific/australia/11411098/Australian-broadcaster-bans -unsuitable-Peppa-Pig-episode-featuring-a-friendly-spider.html.

26. "And The Winner Is. . . ." *BBC News*. 28th March 2006. Accessed 15th January 2018. http://news.bbc.co.uk/1/hi/magazine/4853042.stm.

27. There are literally stacks of Disney scares to choose from, but here are a few choice cuts: the attempted knife murder of a little girl, who escapes into a wailing, haunted forest (*Snow White and the Seven Dwarfs*, 1937); a giant horned demon raising the demonic spirits (*Fantasia*, 1940); and the subtle, but ominous drowning of two girls' parents in a ship engulfed by an ocean storm (*Frozen*, 2013).

28. GravyEvans. "AIBU to think it's silly that DS can't wear these to nursery?" *Mumsnet*. November 2016. Accessed 17th February 2017. https://www.mumsnet .com/Talk/am_i_being_unreasonable/2792583-aibu-to-think-it-s-silly-that-ds -can-t-wear-these-to-nursery?messages=100&pg=1.

29. Lewis, C.S. *On Stories: And Other Essays on Literature*. New York: Harvest Books, 2002. pp39–40.

30. You can find an audio recording, as well as transcript of Gaiman's TED Vancouver talk on Maria Popova's Brain Pickings site. "Neil Gaiman on Why Scary Stories Appeal to Us, the Art of Fear in Children's Books, and the Most Terrifying Ghosts Haunting Society." 20th March 2014. Accessed 26th January 2018. https://www.brainpickings.org/2014/03/20/neil-gaiman-ghost-stories/.

31. Adults find this difficult sometimes. In 2015, a little girl was reportedly sent home from pre-school for bringing in a Wonder Woman lunchbox. The letter home said the school dress code banned violent characters. "We have defined "violent characters" as those who solve problems using violence," the letter said. They believed that superheroes fell into that category. In reporting the story, the *National Review* pointed out that, by that standard, every US President should be banned from the school too, including Barack Obama, who "solved the problem of Osama bin Laden with SEAL Team Six." Goldberg, Jonah. "A School's Rationale for Banning Superhero Lunchboxes Couldn't Be More Morally Confused." *National Review*. 2nd September 2015. Accessed 3rd December 2017. http://www.nationalreview.com/article/423439/schools-rationale-banning -superhero-lunchboxes-couldnt-be-more-morally-confused-jonah.

32. I never threw her as a grenade though. Thought I'd better make that clear.

33. Schechter, Harold. *Savage Pastimes*. New York: St. Martin's Press, 2005. p85.

34. Fisher, Marc. "Bang: The Troubled Legacy of Toy Guns." *Washington Post*. 22nd December 2014. Accessed 5th December 2017. https://www.washingtonpost .com/lifestyle/style/bang-the-troubled-legacy-of-toy-guns/2014/12/22 /96494ea8-86f8-11e4-9534-f79a23c40e6c_story.html?utm_term=.d6a1fdcd07f9.

35. Jay Mechling suggests that up until the 90s, the public hadn't been as bothered about the daily reports of teenagers shooting other teenagers. He suggests that was because so often it seemed to be "urban black-on-black crime;" but "boys and guns became a significant social problem when it was white kids killing white kids." "Gun Play." In *The American Journal of Play*, Vol. 1, No. 2, Fall 2008. p201. http://www.journalofplay.org/sites/www.journalofplay.org/files/pdf -articles/1-2-article-gun-play.pdf.

36. Schmidt, Samantha. "5-year-old Girl Suspended from School for Playing with "Stick Gun" at Recess." *Washington Post*. 30th March 2017. Accessed 5th December 2017. https://www.washingtonpost.com/news/morning-mix/wp /2017/03/30/5-year-old-girl-suspended-from-school-for-playing-with-stick -gun-at-recess/?utm_term=.3c0aed2af2d8.

37. He replaced them with walkie-talkies. Later, in 2011, he admitted to a press crowd that he regretted having altered the film. He promised to re-instate the guns for the 30th-anniversary edition. *Slash Film*. http://www.slashfilm.com /steven-spielberg-regrets-altering-et-raiders-hit-bluray-original-forms/.

38. Rich, Diane. "Bang! Bang! Gun Play and Why Children Need It." *Early Education*, Summer 2003. http://dianerich.co.uk/pdf/bang%20bang %20gun%20play%20and%20why%20children%20need%20it.pdf.

39. Mechling, Jay. "Gun Play." In *The American Journal of Play*, Vol. 1, No. 2, Fall 2008. pp205–8. http://www.journalofplay.org/sites/www.journalofplay.org /files/pdf-articles/1-2-article-gun-play.pdf.

40. Though not an officially licensed tie-in, the game used the name and methodology of the 1975 Roger Corman movie *Death Race 2000*—a cult dystopian satire in which race-drivers like Sylvester Stallone got points for running down pedestrians. (If you're keeping score, it's 10 points for men, 40 for

teenagers, and toddlers rack up a whopping 70 points—but if you want to score high, aim for the over-75s. They're 100 points each!)

41. Kocurek, Carly A. "The Agony and the Exidy: A History of Video Game Violence and the Legacy of Death Race." *Game Studies*. Volume 12, Issue 1. September 2012. Accessed 3rd December 2017. http://gamestudies.org/1201 /articles/carly_kocurek.

42. "Violent Video Games Make Teenagers More Aggressive, Study Finds." *Telegraph*. 8th October 2017. Accessed 2nd December 2017. http://www .telegraph.co.uk/technology/video-games/9593188/Violent-video-games-make -teenagers-more-aggressive-study-finds.html.

43. Bodkin, H. "Violent Video Games Like Grand Theft Auto Do Not Make Players More Aggressive, Major New Study Finds." *Telegraph*. 8th March 2017. Accessed 2nd December 2017. http://www.telegraph.co.uk/science/2017/03/08/violent -video-games-like-grand-theft-auto-do-not-make-players/.

44. Wofford, Taylor. "APA Says Video Games Make You Violent, But Critics Cry Bias." *Newsweek*. 20th August 2017. Accessed 2nd December 2017. http://www .newsweek.com/apa-video-games-violence-364394.

45. McDonald, Emma. "The Global Games Market Will Reach $108.9 Billion in 2017 With Mobile Taking 42%." *Newzoo*. 20th April 2017. Accessed 25th January 2018. https://newzoo.com/insights/articles/the-global-games-market-will-reach-108 -9-billion-in-2017-with-mobile-taking-42/.

46. Nath, Trevir. "Investing in Video Games: This Industry Pulls in More Revenue Than Movies, Music." *Nasdaq*. 13th June 2016. Accessed 2nd December 2017. http://www.nasdaq.com/article/investing-in-video-games-this-industry-pulls -in-more-revenue-than-movies-music-cm634585.

47. McKane, Jamie. "There Are 1.8 Billion Gamers in the World, and PC Gaming Dominates the Market." *My Gaming*. 26th April 2016. Accessed 6th December 2017. https://mygaming.co.za/news/features/89913-there-are-1-8-billion -gamers-in-the-world-and-pc-gaming-dominates-the-market.html.

48. Ford, Matt. "What Caused the Great Crime Decline in the US?" *Atlantic*. 15th April 2016. Accessed 2nd December 2017. https://www.theatlantic.com /politics/archive/2016/04/what-caused-the-crime-decline/477408/.

49. Petit, Harry. "Countries That Play More Violent Video Games Such as Grand Theft Auto and Call of Duty Have FEWER Murders." *Daily Mail*. 2nd March 2017. Accessed 2nd December 2017. http://www.dailymail.co.uk/sciencetech /article-4275262/Countries-play-violent-video-games-safer.html.

50. Merrill, Paul. "Why Violent Video Games Are Good for Kids." *Kidspot*. Accessed 13th February 2017. http://www.kidspot.com.au/parenting /parenthood/parenting-style/why-violent-video-games-are-good-for-kids.

51. Jones, Gerard. *Killing Monsters: Why Children Need Fantasy, Super Heroes and Make-Believe Violence*. New York: Perseus Books Group, 2002. p28.

52. I personally think that in the coming years we'll get better long-term data on video game use. I suspect that the data will show more positive effects than negatives.

53. Gander, Kashmira. "How Easily Can a Parent Psychologically Damage Their Child?" The *Independent*. 9th January 2016. Accessed 2nd December 2017. http://www.independent.co.uk/life-style/health-and-families/features/how -easily-can-a-parent-psychologically-damage-their-child-a6802941.html.

54. Muller, Robert T. "Children Who Kill Are Often Victims Too." *Psychology Today*. 5th Feb 2015. Accessed 2nd December 2017. https://www .psychologytoday.com/blog/talking-about-trauma/201502/children-who-kill -are-often-victims-too.

55. Surgeon General. "Youth Violence: A Report of the Surgeon General." *NCBI*. 2001. Accessed 15th February 2017. https://www.ncbi.nlm.nih.gov/books /NBK44293/.

56. Ladd, Gary W. *Children's Peer Relations and Social Competence: A Century of Progress*. New Haven: Yale University Press, 2005.

57. Rich, Diane. "Bang! Bang! Gun Play and Why Children Need It." *Early Education*, Summer 2003. http://dianerich.co.uk/pdf/bang%20bang%20gun %20play%20and%20why%20children%20need%20it.pdf.

58. Tufekci, Zeynep. "The Virginia Shooter Wanted Fame. Let's Not Give It to Him." *The New York Times*. 27th August 2015. Accessed 2nd December 2017. https://www.nytimes.com/2015/08/27/opinion/the-virginia-shooter-wanted -fame-lets-not-give-it-to-him.html.

CHAPTER NINE: THE HAUNTED

1. "Lamentable Discovery." *Hull Daily Mail*, 4th March 1908.

2. "Barrister's Tragic End." *Hull Daily Mail*, 27th January 1919.

3. "Tragedy at a Hull Hotel." *Hull Daily Mail*, 3rd March 1921.

4. "Bertram Lund Holmes Report." *Black Kalendar*. Accessed 2nd May 2017. http:// www.blackkalendar.nl/content.php?key=25572. See also http://discovery .nationalarchives.gov.uk/details/r/C11606060.

5. An online directory of paranormal societies (paranormalsocieties.com) lists 4,487 registered global groups as of early 2018. The vast majority are in the US (4,235) with a decent number in the UK (76). However, the paranormal investigators I've met suggest this figure is way too small, since many groups don't choose to register with directories.

6. Mike Covell runs ghost tours, and he tells me that the rapidly growing ghost hunting industry is becoming something of a Wild West. "It's so big today," he says, "that competition gets out of hand." He's had death threats from rival groups and promoters, mainly because if he ever spots them making false historical claims to spice up their venues, he'll tell them. The threats, he says, have been numerous. He insists that most groups are professional and treat the industry with respect, but he's also seen "physical assault, theft and violence between groups and investigators," as well as "backstabbing, bitching and general nastiness."

7. https://www.hauntedrooms.co.uk/. Accessed 8th December 2017.

8. I got in touch with the Amityville Police Department to ask if they could talk to me about the ghost tourism there. They refused to comment, perhaps because they don't want to encourage any more gawkers.
9. Millar, Leisa. "Miley Cyrus" Haunted House Drama." *Elle*. 8th May 2013. Accessed 8th March 2017. http://www.elleuk.com/fashion/celebrity-style /articles/a3541/miley-cyrus-rented-haunted-flat-in-london/#image=1.
10. "McConaughey Believes His House Is Haunted." *Irish Examiner*, 25th February 2003. Accessed 8th March 2017. http://www.irishexaminer.com/breakingnews /entertainment/mcconaughey-believes-house-is-haunted-89584.html?utm _source=link&utm_medium=click&utm_campaign=nextandprev.
11. Sitzer, Carly. "Kesha Tells Jimmy Kimmel There's a Ghost in Her Vagina." *In Touch Weekly*. 5th February 2014. Accessed 8th March 2017. http://www .intouchweekly.com/posts/kesha-tells-jimmy-kimmel-there-s-a-ghost-in-her -vagina-27075.
12. Ling, Thomas. "The Spooky Death—and Future Resurrection—of Paranormal TV." *Radio Times*. 31st October 2017. Accessed 8th December 2017. http:// www.radiotimes.com/news/tv/2017-10-31/the-spooky-death-and-future -resurrection-of-paranormal-tv/.
13. Black, John. "Unravelling the mystery of disease in ancient Mesopotamia." *Ancient Origins*. 23rd February 2014. Accessed 18th October 2017. http://www .ancient-origins.net/news-general/unravelling-mystery-disease-ancient -mesopotamia-001378.
14. Gardiner, Alan H. *The Attitudes of the Ancient Egyptians to Death and the Dead.* Cambridge: University Press, 1935. pp20–22.
15. Mark, Joshua J. "Ghosts in the Ancient World." *Ancient History Encyclopaedia.* 30th October 2014. Accessed 13th March 2017. http://www.ancient.eu/ghost/.
16. Mark, Emily. "Ghosts in Ancient China." *Ancient History Encyclopaedia.* 20th April 2016. Accessed 6th December 2017. https://www.ancient.eu/article/892 /ghosts-in-ancient-china/.
17. Righi, Brian. *Ghosts, Apparitions and Poltergeists.* Woodbury: Llewellyn Publications, 2008. p9.
18. Newman, Paul. *A History of Terror: Fear and Dread Through the Ages.* Stroud: Sutton Publishing, 2000. p62.
19. Laskey, Mark. "Rites of Desecration: Suicide, Sacrilege and the Crossroads Burial." *Cvlt Nation.* 8th September 2014 Accessed: 18th October 2017. http:// www.cvltnation.com/rites-of-desecration-suicide-sacrilege-and-profane-burial -at-the-crossroads/.
20. Righi, Brian. *Ghosts, Apparitions and Poltergeists.* Woodbury: Llewellyn Publications, 2008. p13.
21. The Fox sisters were important figures in the growth of Spiritualism, which has since grown into a significant and global new religious movement. The central idea of Spiritualism is not only that talking to the dead is possible, but that to do so is beneficial to us.

22. Many (but not all) Christians tend to think communicating with the dead is a sin. They base this on biblical texts like Deuteronomy 18:9–13 that describe it as a "detestable" practice.

23. YouTube Video. "Professor Ruth Robbins—The Victorian Ghost." From Leeds Becket University. Accessed 26th January 2018. https://www.youtube.com /watch?v=Bg94bRJLLj4.

24. Murch, Robert. "A Brief History of the Ouija Board." *The Fortean Times*. Issue 249. London: Dennis Publishing, June 2009.

25. *New York Tribune*. 28th March 1886. p9. Accessed through *Chronicling America: Historic American Newspapers*. Lib. of Congress. Accessed 6th December 2017. https://chroniclingamerica.loc.gov/lccn/sn83030214/1886-03-28/ed-1 /seq-9/#.

26. According to the article, the Ouija city-hotspots of Ohio 1886 were Youngstown, Canton, Warren, Tiffin, Mansfield, Akron, Elyria and "a number of other places."

27. "History of the Talking Board." The Museum of Talking Boards. Accessed 6th December 2017. http://museumoftalkingboards.com/history.html.

28. Woods, Baynard. "The Ouija Board's Mysterious Origins: War, Spirits and a Strange Death." *Guardian*. 30th October 2016. Accessed 6th December 2017. https://www.theguardian.com/lifeandstyle/2016/oct/30/ouija-board-mystery -history.

29. For those who were looking for a more serious, scientific exploration of the supernatural, learned research groups also developed: like the Society of Psychical Research (SPR). Set up in London in 1882, it scientifically examines paranormal claims to this day.

30. Parry, Hannah. "Amazon Selling Controversial Ouija Board Games for Children as Young as EIGHT—Including a Pink Version Aimed at Girls." *Daily Mail*. 12th June 2015. Accessed 6th December 2017. http://www.dailymail.co.uk/news /article-3121265/Amazon-selling-controversial-Ouija-board-games-children -young-EIGHT-including-pink-version-aimed-girls.html.

31. Goode, Erich. *The Paranormal: Who Believes, Why They Believe and Why It Matters*. New York: Prometheus Books, 2012. p225.

32. Bainbridge, William Sims and Rodney Stark. "Superstitions: Old and New." *Skeptical Inquirer*. Vol 4 Number IV (Summer) 1980. pp18–31.

33. Debunking paranormal stories *can* be newsworthy, occasionally, but only if they have gone through a sufficient period of being presented as potentially real. For example, serious proof that the Amityville haunting or the Enfield Poltergeist case was faked would be newsworthy. But only because the public were so open to it being true.

34. Goode, Erich. *The Paranormal: Who Believes, Why They Believe and Why It Matters*. New York: Prometheus Books, 2012. p236.

35. Meyjes, Toby. "Ghost Hunters Stumble Across Graveyard Porn Shoot." *Metro*. 31st May 2016. Accessed 6th December 2017. http://metro.co.uk/2016/05/31 /ghost-hunters-stumble-across-graveyard-porn-shoot-5914852/.

Notes

CHAPTER TEN: SISTER

1. Cordovani, Rinaldo. *The Capuchin Crypt—A Short Guide (English Translation Version)*. 4th Edition. Rome: Roman Province of the Capuchin Friars Minor, 2015. p3.
2. I'm using the shorthand pronoun of "he" in line with both the biblical texts and the incarnation of Jesus, but technically speaking the biblical God transcends gender labels.
3. Kermode, Mark. *The Exorcist (BFI Modern Classics)*. London: British Film Institute, 1997. p45.
4. Kermode, Mark. "The Exorcist—hype or horror?" *BBC*. 2nd November 1998. Accessed 19th October 2017. http://news.bbc.co.uk/1/hi/entertainment /206337.stm.
5. Shreck, Nikolas. *The Satanic Screen: An Illustrated Guide to the Devil in Cinema*. Powder Springs, GA: Creation Books, 2001. p168.
6. 1 John 4:8
7. Some seem to think that the Old Testament God was a grumpy, nasty deity, while the New Testament flips to the more PR-friendly, chilled-out hippy-Lord. It's almost as if between the testaments the Almighty bought a pan pipe CD, took an Alka-Seltzer and generally chilled out. Yet the two testaments are more consistent than many think—both contain light and darkness.
8. Judges 4:21 (tent peg); 2 Kings 2:23–24 (teenagers mauled by bear—after jeering at a prophet saying, "Get out of here, baldy!") Judges 19:29 (rape victim dismembered into twelve parts) Judges 3:22 (stabbing with discharged bowels).
9. Acts 1:18 (New International Version, NIV, Translation)
10. Matthew 13:42 (fiery furnaces and gnashing teeth) Matthew 22:13 (bound, cast out, also with weeping and gnashing of teeth).
11. Matthew 21:44
12. Exodus 32
13. 1 Kings 18:28
14. Hawthorne, Nathaniel. *The Marble Faun*. Susan Manning (ed.). Oxford: Oxford University Press, 2008. p150.
15. Cordovani, Rinaldo. *The Capuchin Crypt—A Short Guide (English Translation Version)*. 4th Edition. Rome: Roman Province of the Capuchin Friars Minor, 2015. p4.
16. Allen, Paul Marshall and Joan deRis. *Francis of Assisi, Canticle of the Creatures: A Modern Spiritual Path*. New York: Continuum, 1996. p136.
17. This phrase features in both *The Nameless City* (1921) and *The Call of Cthulhu* (1928).

ACKNOWLEDGEMENTS

When you write novels, which is my main job these days, you tend to hang out with yourself. A *lot*. Yeah, every now and again you ping off an email to a publisher or an agent and ask about deadlines and covers and funky stuff like that. And when the novel actually comes out, you even get to crawl out of your writey-hole, comb your Morlock hair over and interact with real-life humans. But on the whole, when you write fiction it's about the people in your head. They say stuff, they do stuff, they make you wince or chuckle. But what they don't do is pop open an actual bottle of red wine, so you can chat into the early hours; or drag lumps of steak along canals by your side; or let you sleep on their spare bed for the night.

However, it turns out, when you write a non-fiction book, that's exactly the kind of thing that happens. You romp across the world having adventures with people who are wonderful, wild and—hold the phone— really there. Now that you've read this book, you've met these characters too, so I won't rename them all here. But how about you join me in a metaphysical glass-clink to every expert, interviewee, werewolf, vampire and every other character who have made the last eighteen months of macabre research such a blast. Some of them even read through the manuscript in its earliest, most unkempt form. So, applause please for Matt Arnold, Mike Covell, Alan Murdie, Maryla Carter, Lucas de Winter and Jon Kaneko-James. You all have beautiful, beady-eyes—in the literary sense, of course.

Thanks also to the gems I met on the Frighteners Road Trip. That's right. A bunch of the experiences in this book happened during an unforgettable week of research where I drove around the UK hunting werewolves, meeting Whitby vampires, handling serial killer hair and shivering with fright in a haunted hotel. A broken-down car right in the middle of that week only added to the atmos. I loved the entire trip, and I thank everybody I met on it, including the lovely Keith Bound, who uses psychological data to make scary movies even scarier, and Elaine and Lous Edmunds, with whom I chatted for hours in their Whitby home, bulging with Gothic art. The vintage crucifix collection in the toilet was a particular treat. I also want to thank Jez Allen and Di Stockham, who run the Secret Transylvania company. *What* a way to spend my 40th.

Thanks also go to the literary crew without whom my kooky thoughts would never have melded into yours. To my brilliant agent Joanna Swainson, who pushed so hard for *The Frighteners*, as well as for my novels. She rocks. And for everybody at Icon Books, who agreed with me that probing the strange depths of "Morbidology" (an early title idea I had), was worth a shot. Particular thanks to Nira Begum, who first said yes to the book—what a smile I had after *that* email! Then a huge, quaking thank you goes to Kiera Jamison, who did a jaw-dropping job of editing this thing. Her input and expertise was wise, detailed and vital, and her comments sometimes made me laugh out loud, too. Like this one: "Saying that TV chef Jamie Oliver is a vampire could be legally troublesome.

Acknowledgements

Suggest removing?" Lol. I did remove it. Because sadly, he isn't. Thanks to Dan Mogford, for his fantastic design work—my first ever hardback. And to Therese Cohen, for taking my humble, freaky words to other, far flung countries. The language might be different over there, but the nightmares remain the same. Thanks also to the book publisher and editor Alison Hull, who took me to lunch after reading an article on my love of faith and horror. She asked if I might consider writing a book on the subject. So, if you want to blame anybody, blame her.

An important nod of thanks goes to any friends, family or colleagues who find my interest in the macabre a bit . . . ahem . . . bizarre. The fact that they love me anyway means a lot. I hope this book counts as a long, but honest, answer to your simple question: "How on earth can you love God AND horror?" Thanks also go to my mum, dad, sister and brother, who didn't freak out when I melted down action figures, or rigged impromptu poltergeists with paper sheets and invisible string. None of them had me incarcerated after that, which I appreciate very much. A huge, hugging, heartfelt thanks goes to my premium-deluxe family. To my wife Joy, who isn't into horror much, but that's okay . . . she's still into me. And to my kids, Emma and Adam. This book is for you. And also, a super-charged thank you goes to Jesus. Yep, *that* guy. I'm into him for lots of reasons, but one of my favourites is that he didn't just create fluffy rabbits and gentle birdsong. He also made howling wolves and creepy clouds across the moon.

And finally, my biggest thanks go to the monster kids out there. The ones who, like me, have always been drawn to the shadows, perhaps for as long as they can remember. It's a lonely life sometimes, especially if you're a churchy type. It's easy to be misunderstood or rejected as a vile, dangerous freak. I hope this book reminds you that you're wonderfully, brilliantly valuable and loveable . . . creepy thoughts and all. A particular thank you goes to the author Lint Hatcher, a Christian horror fan who wrote a book called *The Magic Eight Ball Test: The Christian Defence of Halloween*. I read that during my days of horror cold-turkey, and, dagnabbit, that thing made me cry. For the first time, I realised there were other swivel-eyed folks like me, who loved both the scared and the sacred. This book is basically me passing that message on . . . that none of you should feel weird, because you're not alone.

In fact, you really *aren't* alone. Because there's a very thin old woman with yellow eyes (and many teeth) who lives in your attic. She got there the moment you bought this book and she's been crawling into your room each night, just to stroke your hair. It's an added extra me and the publishers cooked up to help reinvigorate the humble book market. We call it "BookGhoul" and we're really proud of the scheme. However, now that you've finished reading *The Frighteners*, the time for stroking is over. Tonight, she'll crawl into your room for the last time, but before you scream, and before she takes your eyes, please tell her that I, and everybody at the office, say hi, and that we think she's doing a stellar job.

High fives and blessings to all!

Peter Laws, in my kitchen, eating chocolate biscuits, January 2018